EDITORIAL RESEARCH REPORTS ON

THE

CHANGING AMERICAN FAMILY

Timely Reports to Keep
Journalists, Scholars and the Public
Abreast of Developing Issues, Events and Trends

Published by Congressional Quarterly Inc.
1414 22nd Street, N.W.
Washington, D.C. 20037

About the Cover

The cover was designed by Staff Artist Gwendolyn Hammond, under the supervision of Art Director Richard Pottern.

Copyright 1979 by Congressional Quarterly, Inc.
published by Editorial Research Reports

The right to make direct commercial use of material in Editorial Research Reports is strictly reserved for magazine, newspaper, radio and television clients of the service.

PRINTED IN THE UNITED STATES OF AMERICA
MAY 1979

Editor, Hoyt Gimlin
Associate Editor, Sandra Stencel
Editorial Assistants, Patricia Ochs, Diane Huffman,
Production Manager, I. D. Fuller
Assistant Production Manager, Maceo Mayo

Library of Congress Cataloging in Publication Data

Congressional Quarterly, inc.
    Editorial research reports on changing American family.

    Ten reports originally published as separate issues of Editorial research reports.
    Bibliography: p.
    Includes index.
    1. Family — United States. 2. Family life surveys — United States. 3. United States — Social conditions — 1960- I. Editorial research reports. II. Title. III. Title: Changing American family.
HQ 536.C745   301.420973   79,12753
ISBN 0-87187-149-1

Contents

Foreword	v
The Changing American Family	1
Violence in the Family	21
Teenage Pregnancy	41
Single Parent Families	61
Women in the Work Force	81
Youth Unemployment	103
College Tuition Costs	123
Housing Outlook	143
Mandatory Retirement	163
Physical Fitness Boom	183
Index	203

Foreword

The decline of the American family has been a popular theme in recent years. Evidence of stress in the family is not hard to find. The U.S. divorce rate has more than doubled since the 1960s. The number of households headed by single or divorced women has increased by 46 percent since 1970. In 1977 almost 18 million children were living in single-parent homes in the United States, a 100 percent increase since 1960. A recent report by Paul C. Glick, senior demographer for the U.S. Census Bureau, estimated that 45 percent of the infants born in the United States in 1978 are destined to spend at least part of their childhoods with only one parent.

One of the most disturbing signs of deep, underlying stress within the family is evidence of violent confrontations among family members. In any one year, approximately 1.8 million wives are beaten by their husbands, according to one study. Over one million children are abused each year, physically, sexually or through neglect, and at least 2,000 of them die of their injuries. "Violence in the home is a far more serious problem than violence in the streets, in the classrooms or any where else," Professor Murray A. Strauss of the University of New Hampshire told the America Psychological Association last year.

Despite these and other signs of family discord, most sociologists and psychologists believe that the American family will prevail. "Families are changing, but it is a mistake to confuse change with collapse," said Kenneth Keniston, chairman of the Carnegie Council on Children and the principal author of the council's 1977 report, *All Our Children: The American Family Under Pressure*.

The council attributed the current wave of pessimism about the family's future to "an outmoded set of views about how families work." Chief among them were the "myth of the self-sufficient family" and the still widely held belief that parents alone are responsible for what becomes of their children. "Families are not now, nor were they ever, the self-sufficient building blocks of society...," the council concluded. "They are deeply influenced by broad social and economic forces over which they have no control."

This book of ten reports issued since 1976 details many of the social and economic forces that have effected family life and examines some of the suggestions for easing the burdens of today's families.

         — Sandra Stencel
           Associate Editor

May 1979
Washington, D.C.

THE CHANGING AMERICAN FAMILY

by

Sandra Stencel

	page
SIGNS OF FAMILIES IN TRANSITION	3
Evidence of Stress in American Homes	3
Conflicting Views Over Family Stability	4
The Implications of Women's Employment	5
Changing Attitude Toward Child-Rearing	6
Rise in Number of Childless Marriages	8
Diminishing Influence of Parents on Teens	10
HISTORIC FORCES AND HOME LIFE	12
Early Treatment of Women and Children	12
Liberalization of Courtship and Sex Mores	13
Impact of Depression and World War II	14
NATIONAL FAMILY POLICY PROPOSALS	15
Fragmentation of Government Programs	16
Visions of Future Marriage and Family	17
Predictions for Another U.S. Baby Boom	18

**June 3
1977**

Editor's Note: The White House Conference on Families discussed on p. 15 has been postponed from 1979 to 1981.

THE CHANGING AMERICAN FAMILY

JOHN AND MARY Smith are getting a divorce. Smith's frequent business trips and long work hours were a source of friction. Despite his frequent absences, he was upset when his wife announced that she was going back to work, especially when she said it would mean that Grandpa Smith would have to go to a nursing home. Tensions in the Smith household increased when their oldest daughter got divorced and moved back home with her two young boys. Then the youngest daughter left home to live with her boyfriend. And just recently, the son dropped out of college and joined a religious commune.

This fictional family may sound like it sprang from the script for "Mary Hartman, Mary Hartman." But similar scenarios are being played out in millions of real households across the nation. Caught in the middle of broad social and economic changes, American families are finding it increasingly difficult to cope with their problems. Rapidly changing values are creating uncertainties and doubts in parents and children. Traditional notions of parental authority and responsibility are being questioned. Old taboos on sexual conduct in and out of marriage are breaking down. Men and women's roles in the home and in the work force are being redefined.

In the face of all these changes, observed Alan Pifer, president of the Carnegie Corporation, "important governmental and private-sector policies that intimately affect the family...are still in the main geared to earlier value systems and beliefs. Social policies have not yet caught up with changing social practice."[1] Evidence of stress in the family is not hard to find.

> The divorce rate in the United States is the highest in the world. Nearly 40 per cent of all marriages now end in divorce. Census Bureau statistics show that the U.S. divorce rate more than double between 1963 and 1975 *(see table, p. 5).*[2]
>
> Over 11 million children—more than one out of six children under age 18—live in single-parent homes. Since 1960, the number of such families has grown seven times as fast as the number of two-parent families.[3]

---

[1] Alan Pifer, "Women Working: Toward a New Society," *1976 Annual Report of the Carnegie Corporation of New York.*
[2] Bureau of the Census, "Marital Status and Living Arrangements: March 1976," *Current Population Reports,* Series P-20, No. 306, January 1977, p. 2.
[3] See "Single-Parent Families," *E.R.R.,* 1976 Vol. II, pp. 661-680.

The number of marriages performed in the United States declined about 7 per cent from 1973 to 1975, according to a 1976 study by the National Center for Health Statistics. On the other hand, the number of couples living together out of wedlock more than doubled between 1970 and 1975. Today approximately 1.3 million unmarried Americans share living quarters with a member of the opposite sex, the Census Bureau calculates.

"The change in family life under way today," declared Edward Shorter, professor of history at the University of Toronto, "is of no less magnitude, and will have no less importance in the lives of common, everyday people than did the great industrial revolution of the last century."[4]

Conflicting Views Over Family Stability

Experts agree that the family as an institution is facing many new challenges. But they are divided on the question of how well the family is meeting them. Some, like Drs. Urie Bronfenbrenner of Cornell University and Amitai Etzioni of Columbia University, point to the rising divorce rate, declining marriage and fertility rates, and rising numbers of women leaving home for paid work as symbols of the deterioration of the American family. "At the present accelerating rate of depletion, the United States will run out of families not long after it runs out of oil," Etzioni wrote recently in *Science* magazine.[5]

Etzioni and Bronfenbrenner's concerns are shared by President Carter. In a campaign speech last August in Manchester, N.H., Carter said: "[T]he breakdown of the American family has reached extremely dangerous proportions." He pledged that his administration would do everything in its power to reverse this trend *(see p. 15)*. Shortly after taking office, Carter urged his staff members not to neglect their family responsibilities despite job pressures. He admonished federal workers to marry rather than join the growing ranks of couples "living in sin."

Bruno Bettelheim, director emeritus of the Orthogenic School at the University of Chicago, has said that the most serious problem facing today's family is "the discrepancy between its present reality and expectations of what it ought to be." In his opinion these expectations are completely unrealistic and antiquated. "The false expectation is that today's family should function as well as families in the past," he wrote. "The fact is that the conditions which gave substance to the earlier family and made for its cohesion...are no longer present."[6]

---

[4] Edward Shorter, "Changing from Nuclear Nest to Intimate Couple," *Journal of Current Social Issues*, winter 1977, p. 10. The *Journal* is published by the United Church of Christ.
[5] Amitai Etzioni, "Science and the Future of the Family," *Science*, April 29, 1977, p. 487. Etzioni is professor of sociology at Columbia and director of the Center for Policy Research. Bronfenbrenner is professor of human development and family studies at Cornell.
[6] Bruno Bettelheim, "Untying the Family," *The Center Magazine*, September-October 1976, p. 5.

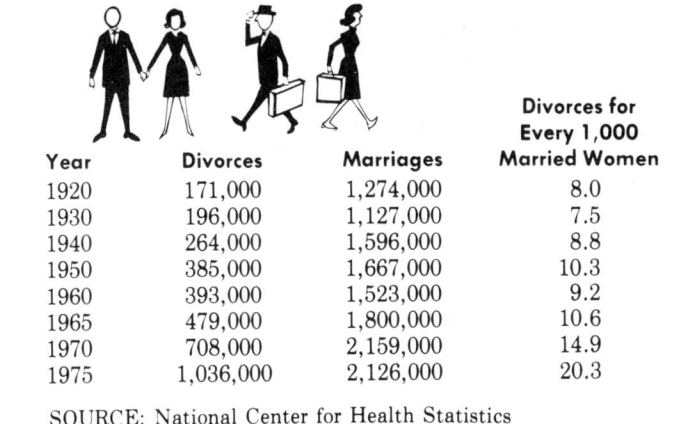

Year	Divorces	Marriages	Divorces for Every 1,000 Married Women
1920	171,000	1,274,000	8.0
1930	196,000	1,127,000	7.5
1940	264,000	1,596,000	8.8
1950	385,000	1,667,000	10.3
1960	393,000	1,523,000	9.2
1965	479,000	1,800,000	10.6
1970	708,000	2,159,000	14.9
1975	1,036,000	2,126,000	20.3

SOURCE: National Center for Health Statistics

A different view of today's family was presented by Mary Jo Bane, a professor at Wellesley College, in her book *Here to Stay: American Families in the Twentieth Century* (1976). She concluded that American families are as strong as ever. Many of the trends in family life which Bronfenbrenner, Etzioni and others found disturbing were, she thought, positive changes. Professor Bane found notions of the good old days romanticized; those happy extended families of assorted relatives living under one roof, as portrayed in Norman Rockwell paintings, were rare. "The nuclear family, consisting of parents living with their own children and no other adults, has been the predominant family form in America since the earliest period on which historians have data," she wrote.[7]

Bane argued that what divorce is doing to disrupt families today, death did in earlier times. In fact, she said, the proportion of children affected by "parental disruption" actually has declined over the last century. Even with the rising divorce rate, more children today are living with at least one parent than ever before. One reason for this is the large increase in the proportion of widowed and divorced women who continue living with their children after their marriage has ended rather than sending the children to live with grandparents, other relatives or to orphanages. While the high rate of divorce in the United States is cause for concern, she said, the high rate of remarriage indicates that marriage "is still a pervasive and enduring institution."

The Implications of Women's Employment

In recent years American families have undergone a fundamental change in the manner in which they provide for their economic welfare. Since 1950, the number of families in which both husband and wife work has climbed from 22 per cent to 42

---

[7] Mary Jo Bane, *Here to Stay: American Families in the Twentieth Century* (1976), p. 37. Bane is associate director of Wellesley's Center for Research on Women.

per cent. Last year alone, an additional one million wives joined their husbands in the work force.[8] The prime reason for their working was sheer necessity—to help keep up with family bills.

During the 1950s, the largest increase in labor force participation was among married women beyond the usual childbearing years (20 to 34). In recent years, however, young married women have entered the labor force in large numbers. Half of the working wives in 1975 had children under age 18.[9] The arrival of the two-paycheck family has been accompanied by a redefinition of family roles. A number of studies have found that women who are employed exercise a greater degree of power in their marriages. Most especially, working wives have more say in family financial decisions. Women who are employed full-time have more leverage within the family than women employed part-time, according to a study by Isabel V. Sawhill and Kristin A. Moore of the Urban Institute in Washington.[10]

Closely related to the issue of marital power is the question of how the employment of women affects the division of labor within the home. Sawhill and Moore found that "in general, husbands of working wives engage in slightly more child care and housework than do husbands of nonworking women." But they go on to say that "it does not appear that the rapid movement of women into the labor force has been matched by any significant increase in husbands' willingness to help around the house."[11]

Although most husbands welcome the additional income, many have found it difficult to adjust to their wives' new roles. Being married to a woman with a busy schedule, an income of her own, and outside friendships and commitments may cause a husband to feel insecure and resentful. Numerous studies have shown that there is more divorce among families in which the wife works.[12] Once society has adjusted to women's new roles the divorce rate might decline somewhat. But, according to Sawhill and Moore, "if the economic achievements of women continue to undermine the utilitarian character of traditional marriages, a permanently higher rate of divorce is a likely outcome."

Changing Attitudes Toward Child-Rearing

Today's families are not as child-oriented as they were in the 1950s. Many parents have come to believe that they are entitled to pursue their own interests—even if it means devoting less

---

[8] See "Women in the Work Force," E.R.R., 1977 Vol. I, pp. 121-144. See also Howard Hayghe, "Families and the Rise of Working Wives—An Overview," *Monthly Labor Review*, May 1976, p. 16.

[9] U.S. Department of Labor, "U.S. Working Women: A Chartbook," 1975.

[10] Kristin A. Moore and Isabel V. Sawhill, "Implications of Women's Employment for Home and Family Life," The Urban Institute, August 1975, pp. 7-8.

[11] Ibid.

[12] See Heather L. Ross and Isabel V. Sawhill, *Time of Transition: The Growth of Families Headed by Women*, 1975, pp. 35-66.

1977 G. B. Trudeau (distributed by Universal Press Syndicate)

> Perhaps no one is a better symbol of today's changing values and life-styles than is Ms. Joanie Caucus, the plucky 42-year-old divorcee from Gary Trudeau's daily comic strip "Doonesbury." For the past three years some 60 million readers have followed her bittersweet metamorphosis from runaway wife and mother to day-care center supervisor, law school applicant and student, and live-in lover of hip Washington journalist Rick Redfern. The culmination of Joanie's search for herself came on May 21, when she and her 225 real-life classmates received their diplomas from the law school at the University of California at Berkeley.

time to their children and making fewer sacrifices for them. In return, they expect less from their children later on. These were the findings of a recent survey of parents of children under 13 years of age conducted by Yankelovich, Skelly and White, the national market research and public opinion organization, for the General Mills Consumer Center.[13]

Two out of three parents interviewed for the General Mills survey said that parents should have their own lives and interests even if it means spending less time with their children; 54 per cent said that people have no right to count on their children to help them when they are old or in difficulty; 67 per cent said that children have no obligation regardless of what parents have done for them; and two out of three do not believe a couple should stay married just for the sake of the children.

The emphasis on self-fulfillment was greatest in the group identified by Yankelovich as the "new breed" parents. The "new breed," representing 43 per cent of the parents interviewed, tend to be better educated and more affluent. They stress freedom over authority, self-fulfillment over material success, and duty to self over duty to others—including their own children. The study found that "new breed" parents are loving but take a *laissez-faire* attitude toward child-rearing. "It's not the permissiveness of the '50s," said Yankelovich, "which was child-centered and concerned with the fragility of the child. Today, the parent says in effect, 'I want to be free, so why shouldn't my children be free?'"[14]

[13] "Raising Children in a Changing Society, The General Mills American Family Report 1976-77."
[14] Quoted in *Time*, May 2, 1977, p. 76.

By contrast, the traditionalists, who still represent the majority of parents (57 per cent of those interviewed), are stricter disciplinarians, more demanding of their children and more willing to make sacrifices for them. But Yankelovich found that not even the traditionalists are prepared for the same kind of self-sacrificing approach to child-raising that was common in their parents' time. For example, a solid majority of the traditional parents (64 per cent) agreed that (1) parents should have lives of their own even if it means spending less time with their children, (2) parents should not stay together for the sake of the children, and (3) children have no obligation to their parents regardless of what parents have done for them.

Many social scientists fear that the emphasis on individualism and self-gratification throughout the culture—which author Peter Marin has labeled "the new narcissism"[15]—is harming the family. Another writer saw the family "being destroyed by the egocentricity of each member."[16] Professor Etzioni expanded on this theme. "People must learn to balance the personal rewards of 'doing one's own thing' against the hurt it might entail to others," he wrote. "No relationships, no institution, family or society can survive otherwise."[17]

Rise in Number of Childless Marriages

Some contend that the new narcissism is responsible for the growing number of young married couples who have decided not to have children—ever. In 1955, according to statistics compiled by the Census Bureau, only 1 per cent of all wives between the ages of 18 and 24 expected to have no children. By 1973, that figure had risen to 4 per cent. Today it stands at 5 per cent.[18] Since 1957, the fertility rate *(see explanation, p. 19)* in the United States has dropped from 3.76 children per woman to 1.75 last year. Philosopher Michael Novak has written that the notion of family is so unpopular these days that a decision to have children, formerly a routine event in a young married couple's life, now requires "an act of courage."[19] Disillusionment with parenthood seems particularly strong among college students.

The adage that "having children can bring a couple closer together" has been displaced by statistics showing that child-rearing puts a severe strain on marriage. Separate studies by Dr. Harold Feldman, professor of human development and family studies at Cornell University, and Dr. Charles Figley, a research

---

[15] Peter Marin, "The New Narcissism," *Harper's,* October 1975, p. 45.
[16] Abram Kardiner quoted in *Human Behavior,* May 1977, p. 73.
[17] Amitai Etzioni, "The Family: Is It Obsolete?" *Journal of Current Social Issues,* winter 1977, p. 8.
[18] Bureau of the Census, Current Population Reports, Series P-20, No. 248, p. 19; No. 265, p. 19; and No. 277, p. 17.
[19] Michael Novak, "The Family Out of Favor," *Harper's,* April 1976, p. 37.

> ## Black Families In the United States
>
> The troubles of black families gained much attention in 1965 with the publication of the so-called Moynihan Report. Prepared by the Department of Labor's Office of Policy Planning and Research under the direction of Daniel P. Moynihan, then an Assistant Secretary of Labor, the controversial report argued that the black family was "deteriorating" because women headed about one-fourth of these families. The report also noted that nearly a quarter of urban Negro marriages were dissolved and nearly one-quarter of Negro births were illegitimate. This breakdown of the black family structure, the report said, had led to a "startling increase" in welfare dependency.
>
> Black families continue to suffer from higher rates of dissolution than white families. In 1975, 10 per cent of all persons of ages 25 to 54 who had ever married were either divorced or separated; the corresponding figures for whites and blacks were 8 per cent and 27 per cent, respectively. Only 49.4 per cent of the black children were living in households with both parents present, compared with 85.4 per cent of the white children. Children in black families were three and a half times more likely to be living below the official poverty level as were white children.
>
> There have been some signs of improvement among black middle-class families. A recent study of social mobility by two University of Wisconsin sociologists, Robert M. Hauser and David L. Featherman, found a vast improvement in the black family's ability to pass on to its sons the social advantages it had managed to acquire. In the early 1960s, it did not matter very much whether the family was poor or middle class—the son usually had to start on the bottom rung of the job ladder. By the early 1970s, however, he was much more apt to start out at, or rise to, the status level of his father, and his career was more apt to reflect the advantages bestowed by his parents.

psychologist and marriage counselor at Purdue University, found that generally the sense of satisfaction with the marriage does drop during the child-raising period. A team of researchers at the University of Michigan's Institute for Social Research found that married childless couples were the happiest group in society.

One of the greatest burdens of child-rearing is financial. The U.S. Commission on Population Growth and the American Future reported in 1972 that the average cost of rearing a child to age 18 was $35,000.[20] Today the figure is much higher. The U.S. Department of Agriculture estimated in 1975 that the yearly expense amounted to 15 to 17 per cent of family income. This meant that a family earning between $16,000 and $18,000 a year would spend nearly $50,000 on a child during his or her first 18 years. College costs would add another $20,000.

---

[20] *Population and the American Future: The Report of the Commission on Population Growth and the American Future,* March 1972.

Editorial Research Reports June 3, 1977

A new study by the Population Reference Bureau[21] stated that the average cost of rearing and educating a child in the United States ranged from $44,000 for relatively low-income families (earning $10,000 to $13,500 a year after taxes) to $64,000 for middle-income families ($16,500 to $20,000). What's more, these figures represented only direct costs. Adding in the "lost" earnings of mothers who stayed home to care for young children boosted the average costs to $77,000 for low-income families and $107,000 for middle-income families.

Married couples who choose to remain childless still are a small minority. Most who choose this route complain that it is a tough decision to make because of pressures from friends, neighbors and, most of all, parents who want to be grandparents. And there is indirect pressure—the glorified picture of parenthood presented by the press, television, movies and advertisements. The National Organization for Non-Parents (NON), headquartered in Baltimore, Md., was founded in 1972 to fight this cultural bias against childless couples and to challenge the pro-natalist pressures in society. NON's founder, Ellen Peck, emphasized that the group is not against parenthood—just against the social pressures that pushed people into having children whether or not they really wanted them.

NON also supports the growing number of couples who are choosing to have only one child. In 1975, approximately 11 per cent of all wives aged 18 to 39 said they wanted a one-child family as compared to only 6 per cent in 1967. Various experts have attacked the image of the only child as spoiled, selfish, lonely and isolated. The organization quotes Dr. Murray M. Kappelman, professor of pediatrics at the University of Maryland, as saying: "...[T]here is absolutely no reason why the only child cannot be as emotionally sound and as socially stable as every other well-adjusted child on the block."[22]

Diminishing Influence of Parents on Teens

The high divorce rate and the increase in the number of people postponing or foregoing marriage and child-rearing are not the only signs of families under stress. Incidents of violence within the family have jumped sharply in recent years. According to estimates supplied to the Department of Health, Education and Welfare by the American Humane Association, one million children are the object of neglect or abuse each year, and 2,000 to 4,000 die from circumstances involving neglect or

---

[21] Thomas J. Espenshade, "The Value and Cost of Children," *Population Bulletin,* April 1977.
[22] "The One-Child Family," brochure published by the National Organization for Non-Parents.

The Changing American Family

abuse.[23] According to authors Roger Langley and Richard C. Levy, 28 million American women are "battered wives."[24]

Urie Bronfenbrenner contends that the deterioration of American family life is responsible for the plight of today's youth. Teenage alcoholism and drug abuse are growing problems.[25] The suicide rate for young people 15 to 19 years old more than tripled in the last two decades, climbing from 2.3 per 100,000 in 1956 to 7.1 per 100,000 in 1974. Recently there has been an increase in suicides among younger children, some as young as ten.[26] Crimes by youths under 18 years old have been growing at a higher rate than has the juvenile population. Bronfenbrenner estimates that children are running away from home at the rate of one million a year. He and other social scientists are concerned about the diminishing influence of parents on children and the growing importance of peer group relations and television. "What we are seeing here...are the roots of alienation...."[27]

Christopher Lasch, professor of history at the University of Rochester, argues that the laissez-faire attitude of today's parents toward their children may be responsible for the growing number of youngsters who are turning to Rev. Sun Myung Moon's Unification Church, the Hare Krishnas and other religious cults. "The ease with which children escape emotional entanglements with the older generation leaves them with a feeling not of liberation but of inner emptiness," Lasch wrote recently. "Young people today often reproach their parents with indifference or neglect, and many of them seek warmth and security in submission to spiritual healers, gurus, and prophets of political or psychic transformation."[28]

Bruno Bettelheim has suggested that increased tension between parents and their adolescent children in recent years is the unavoidable consequence of the extension of the age of dependency. Until a few generations ago, he pointed out, most children left home at the beginning of puberty to join the labor force. "It is something entirely new that most children are kept economically—hence also socially—dependent on their parents until they are twenty or older," he wrote.[29]

---

[23] See "Child Abuse," *E.R.R.*, 1976 Vol. I, pp. 65-84.
[24] Roger Langley and Richard C. Levy, *Wife Beating: The Silent Crisis* (1977).
[25] See "Resurgence of Alcoholism," *E.R.R.*, 1973 Vol. II, pp. 987-1007, and Richard C. Schroeder's *The Politics of Drugs* (1975).
[26] Figures cited by Urie Bronfenbrenner in "The Disturbing Changes in the American Family," *Search*, fall 1976. *Search* is published by the State University of New York.
[27] Urie Bronfenbrenner, "The Isolated Generations," *Human Ecology Report*, winter 1976, p. 7.
[28] Christopher Lasch, "The Undermining of the Family's Capacity to Provide for Itself: How Mass Education and Madison Avenue have Replaced Main Street and Mommy and Daddy," published in *The Washington Post*, Feb. 10, 1977.
[29] Bruno Bettelheim, *op. cit.*, p. 9.

Historic Forces and Home Life

FAMILY LIFE in early America was shaped in large part by older European traditions. The colonies retained the patriarchal family patterns and the strict Judeo-Christian sexual codes of their European ancestors. "On the other hand," wrote Professor William M. Kephart of the University of Pennsylvania, "certain circumstances in early America operated to bring about changes in the European family system."[30] For one thing, there was a marked shortage of women. Consequently, women had much choice in the selection of a husband and the dowry system became obsolete. Frontier conditions also favored relative independence for the young.

Households in colonial America generally were larger than in Europe. It was common for a family to have from five to ten children, and 15 or more was by no means rare. Benjamin Franklin, for example, came from a family of 17. But contrary to popular mythology, the extended family household, populated by an assortment of related people of all ages, was never the dominant family form in America. The first U.S. census in 1790 showed the average size of a household was 5.8 people.

The early colonial family tended to be a farm family and thus an economically self-sufficient unit. Although the women occasionally assisted with the heavier duties, tasks generally were divided along sex lines, with the men doing the land clearing and construction and the women doing the cooking and food processing, spinning and weaving, washing and mending and candle-making. Children were expected to assist their parents. Farm tools were both scarce and crude, and the farmer needed all the help he could get. Children were economic assets.

Marriage was considered an obligation as well as a privilege. People were expected to marry, and they normally did so at a young age, girls often in their early teens and boys frequently before they were 20. "There was little place in colonial society for the unmarried...," Kephart wrote. "For a woman, marriage was deemed to be the only honorable state.... Bachelors were suspect, and in most of the colonies were heavily taxed and kept under close surveillance.... Widows and widowers were expected to remarry and they did, usually without much time elapsing."[31]

The position of women and children in colonial America was only slightly better than in Europe. In New England, especially, where the social milieu was heavily patriarchal, wives and children faced severe social and legal restraints. However,

---
[30] William M. Kephart, *The Family, Society, and the Individual*, 2nd ed. (1966), p. 120.
[31] *Ibid.*, pp. 191-192.

The Changing American Family

women were accorded certain legal rights and protection. Husbands were responsible for the support of their wives and for any debts incurred by them. Women had inheritance rights with regard to their husbands' property. Additionally, wives were legally protected against any abuse or maltreatment by their husbands. Strict discipline and parental respect were the hallmarks of child-rearing practices.

Divorce was exceedingly rare. Plymouth—settled in 1620—did not experience a divorce until 1661. In some of the colonies, particularly in the South, there were simply no provisions for divorce. In colonies that did make provisions, the legal grounds were usually confined to adultery or cruelty and often were punishable as criminal offenses. In many of the colonies, the legislatures rather than the courts were empowered to pass on divorce requests.[32]

Liberalization of Courtship and Sex Mores

There were no real changes in the status of American women until late in the 19th century. As late as 1850, a wife had no legal control over her own personal property; all her belongings were legally in the hands of her husband, to dispose of as he saw fit. Her services also belonged to him, and she had no legal rights even to the custody of her own children. Women were not permitted to vote, nor was their education taken very seriously. Female wage earners were looked upon with suspicion. "In general," concluded Professor Kephart, "a woman had little alternative but to marry and fulfill her 'child-bearing and homemaking destiny.' "[33]

The rights of women were gradually broadened under the impetus of the women's rights movement launched in 1848 at a convention in Seneca Falls, N.Y.[34] Eventually women won the right to vote, to negotiate contracts, run their own businesses, keep their own earnings, and to attend institutions of higher learning. Women began entering the work force in increasing numbers. The first large-scale influx of women workers took place in the New England factories of the mid-19th century. During the Civil war more occupations were opened to women, a phenomenon that was to be repeated in World War I and World War II. By 1900 women comprised 18 per cent of the work force.

The folkways and mores of courtship also changed. From the colonial period to the Civil War, the changes were slow, but thereafter, the tempo increased. The use of dowries ceased altogether. Parental permission to begin courtship was no longer

---
[32] Edmund S. Morgan, *The Puritan Family* (1944).
[33] Kephart, *op. cit.*, p. 25.
[34] The Woman's Rights Convention at Seneca Falls is generally cited as the beginning of the woman's suffrage movement, the forerunner of today's women's movement. See "Status of Women," *E.R.R.*, 1970 Vol. II, pp. 582-583.

a strict necessity. While parents still had a fair measure of control over the marriages of their sons and daughters, love matches were growing in favor. A rapidly increasing urban population meant that single people had more leeway in the choice of mates. Urbanization was accompanied by an increase in commercial amusements—theater, athletic events and public dances. "Opportunities for meeting young people of the opposite sex were so widespread...that a new term was coined: dating.[35]

As the 20th century dawned, the same forces that tended to liberalize courtship—emancipation of women, accelerated urbanization, decline in secular and religious controls—served to weaken the existing sex mores. Three additional factors were (1) automobiles, (2) increased availability of contraceptive devices, and (3) a relatively simple treatment for venereal disease. There is general agreement that after World War I there was a substantial increase in premarital petting, premarital intercourse and adultery. Equally important were the changes in attitudes toward sex. The biggest change was that marital intercourse came to be regarded as an activity which was pleasurable for the wife as well as the husband.

There were no nationwide divorce statistics in the United States until the mid-19th century. The very absence of such figures suggests that divorce was rather infrequent. In 1867, the Census Bureau counted 9,937 divorces among the 37 million people in the United States. By 1900, the population had roughly doubled, while the yearly number of divorces had increased to 55,751. By 1950, the population had again doubled, but during that year divorces had soared to 385,144. As the divorce rate increased over the decades, the stigma attached to divorce tended to decline.

Along with changes in courtship, sex behavior, marriage and divorce came striking changes in the functions of the American family. "In the colonial era," Kephart wrote, "the family...was not only economically independent but also served as the center for such activities as education, religion and recreation.... With the disappearance of the frontier, however, together with rapid increases in urbanization and industrialization, traditional family functions were taken over by...institutions or agencies."

Impact of Depression and World War II

Economic and social forces have had a significant impact on family structure in the past 50 years. During the depression years of the 1930s, the average age at marriage rose sharply, and 9 per cent of the women had not married by age 50. Birth rates plummeted. Lifetime childlessness approached 20 per

---

[35] Kephart, op. cit., p. 237.

cent, and many of the children whom some demographers thought were merely being postponed were never born. One explanation for this, according to Census Bureau demographer Paul C. Glick, "is that many of the women who delayed having those other children reached the point where they liked it better without them than they had thought they would."[36]

World War II caused extensive dislocations in family life, particularly among families with husbands—or would-be husbands—of draft age. Marriage and birth rates remained low, and millions of women, married as well as single, were welcomed into the work force. The proportion of women in the labor force reached 36 per cent during the war, and then dropped sharply to 28 per cent with the return of the veterans to civilian jobs.

The postwar period was marked by a sharp, brief increase in marriage and divorce rates, but both quickly fell back down. The mid-1950s were, in Glick's words, "a relatively familistic period." Much emphasis was placed on family-oriented activities. Popular culture, especially the new medium of television, glorified the happy American home. Couples married younger than before, and all but 4 per cent of the women married during their childbearing years. The baby boom that had started with the return of the World War II servicemen reached its peak in 1957; 4.3 million babies were born in the United States that year. The birth rate did not diminish significantly until after 1960. By that time the rate of entry into marriage had already begun to fall and the divorce rate had resumed its long upward trend.

National Family Policy Proposals

THERE CAN BE NO "more urgent priority for the next administration," Jimmy Carter said in his campaign speech in Manchester, N.H., "than to see that every decision our government makes is designed to honor and support and strengthen the American family." Carter repeated this theme in his Inaugural Address: "I...hope that when my time as your President has ended, people might say...that we have strengthened the American family, which is the basis of our society...." To this end, President Carter will convene a White House Conference on Families in 1979. A prime purpose of the conference will be to examine the ways government policies affect family life.

---

[36] Paul C. Glick, "Some Recent Changes in American Families," *Current Population Reports*, Special Studies, Series P-23, No. 52, p. 1.

Sidney Johnson, director of the Family Impact Seminar at George Washington University, will coordinate the White House Conference. Johnson also has been assigned the task of advising all Cabinet departments on ways to be more responsive to the needs and concerns of families. For example, Secretary of Defense Harold Brown will weigh family considerations as part of a coming review of the military's policy of transferring career personnel to different posts every two or three years.

Many organizations and individuals have urged the federal government to develop and adopt a coherent national family policy. Urie Bronfenbrenner said in a recent interview: "The United States is now the only developed country in the world that doesn't have a national program providing child care for working parents, minimum family income, and health care for families with young children.... What's destroying the family isn't the family itself but the indifference of the rest of society."[37]

Fragmentation of Government Programs

One of the leading proponents of a national family policy is Vice President Walter F. Mondale, who, as senator, was chairman of the Subcommittee on Children and Youth. "We need to begin shaping a society that doesn't just tolerate family life or pretend to be neutral toward it," he wrote recently. "We need instead a society that nourishes it and helps it grow."[38] Mondale has said that while the United States has no formal policy, this does not mean that the nation has no family policy at all. "What we have," he wrote, "might best be called a family policy 'by default'—a series of largely unexamined, unarticulated, and largely inconsistent, burdensome policies with respect to families."[39] As examples of government policies that create hardships for families, Mondale cited frequent transfers of military and foreign service personnel and welfare regulations that deny federal AFDC—Aid to Families With Dependent Children—payments to families unless or until the father leaves home.

Mondale has suggested that the United States test the feasibility of developing "family impact statements"—similar to the environmental impact statements that are now required by federal law. "I believe the family impact idea holds great promise," he said, "but I also believe its political, administrative, and substantive feasibility must be carefully tested.... Clearly we do not need a family protection agency or bureaucracies ensuring impact statements on all proposed

---

[37] Interview in *Psychology Today*, May 1977, p. 41.
[38] Walter Mondale, "The Family in Trouble," *Psychology Today*, May 1977, p. 39.
[39] Walter Mondale, "Government Policy, Stress and the Family," *Journal of Home Economics*, November 1976, p. 13.

The Changing American Family

policies or laws.... What we do need instead is to test the idea of a family impact statement on several public policies in a purely advisory fashion. We need to start a public conversation about the impact of legislation on families."

The key to preserving the family, in Bronfenbrenner's opinion, is to require changes in the workplace. He advocates (1) flexible work schedules that allow parents to be home when their children come home from school, (2) fair part-time employment opportunities that do not deprive the worker of fringe benefits, status and seniority, (3) sick leave for working parents when children are ill, and (4) paternity leave as well as maternity leave. Such policy changes will have to be accompanied by changes in attitudes. Americans will have to discard the notion that domestic considerations should give way before the demands of the job. These policy changes also will require more cooperation between men and women in the sharing of family responsibilities.

Many social scientists have advocated creation of an income support system for families. Their proposals include a "negative" income tax, a system of family allowances, or a combination of the two. Nearly all of them contemplate elimination of the present program of aid to families with dependent children. Professor Bane goes a step further and suggests that a form of Social Security be devised to cover the first 20 years of a person's life, those of greatest dependency. The person would repay this amount during his or her working years. Bane conceded that there would be enormous difficulty in establishing such a plan. For one thing, the costs would probably be enormous.

Opponents of family allowances are concerned with more than just the cost. They fear that such a system would lead to public intrusion into child-rearing practices. They also worry about the tendency of such systems to encourage people to have more children. Another argument is that childless people should not be asked to subsidize people who choose to have children.

Visions of Future of Marriage and Family

Bane thinks that family commitments are likely to survive in society because "it seems clear [that they] are not archaic remnants of a disappearing traditionalism, but persisting manifestations of human needs for stability, continuity and non-conditional affection." Her optimistic assessment of the future of the family draws general agreement. But there also seems to be general agreement that the definition of the family needs to be broadened to include not only the nuclear family but also single-parent families, communal families, childless families, homosexual couples, and others. Robert Hill, director of research for the National Urban League, has said: "We must stop confusing the structure or form of family life with the capacity of families to function."[40] Along these lines, the Department of Housing and Urban Development recently announced that it was opening public housing to unmarried couples living together and to homosexual couples if they could show a "stable family relationship."

The wide range of existing family patterns in the United States was disclosed in the following statistics:[41] Three groups—childless couples, couples whose children are grown and households headed by women—now represent nearly a quarter of all family groups; another quarter falls into such categories as communes, affiliated monogamous families sharing a common household, unmarried couples, single persons alone, single persons living together for economic or convenience reasons without forming a true "family," and stable homosexual couples. Finally, 4 per cent of the families still are reported to be "extended," those in which grandparents or such other relatives as uncles or aunts are part of the household. This means that fewer than half of all American families fall into the category of a traditional nuclear family—father, mother and children living together in their own household.

According to Professor Edward Shorter, the "couple-family" will be the predominant family type of the future. The couple-family will differ from the old nuclear family in several ways. There will be fewer children, and those children will have less influence on their parents' emotional lives. The man-woman relationships will be based on a high level of sexual attraction and a desire for intimacy, and consequently the couple-family will be more socially isolated from the rest of the community, be it neighbors, friends or colleagues from work. And because of this sexual intensity, "the couple-family is going to develop the pattern of coming together, revelling for a few years in intense intimacy, then breaking apart again," Shorter wrote.[42]

Predictions of Another U.S. Baby Boom

Some see a different future for the family. Several demographers have predicted that the nation is on the verge of a new baby boom. University of Michigan demographer Ronald Lee has predicted that fertility will start to rise around 1980, increase steadily through the mid-1980s, and peak in the 1990s with women once again bearing an average of more than three children apiece. Lee and other like-minded demographers base their predictions on a perceived relationship between birth

---

[40] Quoted by Joseph Giordano and Irving M. Levine in "Carter's Family Policy: The Pluralist's Challenge," *Journal of Current Social Issues*, winter 1977, p. 51.
[41] Cited by Marvin Sussman, "An Immodest Proposal," *The National Elementary Principal*, May-June 1976, p. 35.
[42] Shorter, *op. cit.*, p. 13.

The Changing American Family

cohorts—the number of people born in any particular year—and earning power. Demographer Richard Easterlin, professor of economics at the University of Pennsylvania and father of today's most accepted baby boom theory, described the relationship in its application to procreation:

> One of the factors that seem to have been important in the last baby boom was the relative [small] number of young people in the labor market.... These people then had lots of children—the baby boom cohorts—so that in the sixties and seventies there was a relative glut of young people on the market and they've had a somewhat rough time.
>
> They had fewer children than their parents had had, and now some of their children—the first of the post-baby-boom cohorts—will soon be entering the labor market. And when they do, there are going to be relatively few of them and they are going to find themselves relatively well off, and thus the baby trend is going to swing upward again.[43]

Recent statistics give some validity to the new baby boom theory. The latest figures from the National Center for Health Statistics show a slight increase in the general fertility rate, which measures the number of births per 1,000 women of childbearing years. The seasonally adjusted general fertility rate rose to 68.3 during January 1977, the highest it had been since October 1974 when it was 69.8. It was 65.1 in January 1976. Two other measurements of the country's childbearing also increased. The birthrate—which measures the number of births per 1,000 population, including everyone of every age, not just women—and the number of live births both increased about 1 per cent in the 12 months ending in January 1977. Population experts said the statistics gave some indication that women in their late twenties and early thirties may be deciding not to put off childbearing any longer.

If a new baby boom does come, it will not necessarily mean a return to the values of the fifties. Women are unlikely again to turn to motherhood as a full-time occupation. Nor will they continue to assume the full burden of childbearing. Women are unlikely to have more children unless men are willing to assume equal responsibility for their care and society is willing to provide adequate family support systems.

---

[43] Quoted by Linda Wolfe in "The Coming Baby Boom," *New York*, Jan. 10, 1977, p. 40. See also Carl L. Larter's "The 'Good Times' Cohort of the 1930s," *PRB Report*, April 1977. *PRB Report* is published by Population Reference Bureau Inc., Washington, D.C.

Selected Bibliography

Books

Bane, Mary Jo, *Here To Stay: American Families in the Twentieth Century,* Basic Books, 1976.
Kay, F. George, *The Family in Transition,* John Wiley & Sons, 1972.
Kephart, William M., *The Family, Society, and the Individual,* Houghton Mifflin, 1966.
Shorter, Edward, *The Making of the Modern Family,* Basic Books, 1975.
The Women's Movement, Editorial Research Reports, 1973.
Yorburg, Betty, *The Changing Family,* Columbia University Press, 1973.

Articles

Bettelheim, Bruno, "Untying the Family," *The Center Magazine,* September-October 1976.
Bronfenbrenner, Urie, "The Disturbing Changes in the American Family," *Search,* fall 1976.
Hayghe, Howard, "Families and the Rise of Working Wives—An Overview," *Monthly Labor Review,* May 1976.
Journal of Current Social Issues, winter 1977 issue.
Kron, Joan, "The Dual Career Dilemma," *New York,* Oct. 25, 1976.
Mondale, Walter F., "Government Policy, Stress, and the Family," *Journal of Home Economics,* November 1976.
——"The Family in Trouble," *Psychology Today,* May 1977.
Novak, Michael, "The Family Out of Favor," *Harper's,* April 1976.
"The American Family: Can It Survive Today's Shocks," *U.S. News & World Report,* Oct. 27, 1975.
Ware, Ciji, "Is A Baby Worth the Price?" *New West,* April 25, 1977.
Wolfe, Linda, "The Coming Baby Boom," *New York,* Jan. 10, 1977.

Reports and Studies

Editorial Research Reports, "Marriage: Changing Institution," 1971 Vol. II, p. 759; "Single-Parent Families," 1976 Vol. II, p. 661; "Women in the Work Force," 1977 Vol. I, p. 121.
Espenshade, Thomas J., "The Value and Cost of Children," *Population Bulletin,* April 1977.
Glick, Paul C., "Some Recent Changes in American Families," *Current Population Reports,* Special Studies, Series P-23, No. 52, 1975.
Moore, Kristin and Isabel V. Sawhill, "Implications of Women's Employment For Home and Family Life," The Urban Institute, August 1975.
Pifer, Alan, "Women Working: Toward a New Society," *1976 Annual Report of the Carnegie Corporation of New York.*
"Raising Children in a Changing Society, The General Mills American Family Report 1976-77."
U.S. Bureau of the Census, "Fertility History and Prospects of American Women: June 1975," *Current Population Reports,* Series P-20, No. 288, January 1976.
——"Marital Status and Living Arrangements: March 1976," *Current Population Reports,* Series P-20, No. 306, January 1977.

VIOLENCE IN THE FAMILY

by

Sandra Stencel

	page
CONCERN OVER DOMESTIC VIOLENCE	23
Severity of Child, Spouse Abuse Problem	23
Increased Attention From the Government	24
Police Response to Wife-Battering Cases	26
Self-Defense Pleas in Wife-Husband Killings	29
GENERATIONAL THEORY OF VIOLENCE	31
Violence as a Learned Pattern of Behavior	31
Tolerance for Violence in Family Setting	32
Society's Mixed Views of Punishing Kids	33
NEW EFFORTS TO HELP ABUSERS	35
Early Detection of Abuse-Prone Parents	35
Preventing Abuse and Treating Abusers	36
Special Aid Programs for Wife Batterers	37
Therapy Techniques for Troubled Couples	38

**Apr. 27
1979**

VIOLENCE IN THE FAMILY

THE IMAGE of the family as a refuge from the strains and stresses of the outside world is one most Americans hold dear. Our unwillingness to abandon this idealized picture of family life, despite rising divorce rates and other signs of family discord,[1] is perhaps an indication that the American family is here to stay. This optimistic assessment of the future of the family draws general agreement. But there also seems to be a growing recognition that this idyllic concept of family life has contributed to the conspiracy of silence that, until very recently, surrounded the problem of violence in the family.

Evidence of violent confrontations among family members, especially extreme cases of child abuse and neglect, were never completely ignored by law enforcement personnel, social workers, psychologists or the news media. But the tendency was to view these cases as abnormalities, as exceptions to the usual state of affairs. Family violence also was seen as primarily a working-class phenomenon. In recent years, however, it has become increasingly apparent that violence in the family is a much more serious problem than many realized — or were willing to admit. Consider these statistics:

> In 1977, according to the FBI Uniform Crime Reports, nearly 20 percent of all murder victims in the United States were related to the assailants. About half of these intra-family murders were husband-wife killings.[2]

> In any one year, according to one study,[3] approximately 1.8 million wives are beaten by their husbands. Over one-fourth of all American couples engage in at least one violent episode during their relationship.

> Over one million children are abused each year, physically, sexually or through neglect, the Department of Health, Education and Welfare (HEW) reports. About 240,000 children are victims of physical abuse and at least 2,000 of them die of their injuries.[4]

---

[1] See "The Changing American Family," *E.R.R.*, 1977 Vol. I, pp. 413-432.
[2] U.S. Department of Justice, "FBI Uniform Crime Reports: Crime in the United States, 1977," Oct. 18, 1978, p. 9.
[3] See Murray A. Straus, "Wife Beating: How Common and Why?" *Victimology: An International Journal*, November 1977, p. 445.
[4] U.S. Department of Health, Education and Welfare, "New Light on an Old Problem: 9 Questions and Answers on Child Abuse and Neglect," 1978, p. 5.

"The family is both the most loving and supportive of human groups and also by far the most physically violent group or institution except for the police or the military during a war," Professor Murray A. Straus of the University of New Hampshire said at a meeting of the American Psychological Association in Toronto, Aug. 29, 1978. "Violence in the home is a far more serious problem than violence in the streets, in the classrooms, or anywhere else."

Violence within the family does not necessarily have to involve physical abuse. While Professor Straus notes that "the most common of all forms of intra-family violence" is the physical punishment of children *(see p. 317)*, psychologists and sociologists also are beginning to recognize the toll so-called "emotional violence" takes on family members. The most common tactics in emotional warfare are the withholding of sex, love or money. An increasingly popular strategy is the "honesty or openness maneuver, where being brutally frank is often times an excuse for being brutal."[5]

Increased Attention From the Government

In recent years the problem of domestic violence has been receiving more attention. Child abuse and wife battering have been the subject of numerous newspaper and magazine articles, radio and television talk shows and even a few made-for-television movies. Social service agencies, church groups, schools, colleges and other organizations are offering courses, seminars and lectures on various aspects of the problem.

The women's movement has encouraged battered women to speak more openly about their predicament and to demand protection from the police and the courts. Some police departments are beginning to train officers in family crisis intervention. Social workers are being trained better to detect domestic violence when rendering other services. And prosecutors show a new willingness to bring domestic violence cases to trial.

Hearings have been held at the state and local level to measure the prevalence of domestic violence and to consider such remedies as legislation and coordination of social services. In the past decade most states have strengthened their laws to encourage prompt reporting of suspected cases of child battering. In many states, telephone "hot lines" have been set up to assist the public in reporting suspected cases of child abuse and to offer advice to victims of domestic violence *(see p. 321)*. Emergency shelters for battered wives and their dependents are being opened in a growing number of communities.

---

[5] Remarks of Barbara O'Connor, a New York social worker, at a seminar on emotional violence within the family held Nov. 18, 1978, at the New School for Social Research in New York.

Murders in the Family

Year	All reported murders	Spouse killing spouse	Parent killing child	Other relative killings
		(in percentages)		
1969	14,680	13.1	3.7	8.4
1970	15,910	12.1	3.1	8.1
1971	17,680	12.8	3.5	8.4
1972	18,570	12.5	2.9	8.9
1973	19,530	12.3	3.2	7.7
1974	20,600	12.1	2.7	8.0
1975	20,510	11.5	3.0	7.9
1976	18,780	*	*	*
1977	19,120	10.6	3.1	5.3

*In 1976 available figures show that a total of 27.2 percent of all reported murders were by relatives.

Source: FBI Uniform Crime Reports

Growing awareness of the problem also prompted action at the federal level. The Child Abuse Prevention and Treatment Act, passed by Congress on Jan. 31, 1974, authorized $85 million over a three-year period for federal aid to programs for the prevention, identification and treatment of child abuse. At least half of the funds were assigned to demonstration programs and to training programs for professionals involved in child abuse work. The National Center on Child Abuse and Neglect was created by the Child Abuse Prevention and Treatment Act to administer these funds. The National Center, within HEW, also is responsible for studying the incidence of child abuse nationwide and for maintaining a central clearinghouse of information on child abuse and neglect.

In 1977 Congress extended the Child Abuse Prevention and Treatment Act for two years, through fiscal 1979. The reauthorization bill broadened the definition of child abuse under the bill to include "sexual abuse and exploitation." Some $2 million was authorized in fiscal 1978 and again in 1979 for programs and projects designed to prevent, identify and treat sexual abuse of children. In a report issued in August 1978, the National Center on Child Abuse and Neglect estimated that the current annual incidence of sexual abuse of children is between 60,000 and 100,000 cases a year.[6]

Last year the Senate passed but the House voted down separate bills to establish a new federal program for financing spouse-abuse shelters and other community activities intended to prevent family violence and treat its victims. The bills pro-

---
[6] National Center on Child Abuse and Neglect, "Child Sexual Abuse: Incest, Assault, and Sexual Exploitation," August 1978, p. 3.

posed to establish a National Center on Domestic Violence within HEW.[7] Women's groups, pushing for reintroduction of the bills this year, cite the continuing need for additional federal funding for spouse abuse shelters.[8] As late as 1976, only 30 such houses were known to exist. By 1978, over 170 shelters were operating in the United States, according to a survey conducted by the Center for Women Policy Studies in Washington, D.C.[9]

Police Response to Wife-Battering Cases

It is generally agreed that available statistics greatly underestimate the extent of violence within the family. Many cases of child abuse and spouse battering still go unreported, even though every state now requires physicians to report suspected cases of child abuse. In most states the reporting requirements also apply to other medical personnel, including nurses, dentists, interns, coroners and medical examiners. Since 1973, according to the National Center on Child Abuse and Neglect, many states have broadened their reporting requirements to cover non-medical professionals, including teachers and law-enforcement and child-care personnel.[10]

States and localities have been slower to respond to the problem of spouse abuse. Police authorities often are reluctant to get involved in such cases since wife beating traditionally has been thought of not as a crime, but as a private marital squabble. Police indifference is thought to have contributed to the reluctance of many battered wives to even call the police. The FBI has said that wife battering may be the most underreported crime in the nation.

Police intervention in domestic violence can be dangerous. About 20 percent of the deaths and 40 percent of injuries suffered by the police occur when officers seek to intervene in such cases. But the primary reason police are reluctant to get involved in domestic fights, according to James Bannon, executive deputy chief of the Detroit Police Department, "is because we

---

[7] The Senate bill was introduced by Alan Cranston, D-Calif.; the House version was sponsored by Reps. George Miller, D-Calif., Lindy Boggs, D-La., Newton Steers, R-Md., and Barbara Mikulski, D-Md. See *CQ Weekly Report* of May 27, 1978, p. 1335, and Sept. 16, 1978, p. 2485.

[8] Some federal funding for shelters is provided under Title XX of the Social Security Act. Title XX, which took effect Oct. 1, 1975, authorized federal payments to the states for provision of social services directed at the goals of (1) economic self-support, (2) personal self-sufficiency, (3) prevention or correction of neglect of children or adults and preservation of families, (4) prevention of inappropriate institutional care through community-based care programs and (5) provision of institutional care where appropriate.

[9] Center for Women Policy Studies, "Programs Providing Services to Battered Women," April 1978. The Center for Women Policy Studies received two grants from the Law Enforcement Assistance Administration (LEAA) to develop a clearinghouse and a newsletter to gather and share information on domestic violence, child sexual abuse and rape. The center recently received another LEAA grant to provide assistance to LEAA-funded Family Violence Programs in 17 communities across the nation.

[10] National Center on Child Abuse and Neglect, "Child Abuse and Neglect: State Reporting Laws," May 1978, pp. 7-8. See also "Child Abuse," *E.R.R.*, 1976 Vol. I, pp. 65-84.

> ### Battered Husbands
>
> "The most unreported crime is not wife beating — it's husband beating," according to University of Delaware sociologist Suzanne Steinmetz. "Unless a man is battered to the degree where he requires medical attention, he is not going to report it." Extrapolating from her studies of domestic quarreling in New Castle County, Del., Steinmetz has estimated that each year at least 250,000 American husbands are severely thrashed by their wives.
>
> "Most battered men are too ashamed to admit they've been beaten by their wives," Roger Langley and Richard C. Levy noted in their book *Wife Beating: The Silent Crisis* (1977). "The humiliation a battered woman suffers is multiplied enormously for a man who must stand before a police sergeant and file a complaint. Not many men have the courage to face the snickers, innuendos, and open sarcasm inherent in this situation."
>
> Langley and Levy also observed that there are few places a battered man can go for help. "When he does reach out," they wrote, "or if circumstances propel the family problem into the public arena, a man can find his life bewildering and frustrating. He can conclude as easily as does the battered wife that the police, the courts, the clergy, and the social-service agencies are all stacked against him."

do not know how to cope with them."[11] To overcome this problem, a growing number of police departments are forming specially trained units. In Atlanta, for example, police are taught through role-playing to defuse family fights by projecting a calm, mediating manner rather than the aggressive posture of an arresting officer.

A training guide on wife beating published by the International Association of Chiefs of Police in 1976 reflected changing police attitudes toward domestic violence. It urged police to distinguish between situations where there is a threat of violence, and where mediation might be effective, and situations where violence already has occurred. "Where an attack has already taken place," it stated, "the police officer must be prepared to conduct an assault investigation. . . . 'Family disturbances' and 'wife beatings' should not be viewed synonymously; nor should wife abuse be considered a victimless crime or solely a manifestation of a poor marriage. A wife beating is foremost an assault — a crime that must be investigated."

Several states have modified their laws to make it easier to arrest wife batterers. An Oregon law that took effect in October 1977 states that a police officer called to a domestic disturbance must take the assailant into custody when the officer has reasonable cause to believe an assault has occurred or a person

---

[11] Quoted by Joan Potter in "Police and the Battered Wife: The Search for Understanding," *Police Magazine*, September 1978, p. 41.

has been placed in fear of injury. A similar law went into effect in Minnesota in April 1978. Until that time Minnesota police could make an arrest for a misdemeanor assault only if the assault was committed in their presence. Under the new law an officer can make an arrest for a domestic assault he did not witness if he has probable cause to believe it happened within the preceding four hours or if there is visible injury to the victim.

Many changes in police attitudes and in domestic violence laws are attributed to a class-action suit filed in December 1976 against the New York City Police Department. The suit was filed on behalf of 71 wives who accused the police of denying them assistance after they reported being assaulted by their husbands. In June 1978 the police department agreed in an out-of-court settlement to arrest wife beaters when there was reasonable cause to believe the men had committed the crime. New York City Counsel Allan G. Schwartz said the new stipulation did not change existing law but "recognizes that, in practice in the past, married women in assault cases have been treated differently from unmarried women."[12]

The out-of-court settlement stipulated that the police department would send one or more officers in response to every call from a woman who said that her husband had assaulted her or was threatening her with assault. The police also agreed to inform a battered wife of her rights; to protect the wife or aid her in getting medical help if she needs it; and to try to locate the assailant if he had left the scene.

One reason police have been reluctant to respond to wife battering cases is that many women are reluctant to prosecute their husbands. Only about 2 percent of the accused males are ever prosecuted. Many feminists argue that this is because prosecutors make it very difficult to press charges. "Prosecutors impose extraordinary conditions on a woman complaining of assaults or harassment by her husband or former husband," wrote Marjory D. Fields, a lawyer with the Brooklyn Legal Services Corporation. "After she passes these tests of her intent to prosecute, pleas to minor infractions are accepted and suspended sentences . . . recommended to the court. Judges impose light or suspended sentences even without the prosecutor's suggestion. Thus, the injured wife who persists does not receive the protection of having her assaultive husband jailed."[13]

According to Fields, "prompt and certain punishment" is the only answer to wife abuse. Others believe that traditional prosecution is not always appropriate. Charles Benjamin Schudson, an assistant district attorney in Milwaukee, Wis., said: "Crimi-

---

[12] Quoted in *The New York Times,* June 27, 1978.
[13] Marjory D. Fields, "Representing Battered Wives, or What To Do Until the Police Arrive," *The Family Law Reporter,* April 5, 1977.

Violence in the Family

nal prosecution is an act of desperation. It's something done when all else has failed. Sometimes it is necessary, sometimes it must be done. But what I'm saying is that ... criminal prosecution does not solve the problem."[14]

Self-Defense Pleas in Wife-Husband Killings

Frustrated by the criminal justice system, some battered wives have taken the law into their own hands — and many of them have gotten away with it, as a number of press reports indicate:

> Marlene Roan Eagle, a pregnant American Indian in South Dakota, stabbed her husband through the heart after he came at her with a broken broomstick. It was established that he had beaten her on several occasions and, in July 1977, she was acquitted of murder on the ground that she acted in self-defense.
>
> Sharon McNearney was found innocent of murdering her husband in November 1977. The Marquette, Mich., housewife fired a shotgun at him as he walked through the front door. Police described her as a battered wife who had long been abused. Marquette County Circuit Court Judge John E. McDonald said the prosecution failed to prove she had not acted in self-defense.
>
> The same month Evelyn Ware was found not guilty of murdering her husband after pleading self-defense in Superior Court in Orange County, Calif. She shot her husband five times. Evidence of past beatings was used as part of her defense.
>
> In the spring of 1977 a jury in Bellingham, Wash., acquitted Janice Hornbuckle of first-degree murder. One night, after her husband beat her and threatened her at knife-point, she grabbed a shotgun from her teenage son and shot her husband. She had sought police protection on several occasions.
>
> In Chicago, Juan Malonado was shot and killed by his wife, Gloria, after he beat his eight-year-old son with a shoe. The State's Attorney's office ruled there was "insufficient evidence" to warrant her prosecution.
>
> In a well-publicized case in Lansing, Mich., Francine Hughes claimed that years of physical abuse drove her to pour gasoline around her sleeping husband and light it. A jury acquitted her of murder on the ground of temporary insanity.

These and other similar cases have attracted national attention and generated considerable controversy. Indeed, it has been suggested that the acquittals could result in an "open season on men."[15] Despite the controversy, lawyers increasingly are using

---
[14] Interview on "The MacNeil/Lehrer Report," Public Broadcasting System, Oct. 19, 1978.

[15] See "Thirteen Ways to Leave Your Lover," *New Times*, Feb. 6, 1978, p. 6. See also "A Killing Excuse," *Time*, Nov. 28, 1977, p. 108; "The Right to Kill," *Newsweek*, Sept. 1, 1975, p. 69; "Wives Who Batter Back," *Newsweek*, Jan. 30, 1978, p. 54; and "Wives Accused of Slayings Turning to Self-Defense Pleas," *The Washington Post*, Dec. 4, 1977.

> ### Marital Rape
>
> One aspect of spouse abuse that until recently received very little attention is marital rape. That was before the celebrated Rideout case in Oregon. Last October, Greta Rideout, then 23, charged her husband John with rape. Filing such a charge would have been unthinkable and, in fact, impossible until the Oregon legislature changed the state's rape law in 1977 to remove marriage or cohabitation as a defense.
>
> John Rideout was acquitted of the rape charge in January. But that did not end the debate on marital rape. Besides Oregon, at least three other states — New Jersey, Delaware and Iowa — have revised their rape laws to allow women to charge their husbands with sexual assault. Several other states, including California, are considering similar legal changes.
>
> The Rideouts, when last heard from, were granted a divorce after a brief reconciliation.

the self-defense plea in wife-husband murders. Two lawyers associated with the Center for Constitutional Rights in New York last year published a report intended to help attorneys representing women who commit homicide after they or their children have been physically or sexually assaulted.[16] "Ten years ago women didn't talk about being raped," said one of the lawyers, Elizabeth M. Schneider. "Ten years ago women didn't talk about being battered. If they fought back, society and they themselves thought they were wrong to do it; they pleaded guilty and they went to jail. The climate of the times now is that more battered women are ready to say, 'It's either him or me at this moment and I choose me.' You can't really assert self-defense until you feel you have a self to defend; that's what women finally are developing."[17]

In many states, to prove self-defense the defendant has to show a reasonable apprehension of imminent danger of great bodily harm. Lawyers have effectively used evidence of past beatings and threats to show reasonable apprehension, even in cases where the husband's actions at the moment of the killing are inconclusive or negligible. Lawyers also have successfully argued that it is not an unreasonable response for a physically outmatched wife to resort to a lethal weapon such as a gun or a knife if a husband comes at her with his fists.

Acceptance of self-defense pleas is not universal. In Birmingham, Ala., Hazel Kontos was convicted and sentenced to life in prison in December 1977 for shooting her husband despite her contention that he had slapped her around and once held

---

[16] Elizabeth M. Schneider and Susan B. Jordan, "Representation of Women Who Defend Themselves In Response to Physical or Sexual Assault," Center for Constitutional Rights, 1978.
[17] Quoted in *The New York Times*, March 10, 1978.

her at gunpoint. In Waupaca, Wis., Jennifer Patri, a Sunday school teacher and PTA president, was convicted and sentenced to 10 years in prison for the shooting death of her auto-repairman husband. Patri had pleaded self-defense. Her lawyer argued that her husband beat and sexually abused her and that he also molested their 12-year-old daughter. Like many battered women, Patri said she had never called the police for help because of feelings of shame.

Generational Theory of Violence

WHAT MAKES someone physically abuse their children or their spouse? No one knows for sure, but recent studies seem to confirm the long-held belief that children who witness violent acts between their parents or who are victims of parental violence themselves often grow up to become the wife abusers and child abusers of their generation. "Family violence is usually a learned pattern of behavior," according to psychologist B.L. Daley. "Often the behavior is modeled on the father or other adult male figures. The mother also contributes by accepting this behavior."[18]

A 1975 British study of 100 abusive husbands indicated that over half of them had witnessed their fathers battering their mothers.[19] A 1975 study by John D. Flynn of Western Michigan University on spouse abuse in the area around Kalamazoo, Mich., indicated that two-fifths of the wife beaters studied had been abused as children.[20] A study by D.G. Gil, author of *Violence Against Children: Physical Child Abuse in the United States* (1970), found that 14 percent of the abusive mothers studied and 7 percent of the abusive fathers had been abused as children.

"The chances of a battered child becoming a battering adult are very, very strong," said sociologist Suzanne K. Steinmetz. "I found that there were patterns that extended over three generations. So that if you had a grandmother and a grandfather who perhaps screamed and yelled at each other and maybe occasionally slapped each other, they tended to use those methods on their children, and their children tended to use those methods

---

[18] Quoted by Roger Langley and Richard C. Levy in *Wife Beating: The Silent Crisis* (1977), p. 50.
[19] J.J. Gayford, "Wife Battering: A Preliminary Survey of 100 Cases," *British Medical Journal*, Jan. 25, 1977, pp. 194-197.
[20] John D. Flynn, "Spouse Assault: Its Dimension and Characteristics in Kalamazoo County, Michigan," Unpublished field studies in research and practice. School of Social Work, Western Michigan University, 1975.

on their brothers and sisters. And then when these children married, they tended to use the same methods on their husbands and wives and similarly on their children, and of course their children repeated it. So for three generations I found very consistent patterns on the way they resolved conflict ... the monkey see, monkey do idea."[21]

According to psychologist Lenore E. Walker, author of *The Battered Woman* (1979), children who live in homes where spouse abuse is a problem "experience the most insidious form of child abuse."

> Whether or not they are physically abused by either parent [she wrote] is less important than the psychological scars they bear from watching their fathers beat their mothers. They learn to become part of a dishonest conspiracy of silence.... Like many children who suffer from overt physical abuse, these children learn to be accommodating and cooperative. They blend into the background. They do not express anger. They do not acknowledge tension. They do expend a lot of energy avoiding problems. They live in a world of make-believe. When the screaming and yelling begin they stare transfixed but inconspicuous, watching in terror.[22]

Tolerance for Violence in Family Setting

According to Murray Straus, the norms within the family are far more accepting of physical violence than are the rules governing behavior outside the family. Straus observed that most parents are much more tolerant of physical fights among their children than they would be if their children got into a fight with someone else's child. A recent study by Straus and others found that the same children are far more violent to their own siblings than they are to other children. For example, 62 percent of the high school seniors they interviewed had hit a brother or sister during the preceding year, but "only" 35 percent had hit someone outside the family during the same year.[23]

Violence generally is tolerated in the family setting when it is labeled as discipline or punishment. "In general," Straus told the American Psychological Association last year, "the rule in the family is that if someone is doing wrong and 'won't listen to reason,' it is OK to hit. In the case of children, it is more than just OK. Most American parents see it as an obligation." A poll taken for the National Commission on the Causes and Prevention of Violence in 1969 found that the overwhelming majority of Americans (93 percent) approved of a parental spanking. About

---

[21] Quoted by Langley and Levy, *op. cit.*, p. 51.
[22] Lenore E. Walker, *The Battered Woman* (1979), pp. 149-150.
[23] Results to be included in a forthcoming book, *Violence in the American Family* by Murray Straus, Suzanne Steinmetz and Richard Gelles.

Disciplinary Measures Used by Parents

Yelled at or scolded the children	52%
Spanked them	50
Made them stay in their rooms	38
Didn't allow them to go out to play	32
Didn't let them watch television	25
Made them go to bed	23
Threatened them	15
Gave them extra chores	12
Took away their allowances	9

Source: "The General Mills American Family Report 1976-77"

20 percent of those interviewed approved of a husband slapping his wife's face in certain circumstances.[24]

After yelling and scolding, spanking still is the principal form of punishment in most families with children under 13 years of age, according to a survey conducted by Yankelovich, Skelly and White, the national market research and public opinion organization.[25] Half of the parents interviewed said they recently had spanked their children. The study found that younger parents (60 percent) were more likely to spank their children than were parents over age 35 (37 percent). Spanking also was slightly more common in families with incomes under $12,000 a year (56 percent).

Society's Mixed Views of Punishing Kids

Most parents are quick to defend their right to raise their children as they see fit. The idea of parental rights has been culturally ingrained in society from the beginning and it includes the widely accepted notion that children are taught acceptable behavior through punishment — including physical punishment. But many psychologists and sociologists have warned that parents who use physical punishment run the risk of teaching their children that the only way to cope with stress is through the use of violence. "Violence begets violence, however peaceful and altruistic the motivation," said a 1974 study.[26]

Another study found that adults who were hit frequently as children were more likely to be violent with their mates than people who were never hit as children. "Not only does the family expose individuals to violence and techniques of violence," it said, "the family teaches approval for the use of violence."[27]

---

[24] See "Violence and the Media: A Staff Report to the National Commission on the Causes and Prevention of Violence," November 1969, p. 343. The National Commission on the Causes and Prevention of Violence was set up by President Johnson in 1968 after the assassinations of Sen. Robert F. Kennedy, D-N.Y., and Dr. Martin Luther King Jr.

[25] "Raising Children in a Changing Society, The General Mills American Family Report 1976-1977," p. 104.

[26] Suzanne K. Steinmetz and Murray A. Straus, eds., *Violence in the Family* (1974), p. 3.

[27] Richard Gelles, *The Violent Home* (1972), p. 171.

Seven years later, Lenore E. Walker wrote: "When we correct our children by hitting them, we teach them that it is possible to love someone and physically hurt the person at the same time, all in the name of discipline. We need to find ways of disciplining our children that do not include transmitting this message to them."[28]

The results of one of the most recent studies on the effects of physical punishment on children were published in the February 1979 issue of *Human Behavior* magazine. Sociologist Brian G. Gilmartin reported that "children who are frequently spanked tend to become highly resentful and distrustful of authority. Indeed, sometimes their often blind feelings of extreme hostility for, and distrust of, any and all authority figures reach the point of being dangerous to both themselves and others." He went on to say that "children who are often spanked tend to be conspicuously quieter, less articulate and more sullen than those who grow up under milder, more democratic forms of discipline. In addition, harshly disciplined offspring tend to display a large amount of negativity in their approach to people and to life."[29]

Evidence of a link between physical punishment and later tendencies toward violence so impressed Swedish legislators that they recently voted to outlaw spanking.[30] The new law is meant to be primarily "educational." The statute carries no penalties for spanking, but it is hoped that it will encourage children and concerned neighbors to file complaints with police or social workers. A similar ban is not likely to be enacted soon in the United States. In April 1977, for example, the U.S. Supreme Court voted 5 to 4 in favor of continuing to permit the use of corporal punishment in public schools *(Ingraham v. Wright).*

The majority held that the Eighth Amendment ban on cruel and unusual punishment "was designed to protect those convicted of crimes ... [and] does not apply to the paddling of children as a means of maintaining discipline in public schools." Commenting on the Supreme Court's decision, Gilmartin wrote: "Banning the use of physical punishment in the schools is not going to end its use in the home. But public schools can and should be expected to set a positive example for parents to follow."

---

[28] Walker, *op. cit.*, p. 252.
[29] Brian G. Gilmartin, "The Case Against Spanking," *Human Behavior,* February 1979, p. 18.
[30] See *Newsweek,* April 16, 1979, p. 63.

New Efforts to Help Abusers

BREAKING the chain of violence from one generation to the next will have to involve efforts to help abusers as well as the victims of family violence. At the National Center for the Prevention of Child Abuse and Neglect in Denver, Colo., professionals directed by Dr. C. Henry Kempe[31] teach lay therapists to work in the home with abusive parents. The therapists try to help the parents become aware of their tendency to react to crises with violence. The center also operates a therapeutic day-care center for abused children, a residential treatment program for parents and children who are undergoing therapy, and a "crisis nursery" open 24 hours a day where parents can leave their children when things get tense at home.

Dr. Kempe and his colleagues have developed a screening method that may help predict which parents will abuse their children. The profile of abuse-prone parents emerged during a four-year study of 150 couples at Colorado General Hospital in Denver. Each mother was observed during labor, delivery and the post-partum period for clues that might determine how she would treat her baby. Among the things researchers were looking for was whether the mother was depressed, not affectionate with the infant, bothered by its cries, disappointed with its sex, quick to make disparaging remarks about its physical characteristics. The researchers also observed each husband, looking to see whether he was supportive and how he reacted during the delivery process.

After interviews and further observation, the mothers were divided into high- and low-risk groups. Half of the high-risk mothers were provided with intensive post-natal help and therapy; the rest received routine care. When the children were a little over two years old, 25 families in each of the three groups were randomly chosen for evaluation. The researchers found that five children in the high-risk/ordinary-care group had required hospitalization for serious injuries that were thought to have involved parental mistreatment. No such injuries were found among the children of the high-risk group that received special help or among the children of the low-risk parents.

Kempe and his colleagues insist that their study has not produced any "magic formula" for detecting parents who might be likely to harm or neglect their children. But they believe the clues they have gathered will make it easier for observant hospital personnel to spot warning signals early and try to help the

---

[31] In a paper presented to the American Academy of Pediatricians in 1961, Dr. Kempe coined the phrase "the battered child syndrome" and described the symptoms of the abnormality.

Editorial Research Reports   *April 27, 1979*

new parents adjust to their new responsibility. "Families identified early as being in need of extra parent-preparedness services must have access to intensive, continuous intervention," said one of the researchers, Dr. Jane Gray. "It makes little sense to provide excellent prenatal, obstetric and neonatal care only to abandon the most needy young families at the hospital door and leave the child rearing to chance."[32]

The National Center on Child Abuse and Neglect has observed that "even if it is possible to identify successfully a high-risk group of parents, the next step, intervention, is by no means easy. Ethical and legal problems involving the rights of parents to privacy versus the rights of children, and the states' right to intervene if parents object, are not easily solved. There is an additional concern about labeling these parents 'potential abusers' and the possibility that this can become a self-fulfilling prophecy."[33]

Preventing Abuse and Treating Abusers

Many people think the best cure for child abuse is a dose of prevention in the form of training for parents. "It's ironic that the most important job many of us will ever do is one for which most of us receive absolutely no training," Kitty Ward of the Massachusetts Society for the Prevention of Cruelty to Children said in 1977.[34] Studies have found that abusive parents often lack specific knowledge of what children do at various stages of their development and therefore have unrealistic expectations for their children. When the children fail to meet these expectations, the parents often erupt in violence.

Many experts think child care should become a required part of the curriculum in high schools. Education for Parenthood, a program sponsored by the Department of Health, Education and Welfare, attempts to teach students the "joys and responsibilities" of being a parent. The course currently is being given to approximately 121,000 high school students across the country.

One of the most successful treatment methods for abusive parents was started in 1970 by a California mother who prefers to be known as Jolly K. She is a former abusive parent who in one instance threw a kitchen knife at her six-year-old daughter and in another tried to strangle her. When Jolly could find no agency providing the kind of help she wanted, she founded her own and called it Mothers Anonymous. Known today as Parents

---

[32] Quoted in *Human Behavior*, May 1978, p. 67. See also Jane Gray et al., "Perinatal Assessment of Mother-Baby Interaction," in *Child Abuse and Neglect: The Family and the Community* (1976) edited by R.E. Helfer and C. Henry Kempe.

[33] National Center on Child Abuse and Neglect: "1977 Analysis of Child Abuse and Neglect Research," January 1978, p. 22.

[34] Quoted in *Newsweek*, Oct. 10, 1977, p. 115.

Violence in the Family

Anonymous, the organization claims to have over 500 chapters in the United States and Canada. Patterned after Alcoholics Anonymous, the group gives parents an opportunity to meet each other and share their problems. "Child abusers are going through hell," Jolly K. said in an interview in 1975. "We have a vision of how powerful our anger can be, a concept of where this anger will take us if we are pushed too far, and the constant dread that we will be pushed that far."[35]

Besides giving psychological support to each other at meetings, members of Parents Anonymous also contact one another by telephone when a crisis develops at home. Emergency "hot lines" are sponsored by many groups interested in helping abusive parents. A survey conducted by the National Center on Child Abuse and Neglect in 1978 found child abuse hot lines in at least 52 communities across the country.[36] According to the center, hot lines "provide isolated parents with a sympathetic, concerned individual who will listen as the caller airs frustrations, vents anger (which might otherwise have been directed at the children), or simply expresses feelings which cannot be confided to friends or relatives."

Besides the emergency hot lines serving the needs of anxiety-ridden parents, there also are a growing number of telephone lines set up to encourage neighbors, relatives, social workers and others to report suspected cases of child abuse. The National Center on Child Abuse and Neglect reports that at least 10 states — Arkansas, Colorado, Iowa, Mississippi, Missouri, New Jersey, New York, Pennsylvania, Virginia and West Virginia — have established these child abuse reporting lines through legislation. Hot line services also are being made available to spouse abusers, according to a recent survey by the Center for Women Policy Studies.[37]

Special Aid Programs for Wife Batterers

A 24-hour-a-day hot line is run by the Victims Information Bureau of Suffolk Inc. (VIBS) in Hauppauge, N.Y. "The majority of women coming to VIBS want to remain in their marriages, but without the violence," said Executive Director James Walsh. "We believe that battering will not stop unless both partners are involved in counseling. The emphasis ... is on restructuring relationships...."

In its survey, the Center for Women Policy Studies found

---

[35] Quoted by Judith Reed in "Working with Abusive Parents; A Parent's View," *Children Today*, May-June 1975, p. 6.

[36] National Center on Child Abuse and Neglect, "Child Abuse and Neglect Helplines," August 1978.

[37] See the October 1978 issue of *Response*, a newsletter published by the Center for Women Policy Studies.

several programs that work exclusively with abusive men. One is EMERGE in Somerville, Mass. It grew out of the concern of women working in local shelters who saw the need for such a service. The program emphasizes that "it is important for men to begin to talk about battering — why it starts, what leads to it, how it affects individuals and relationships, and what can be done to stop it." To encourage this, EMERGE provides "a safe environment for men to explore the roots of their violence and to learn ways to change their behavior."

Another program concerned directly with the abuser is Therapy for Abusive Behavior (TAB) in Baltimore, Md. The program is run by three women volunteers with the assistance and cooperation of the Southern Baltimore Police District commander and one of his community relations officers. It was started to give abusers the "opportunity for self-help in the areas of personal growth and development by actively participating in a program designed to identify and change violent behavior patterns." TAB teaches men more effective techniques for handling situations and relationships, while it provides a supportive network for the men during and after the program.

According to the Center for Women Policy Studies, the TAB program "is unique in that it intervenes to help the abuser at the initial stages of his contact with the courts.... Instead of allowing the litigation to continue, a judge may place the abuser in the TAB program, under the condition that he attend the program regularly or else re-enter the judicial system."

Minneapolis, Minn., has several programs to help spouse abusers. These include the Citizens' Dispute Settlement Project, the Walk-in Counseling Center, the Twin Cities Men's Center and men's groups within the state's Family and Children's Services department. Other efforts to help spouse abusers have been established in Seattle, Wash., Portland, Ore., and Pittsburgh, Pa. The relatively small number of programs operating to help abusive husbands is perhaps an indication of the reluctance of many men to seek help. "It must be understood that the husband is caught by the same societal values as his wife," explained James Walsh of the VIBS program. "He has been taught that men are not supposed to express feelings and that he must handle his own problems and not ask for help."

Therapy Techniques for Troubled Couples

If the husband is willing to undergo treatment or counseling, successful changes in his behavior can be accomplished in up to 80 percent of the cases, according to Sanford Sherman, executive director of Jewish Family Services in New York.[38] Sherman

[38] Quoted in Langley and Levy, *op. cit.*, p. 201.

Violence in the Family

recommends having the husband and wife visit the therapist together. "It's important for both partners to understand that [the husband is] afraid. He fears loss of status, loss of life, and paradoxically, loss of his wife. The fear is intolerable to him. He must choose either fight or flight. With a vulnerable woman present, the tendency is to fight." Sherman said the man must be taught non-violent ways of behaving when he is enraged, to get him to translate his anger into words or to take it out on objects rather than people.

The assumption that most men will stop their abusive behavior if they participate in therapy is not universally accepted. Among those who disagree is Lenore E. Walker. "Very few traditional techniques of couples therapy apply to battering couples," she wrote. "Many of these methods include teaching couples how to fight fairer and better.... Battering couples do not need to learn new fighting behavior. Rather, they need to learn to control their anger."[39]

Another problem with traditional couples therapy, Walker said, is that its primary goal is to make the relationship better. "With battering couples, the survival of the relationship [should be] secondary. The goal is to strengthen each individual to be able to build a new, healthier relationship. Success is achieved if the individuals are strengthened, even if the relationship itself is not able to survive." Walker and her late husband, Dr. Morton Flax, a psychologist, developed a technique which, she said, "has been successful in limiting the severity of battering incidents, although it has not yet eliminated battering incidents completely." Most couples in a battering relationship have extremely poor communications skills. "Their verbal and nonverbal communication is fraught with distortion and misinterpretation...," Walker said. "We begin by teaching the couple a signal to use with each other when either one begins to feel tension rising.... Often it takes a lot of work to teach the couples to recognize their own cues. Once they learn to feel their tension at minimum levels, we can begin to prevent the tension build-up that causes an acute battering incident."

Dr. Walker admitted that this type of therapy is "time-consuming, expensive and exhausting for both the couple and the therapists." And while it may help the two parties involved, therapy does little to address the broader problem of violence in the family. Both spouse abuse and child abuse are symptomatic of deep, underlying stress within the family. Until the dynamics of the problem are better understood, more support systems must be provided the growing number of victims of domestic violence.

---

[39] Walker, *op. cit.*, p. 245.

Selected Bibliography

Books

Gelles, Richard J., *The Violent Home: A Study of Physical Aggression Between Husbands and Wives,* Sage Publications, 1972.

Langley, Roger and Richard C. Levy, *Wife Beating: The Silent Crisis,* E.P. Dutton, 1977.

Martin, Del, *Battered Wives,* Glide Publications, 1976.

Pizzey, Erin, *Scream Quietly or the Neighbors Will Hear,* Anchor Press, 1974.

Steinmetz, Suzanne K. and Murray A. Straus, eds., *Violence in the Family,* Harper & Row, 1974.

Walker, Lenore E., *The Battered Woman,* Harper & Row, 1979.

Walters, David R., *Physical and Sexual Abuse of Children: Causes and Treatment,* Indiana University Press, 1975.

Articles

"Authorities Face Up to the Child Abuse Problem," *U.S. News & World Report,* May 3, 1976.

Eisenberg, Susan and Patricia Micklow, "The Assaulted Wife: 'Catch 22' Revisited," *Women's Rights Law Reporter,* spring-summer 1977.

Fields, Marjory D., "Wife Beating: the Hidden Offense," *New York Law Journal,* April 29, 1976.

Franke, Linda Bird, "Battered Women," *Newsweek,* Feb. 2, 1976.

Gelles, Richard J., "Abused Wives: Why Do They Stay," *Journal of Marriage and the Family,* November 1976.

Gingold, Judith, "One of these days — Pow — right in the kisser," *Ms.,* August 1976.

Jacobson, Beverly, "Battered Women," *Civil Rights Digest,* summer 1977.

Potter, Joan, "Police and the Battered Wife: The Search for Understanding," *Police Magazine,* September 1978.

Shiels, Merrill, "The Battered Children," *Newsweek,* Oct. 10, 1977.

Straus, Murray A., "Wife Beating: How Common and Why?" *Victimology,* November 1977.

"The Battered Husbands," *Time,* March 20, 1978.

Reports and Studies

"Battered Women: Issues of Public Policy," A Consultation Sponsored by the U.S. Commission on Civil Rights, Washington, D.C., Jan. 30-31, 1978.

Editorial Research Reports: "Child Abuse," 1976 Vol. I, pp. 65-84; "The Changing American Family," 1977 Vol. I, pp. 413-432.

National Center on Child Abuse and Neglect, "1977 Analysis of Child Abuse and Neglect Research," January 1978.

Schneider, Elizabeth M. and Susan B. Jordan, "Representation of Women Who Defend Themselves In Response to Physical or Sexual Assault," Center for Constitutional Rights, 1978.

Straus, Murray A., Suzanne K. Steinmetz and Richard J. Gelles, "Violence in the Family: An Assessment of Knowledge and Needs," paper presented to the American Association for the Advancement of Science, Feb. 23, 1976.

TEENAGE PREGNANCY

by

Sandra Stencel

	page
EPIDEMIC OF TEENAGE PREGNANCY	43
Concern for Welfare of Pregnant Teens	43
Grim Prospects Faced by Young Mothers	44
Administration's Response to the Problem	46
Criticisms of Family Planning Strategies	48
SOCIAL AND PUBLIC POLICY FACTORS	49
Early Puberty Among Adolescents Today	49
Young Parenthood as a Social Problem	50
Federal Intervention in Family Planning	51
Increased Sexual Activity Among Teens	53
Teenage Attitudes Toward Birth Control	54
SEX EDUCATION FOR ADOLESCENTS	56
Drawbacks of Classroom Sex Education	56
Promoting Contraception Through Radio	57
Laws Affecting Access to Birth Control	57
Criticism of a Contraceptive Orientation	58

**Mar. 23
1 9 7 9**

TEENAGE PREGNANCY

THE BIRTH of a child usually is an occasion of great joy. But for thousands of teenagers, especially those who are unmarried, childbirth can usher in a dismal future of unemployment, poverty, welfare dependency, emotional stress and health problems for mother and child. "The girl who has an illegitimate child at the age of 16 suddenly has 90 percent of her life's script written for her," population expert Arthur A. Campbell has written. "Her choices are few and most of them are bad."[1]

President Carter's proposed budget for fiscal year 1980, sent to Congress Jan. 22, included a $60 million request for a new program to provide medical and other supportive services to pregnant teenagers, adolescent parents and their babies *(see p. 46)*. The fact that Carter requested funding for the teenage pregnancy program, at a time when he is calling for restraint in spending for most social-welfare programs, reflects his deep concern for what the Secretary of Health, Education and Welfare, Joseph A. Califano Jr., has called "one of the most serious and complex social problems facing our nation today."[2] Carter and Califano's concern is shared by most family planning and child welfare organizations, even those that have reservations about the administration's approach to the problem.

Each year about one million teenagers become pregnant; about 600,000 actually give birth. Nearly a quarter-million of these births are to girls between the ages of 15 and 17, while over 12,000 are to girls under the age of 15. With birth rates declining for women over 20, teenagers now account for nearly one in every five births in the country.

Thousands of adolescent pregnancies are terminated by abortion. About one-third of all legal abortions performed in the United States involve teenagers. The pregnant adolescent who does not opt for abortion is far less inclined than her counterpart of a generation ago to get married, and she is far more likely to keep her baby. Nearly two in five (39 percent) of all births to adolescents are out of wedlock. In 1975, the latest year for which such statistics are available, one in five babies born to white teenagers and three in four babies born to black teenagers were illegitimate.

---

[1] Arthur A. Campbell, "The Role of Family Planning in the Reduction of Poverty," *Journal of Marriage and the Family*, Vol. 30, 1968, p. 236.
[2] "HEW News," April 13, 1978.

Editorial Research Reports   *Mar. 23, 1979*

According to Zero Population Growth Inc., 87 percent of all teenagers who give birth out of wedlock keep the child; 5 percent send the baby to live with others; only 8 percent give the baby up for adoption.[3] "The pressure now, at least from their peers, is to prove that they're responsible adults by raising the child themselves, whether they are capable or not," explained Denese A. Shipp, director of prenatal programs at the Johns Hopkins Center for School-Age Mothers in Baltimore, Md.[4]

Grim Prospects Faced by Young Mothers

Why in this age of The Pill has there been such a sharp rise in teenage pregnancies? Family planning experts point to two primary factors: (1) increased sexual activity among young people *(see p. 53)* and (2) non-use or improper use of contraceptives *(see p. 54)*. Some girls get pregnant because they want to have a baby. It is surmised that these girls believe a baby will bring them the love and affection their parents have failed to provide. Such hopes usually are unfulfilled.

Janet Forbush, director of the National Alliance of Concerned School-Age Parents, asserts that most unwed teenage mothers "have the baby and then ... whammy." The "whammy" turns out to be 2 a.m. feedings instead of Saturday night dates. It may mean dropping out of school to pay the pediatrician's bills. It also may mean conflict between the girl and her parents if she continues to live at home.

It is the babies who most often bear the brunt of these frustrations. According to one expert on the problem of child abuse, Dr. Vincent J. Fontana, medical director of the New York Foundling Hospital, "Troubled parents, particularly single adolescent mothers, become saturated with a sense of desperation, alienation and anger that during stressful situations leads them to lose control and strike out at what is closest to them — their child."[5]

For some girls the problems start even before the baby is born. Pregnant teenagers face far greater health risks than women in their twenties. The most common complications are toxemia, iron-deficiency anemia, bleeding in the late stages of pregnancy and prolonged labor. Some of these problems are due to physical immaturity, others to the fact that many young girls do not seek or receive prenatal care, including special attention to nutritional needs.

Children born to teenage mothers also face health risks. They are two to three times more likely to die in their first year than

---

[3] Zero Population Growth Inc., "Teenage Pregnancy: A Major Problem for Minors," August 1977. Zero Population Growth is a national membership organization which advocates world population stabilization.
[4] Quoted in *U.S. News & World Report*, June 26, 1978, p. 60.
[5] Quoted in "The Teenage Pregnancy Epidemic," *McCall's*, July 1978, p. 48.

Outcome of Teenage Pregnancies

	Under 15	15-19 Years
Postmaritally Conceived Marital Births	45.2%	27.6%
Abortions		27.4%
Out-of-Wedlock Births	35.4%	20.6%
Miscarriages	13.0%	14.4%
Premaritally Conceived Marital Births	6.4%	10.0%

SOURCE: Alan Guttmacher Institute, 1974

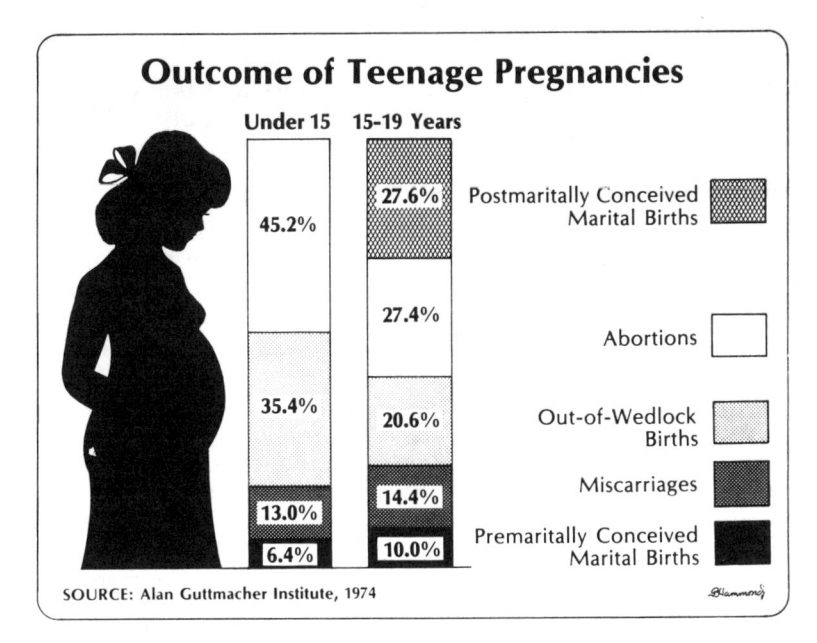

babies born to women in their twenties. About 6 percent of the first babies born to girls under age 15 die in their first 12 months. Prematurity and low birth weights, common in the children of adolescents, increase the chances of epilepsy, cerebral palsy and mental retardation.

Even mothers who deliver without health complications are more likely than older women to be headed for difficulty. Pregnancy and motherhood are the most common causes of young girls dropping out of school. Despite legislation and court decisions upholding the right of school-age parents to education, eight out of 10 who become pregnant at 17 or younger never complete high school, according to a 1976 study by the Alan Guttmacher Institute, the research division of the Planned Parenthood Federation of America.[6]

Unemployment is a severe problem for young mothers. According to a study conducted in New York City in 1973 and 1974, over 90 percent of the mothers who gave birth at age 15-17 were unemployed and 12 percent were receiving welfare; 41 percent of the 18- and 19-year-old mothers also were receiving welfare. Kristin A. Moore of the Urban Institute in Washington, D.C., estimates that half of the $9.4 billion spent on Aid to Families With Dependent Children in the United States goes to households in which there are women who first become mothers while still in their teens.[7] "There is definitely a high correlation

---

[6] "11 Million Teenagers: What Can Be Done About the Epidemic of Adolescent Pregnancies in the United States," the Alan Guttmacher Institute, 1976, p. 25.

[7] Testimony before the House Select Committee on Population, Feb. 28, 1978. See also Kristin A. Moore, et al., "Teenage Motherhood — Social and Economic Consequences," The Urban Institute, January 1979.

between out-of-wedlock births, welfare costs and many of our most pressing social problems," Peter Schuck, deputy assistant secretary of Health, Education and Welfare, said last year.[8]

Administration Response to the Problem

In June 1977 Schuck was designated by HEW Secretary Califano to head a special task force to study the problem of teenage pregnancy. Since Califano and President Carter both opposed the use of public funds to finance abortions, they were under political pressure to come up with alternative programs to deal with unplanned pregnancies. "There is no question that their position on abortion vastly increased the incentives to address the problem in other ways," Schuck told *New York Times* reporter Steven V. Roberts.[9] Califano and Carter also were said to be alarmed by the statistics in the 1976 report published by the Alan Guttmacher Institute. Roberts quoted an unidentified administration official as saying: "Our earliest concern in part reflected our concern over abortion, but the more we looked into it, we saw that the problem far transcends abortion."

Schuck's task force submitted its report to Califano in August 1977. After outlining various policy options, the task force recommended a combination of services to encourage pregnancy prevention and improve services to pregnant teenagers and adolescent parents. After reviewing the report, the administration drew up a "teenage pregnancy initiative," for which President Carter requested $142 million in his budget for fiscal year 1979. The amount included the addition of $64 million to existing family planning and child care programs, on the understanding that the added funds would aid teenagers. The budget request also included $18 million in federal assistance to state Medicaid plans to help teenagers while they were pregnant and after they gave birth.

The centerpiece of the administration's "initiative" was a bill called the Adolescent Health, Services and Pregnancy Prevention and Care Act. Its provisions, accounting for the final $60 million of the $142 million budget request, would establish or coordinate existing community-based services "to prevent initial and repeat pregnancies among adolescents and to provide care to pregnant adolescents...." These services included family planning, education about sexuality and responsibility of parenthood, mental health programs, nutritional education and counseling, vocational and employment counseling, prenatal and postpartum health care, residential care for pregnant teenagers, and services to help pregnant girls stay in school.

---

[8] Quoted in *U.S. News & World Report,* June 26, 1978, p. 59.
[9] *The New York Times,* Jan. 24, 1978.

Births to Teenage Girls, 1977

	Total	Out of Wedlock
Under 15	11,455	10,100
Age 15	30,956	23,000
Age 16	70,050	42,400
Age 17	112,782	55,500
Age 18	153,537	60,800
Age 19	191,829	57,900
Total	570,609	249,800

Source: National Center for Health Statistics

Even before the bill was introduced on April 13, 1978, it had come under attack from a coalition of family planning and child welfare organizations. They complained that the bill was vague and underfunded, and that it did not specify the percentage of funds to be allotted to pregnancy prevention, as opposed to the care of pregnant girls and their families.

Much of the criticism was aimed at the bill's emphasis on coordination of existing services. Fay Wattleton, the president of Planned Parenthood, criticized the administration for assuming that "most of the needed services are available ... at the community level." They are "inadequate or non-existent," she testified before the House Education and Labor Select Education Subcommittee on July 24.

The final version of the Adolescent Health, Services and Pregnancy Prevention and Care Act, which passed in the closing hours of the 95th Congress,[10] differed slightly from the administration's original proposal. The scope of the legislation was narrowed, focusing primarily on pregnant teenagers and parents who are under age 18. A provision requiring that at least half the funds be used to coordinate existing services was deleted. Public and private non-profit agencies receiving funding under the act must provide certain "core" services, including pregnancy testing, maternity counseling and referral, and nutritional information and counseling.

Although the use of funds authorized under the program for abortions was prohibited, the act required grant recipients to inform pregnant teenagers of the availability of abortion counseling. Grant recipients would not be required to provide the counseling themselves, but they would be required to refer girls to facilities that did such counseling. Eliminated from the final version of the bill was a Senate amendment to require parental notification prior to prescribing any contraceptive drug or device to persons under 16.

---

[10] It was included as an amendment to the Health Services Act, which Congress passed during a round-the-clock session, Oct. 14-15, 1978.

Funding for Title X Family Planning Services and Research
(in millions)

Services	Fiscal 1978	Fiscal 1979	Fiscal 1980	Fiscal 1981
Authorization	$140.0	$203.8	$234.4	$269.5
Appropriation	135.0	—	—	—
Carter's Budget Request	—	145.0	145.0	—
Research				
Authorization	68.5	105.0	120.8	138.9
Appropriation	66.0*	—	—	—
Carter's Budget Request	—	76.7	82.3	—

* Estimated spending level.
Source: Alan Guttmacher Institute

Critics of the administration's original bill were almost as unhappy with the final version. Many agreed with Planned Parenthood that the bill would "do very little to help pregnant teenagers." Many were especially disappointed that some form of infant day care, considered to be essential to any program designed to keep pregnant teenagers and young parents either in school or working, was deleted from the list of mandated core services.

Criticisms of Family Planning Strategies

Behind the criticism of the new law lies a more general dissatisfaction with the Carter administration's overall family planning effort. Critics accuse the administration of making inadequate requests for family planning programs authorized under Title X of the Public Health Services Act of 1970. Planned Parenthood has called Title X "the cornerstone of our national effort to prevent teenage pregnancies."[11] The organization estimated that almost one-third of the persons served by Title X programs are under 20 years of age.

Congress, on Oct. 15, extended Title X programs through 1981.[12] The extension bill authorized substantial funding increases for population research and family planning services, including special programs for teenagers. President Carter's fiscal 1980 budget, on the other hand, called for no funding increase for family planning services and only a small increase for

---
[11] "Planned Parenthood-World Population Washington Memo," Oct. 10, 1978.
[12] See *CQ Weekly Report,* Nov. 18, 1979, pp. 3323-3324.

research programs *(see table, opposite)*. According to Fay Wattleton, Carter's budget recommendations would result in a substantial decrease in the number of clients served by family planning programs in 1980. "Such a move would be bad social policy, false economy and even self-defeating of the president's own objective to reduce the need for abortions."[13]

In past years Congress has appropriated more money for Title X programs than the various administrations have requested. But according to Planned Parenthood, this year the situation could be different. "Both the president and Congress will have inflation uppermost in their minds and will be trying very hard to hold expansion of the entire federal budget to an absolute minimum. Because of perceived military commitments, the budget for domestic programs will be especially tight."[14]

Social and Public Policy Factors

BEFORE the early decades of this century there was virtually no teenage pregnancy problem. Aside perhaps from Victorian constraints, the reason can be found in statistics indicating that the average age at which girls can become pregnant has been dropping decade by decade. Anne C. Peterson, an assistant professor of psychiatry at the University of Chicago, reports that at the turn of the century the average age of first menstruation was about 14. Today, in contrast, one-third of the girls in America reach puberty before or during their twelfth year — a fact that is attributed to improved nutrition and health. "What we are facing in this country is not a sexual revolution but a biological one," said Sheri Tepper, director of Rocky Mountain Planned Parenthood in Denver, Colo.[15]

Few societies encourage childbearing at the time of puberty. "Even in traditional social systems, in which family formation tends to occur earlier, the age at marriage is likely to be postponed beyond the point at which individuals are biologically capable of becoming parents," Frank F. Furstenberg Jr. wrote in *Unplanned Parenthood* (1976). "The scheduling of marriage and parenthood will depend on the type of kinship system, on the social and economic value of children, and probably on demographic constraints on population growth." At no time has early childbearing been socially acceptable in the United States.

[13] Statement issued Jan. 20, 1979.

[14] "Planned Parenthood-World Population Washington Memo," Jan. 19, 1979.

[15] Quoted in *Parade*, Jan. 7, 1979, p. 20. Peterson's figures are cited in her article, "Can Puberty Come Any Earlier?" in *Psychology Today*, February 1979, p. 45.

"Contrary to popular impression," Furstenberg wrote, "parenthood before the age of 18 has never been common in this country."

> Reliable data on the fertility patterns of youth prior to the Civil War are extremely difficult to come by [he continued], but scattered statistical evidence on family formation in the 17th and 18th centuries suggests that women typically married in their early twenties. Marriage prior to age 18 was unusual and generally confined to the affluent. Census data collected in the late 19th century reveal that teenage marriage occurred only infrequently and that the overwhelming majority of women did not have their first child until they reached their twenties.[16]

The government began publishing birth statistics on a regular basis after 1915. These records show a constant pattern of teenage fertility during the first half of the 20th century. The birth rate among 15- to 19-year-olds remained essentially unchanged until the end of World War II, fluctuating between 50 and 60 births per 1,000 women. Furstenberg noted that it was impossible to determine how many of these births occurred among women who were not yet 18 "since no specific information was published on this age group, an indication perhaps of how rare early childbearing was."

After World War II, there was a sharp rise in the rate of teenage marriages and, accordingly, a substantial increase in the number of births to teenagers. The birth rate climbed from 51.1 to 1,000 teenage women in 1945 to 96.3 by 1957, the peak year of the post-war baby boom. "Thus, the trend in the teenage population paralleled that in other age groups except that the birth rate shot up much more rapidly for teenagers than for the rest of the population," Furstenberg wrote. Births to very young girls still accounted for only a small proportion of teenage births. Of the 484,000 teenagers who produced children in 1955, less than one-third (132,000) were younger than 18. Although the number of teenage births has risen since the end of the baby boom, the birth rate among those between 15 and 19 has steadily and sharply declined since the 1950s

Young Parenthood as a Social Problem

The convergence of several factors in the late 1950s and 1960s aroused public concern about adolescent parenthood. As the first of the baby boom children entered adolescence, there was a significant increase in the number of teenage mothers. This sharp rise offset and obscured the concurrent decline in the teenage birth rate, "conveying the false impression that women

---

[16] Frank F. Furstenberg Jr., *Unplanned Parenthood: The Social Consequences of Teenage Childbearing* (1976), p. 6.

Birth Rate for Teenagers 15-19

1950	81.6	1970	68.3	1974	58.1
1955	90.3	1971	64.7	1975	56.3
1960	89.1	1972	62.0	1976	53.5
1965	70.5	1973	59.7	1977	53.7

Source: National Center for Health Statistics

under age 18 actually were producing more babies than ever before."[17]

Growing apprehension about overpopulation in the 1960s also intensified concern about teenage pregnancy. Family planning experts were particularly concerned by the high proportion of teen births that occurred out of wedlock. "This pattern always has been evident," Furstenberg wrote, "but during the late fifties the 'illegitimacy' ratio ... began to rise throughout the population. Teenagers by virtue of their marital status had the greatest potential for producing out-of-wedlock children, and therefore the rising ratio among this group inevitably attracted most attention."

During the 1960s, as Congress and the White House began addressing the problems of racial and economic inequality in the country, attention was drawn to the links between teenage pregnancy, poverty and welfare dependency. In this vein, a report issued by the Department of Labor's Office of Policy Planning and Research in 1965 argued that the black family was "deteriorating" because nearly one-fourth of all Negro births were illegitimate. The report, "The Negro Family: The Case for National Action," was prepared under the direction of then-Assistant Secretary of Labor Daniel Patrick Moynihan, currently a U.S. senator from New York. It also noted that nearly one-fourth of the urban Negro marriages were dissolved and that women headed about one-fourth of the Negro families.[18]

Federal Intervention in Family Planning

Despite the growing awareness of the relationship between unplanned childbearing and poverty, the federal government was slow to intervene in family planning. As late as 1959 President Eisenhower had said he "could not imagine anything more emphatically a subject that is not a proper political or governmental activity or function or responsibility" than birth control. Before 1965 the federal government participated in birth control programs only indirectly.

---
[17] *Ibid.*, p. 9.

[18] The report was issued in March 1965, intended solely as an internal policy paper. It was made public in August 1965 after some of its contents had been leaked to newsmen. Its release generated a storm of controversy. A detailed account of the genesis of the report and ensuing controversy were the subject of a book published in the spring of 1967, *The Moynihan Report and the Politics of Controversy* (Massachusetts Institute of Technology Press), by sociologists Lee Rainwater and William L. Yancey.

Editorial Research Reports   *Mar. 23, 1979*

Federal funds and technical assistance, both at home and abroad, went for research and training in demography and reproductive biology rather than for spreading information about birth control and providing contraceptive materials. Although federal funds authorized by the public assistance provisions of the Social Security Act of 1935 had been used by health and welfare agencies for birth control programs since the late 1930s, particularly in the South, there was no explicit or direct authority for a government role in family planning.[19]

During 1965 the government took a more active, though still largely indirect, role in family planning, notably through the federal anti-poverty program. Early that year, the Office of Economic Opportunity indicated it would provide funds for local birth-control projects, if locally approved, and by the end of November it had approved 17 grants for family planning services. Funds were used for information, mobile clinics and medical supplies, including contraceptives. But OEO policy stipulated that the projects must assist married women only. Other birth-control aid was provided by HEW grants to state and city hospitals and clinics.

President Johnson, in his 1965 State of the Union address, became the first American president to indicate that federal support of population control was under consideration. "I will seek new ways to use our knowledge to help deal with the explosion in world population and the growing scarcity of world resources," he said. Later in the year the U.S. Supreme Court struck down a Connecticut law banning the use of, and the distribution of information on, contraceptive devices. In *Griswold v. Connecticut,* the court held the state law unconstitutional and in violation of a married couple's right to privacy.

The following year, in a message on health and education, Johnson told Congress: "It is essential that all families have access to information and services that will allow freedom to choose the number and spacing of their children within the dictates of individual conscience." Several measures enacted by Congress in 1966 contained birth-control provisions. Birth control was among the special health problems for which states could receive federal grants. The Economic Opportunity Act was amended to let community action agencies decide whether unmarried women would be eligible for family planning information. The various agencies of HEW were also told they could distribute birth-control information, but not contraceptive devices.

Congress in 1970 passed the Family Planning Services Act to

---

[19] See Congressional Quarterly, *Congress and the Nation, Vol. II* (1969), pp. 676-677.

Teenage Pregnancy

coordinate and expand the family planning services and population research activities of the federal government. The law has been "the core of the nation's program of subsidized family planning services for low-income women and teenagers, as well as for the biomedical and social sciences research efforts in population, human reproduction, contraceptive development and evaluation sponsored by the National Institutes of Health."[20]

Increased Sexual Activity Among Teens

Despite the government's growing interest in population problems, family planning for teenagers remained a controversial issue in the early 1970s. President Nixon, on May 5, 1972, rejected a proposal of the Commission on Population Growth and the American Future[21] that all states make contraceptive devices and other family-planning services available to teenagers. Nixon also rejected the suggestion that states permit a doctor to perform abortions at a patient's request. Nixon said he regarded abortion as an "unacceptable means of population control" and that the widespread distribution of contraceptives to minors would "do nothing to preserve and strengthen close family relations."

The commission's recommendation that contraceptives be made more readily available to teenagers was based in part on a report prepared by two Johns Hopkins University professors, Melvin Zelnik and John F. Kantner.[22] Their survey of more than 1,000 indicated that nearly half of all unmarried women had sexual relations by the time they were 19 and that over 75 percent of those who had relations never used contraceptives or used them only occasionally.

Subsequent findings indicate that sexual activity among young people has become even more widespread. "There just aren't any supports for those who want to be virgins," Kristin A. Moore of the Urban Institute said recently. "It really is harder to say no."[23] A follow-up survey by Zelnik and Kastner indicated that the number of single teenage girls having experienced sexual intercourse rose from 27 percent in 1971 to 35 percent in 1976. They found that only about one girl in five (18 percent) had ever had intercourse at age 15. But by age 17 the number

---

[20] "Planned Parenthood-World Population Washington Memo," Jan. 19, 1979.

[21] The commission was set up by President Nixon in 1971 to study the effects of U.S. population growth on government activities, the impact of population growth on the environment and the means by which the country could achieve a population level suited to its resources. John D. Rockefeller III, a long-time advocate of population control, was named chairman of the commission. The commission issued its report in March 1972.

[22] Melvin Zelnik and John F. Kantner, "Sexuality, Contraception and Pregnancy Among Young Unwed Females in the United States," in *Research Reports*, Vol. I, Commission on Population Growth and the American Futures (1972), pp. 355-374. See also "Contraceptives and Society," *E.R.R.*, 1972 Vol. I, p. 422.

[23] Quoted in *The New York Times*, June 18, 1978.

had doubled (more than 40 percent) and by age 19 had climbed to 55 percent.[24] The researchers also said the average age at which women first had sexual intercourse had declined from 16.5 in 1971 to 16.2 in 1976.

Zelnik and Kastner emphasized that teenage sexual activity is sporadic. About 15 percent of the girls surveyed said they had experienced sex only once, while 40 percent said they had been sexually inactive in the four weeks preceding the interview. Proportionally far more blacks (63 percent) than whites (31 percent) reported being sexually experienced, but the racial gap had narrowed since 1971. Along with increasing sexual experience, teenagers of both races are contracting venereal diseases in growing numbers. Persons of ages 15 to 19 are three times more likely to contact gonorrhea than those over 20, while the risk of syphilis is 61 percent greater for teenagers.[25]

Teenage Attitudes Toward Birth Control

There is no single explanation for the increase in teenage sexual activity, but there seems to be a simple reason for the increase in adolescent pregnancies — many teenagers do not practice birth control. Zelnik and Kastner reported that the number of sexually active teenage girls who never used contraception increased from 17 percent in 1971 to 26 percent in 1976. About 45 percent of the girls interviewed for the 1976 study said they used contraceptives only occasionally. However, the proportion of teenage girls who always practiced contraception increased from 18 to 30 percent between 1971 and 1976.

Those teenagers who practice birth control are selecting more effective methods today than they did in 1971. The Pill was named the "most recently used" method by 47 percent; others listed the condom (21 percent), withdrawal (17 percent), foam, cream, diaphragm or rhythm (8 percent), douche (4 percent) and IUD (3 percent). In 1971 the "most recently used" methods were the condom (27 percent), withdrawal (24 percent) and The Pill (21 percent).

Most girls who do not use any form of birth control are poorly informed about the risks of pregnancy. Many parents today are skipping the traditional facts-of-life lecture in the belief that their children already know it all. But despite sex education classes in the schools, many teenagers are ignorant or misinformed about the basic facts of reproduction.

Some girls believe they are too young to get pregnant, or that

---

[24] Melvin Zelnik and John F. Kastner, "Sexual and Contraceptive Experience of Young Unmarried Women in the United States, 1976 and 1971," *Family Planning Perspective*, Vol. IX (1977), p. 55. The corresponding figures for 1971 were 14 percent for 15-year-olds, 26.6 percent for 17-year-olds, and 46.1 percent for 19-year olds.

[25] See "Venereal Disease: Continuing Problem," *E.R.R.*, 1979 Vol. I, pp. 45-64.

Teenage Pregnancy

they are protected because they have sex infrequently. Others believe they cannot become pregnant the first time they have intercourse. One of the most common reasons girls give for not using birth control is that they had intercourse at the "safe time of the month." Yet according to one survey, only 38 percent could identify the time of the menstrual cycle when pregnancy is most likely to occur.[26]

Some teenagers attribute their failure to use birth control to its unavailability. But in most cases they know they can obtain a contraceptive, but are afraid or embarrassed to ask for it or worried about their parents' reaction if the contraceptive is discovered. Adolescent attitudes toward sex also interfere with their use of birth control. Many teenagers think sex should be spontaneous and that planning for it makes it calculated and unromantic. "Girls often don't want to admit to themselves — or their partners — that they're sexually active," said Dr. Takey Crist, director of the Crist Clinic for Women in Jacksonville, N.C. "If they consider birth control, that would affirm the fact that they have sex — and are bad."[27]

The persistence of a double standard regarding sexual activity complicates the problem. Young men often leave contraceptive responsibility wholly up to the female partner. About 43 percent of 1,000 boys who answered a recent Chicago Planned Parenthood questionnaire considered contraception the girl's responsibility; 61 percent said it was all right to tell a girl you loved her in order to have sexual relations with her.

Another reason teenagers make inadequate use of birth control, according to Andrew Cherlin, assistant professor of social relations at Johns Hopkins University, is that the most effective methods are inappropriate for them. "To a young woman whose sex life is irregular," he wrote, "taking a birth control pill every day makes little sense, nor is she apt to go to the trouble of having an IUD [intrauterine device] inserted.... One solution to this problem is more funds for research on a contraceptive suitable for teenagers — such as a pill which can be taken safety after intercourse."[28] A "morning-after pill" suitable for use as an emergency medication in cases such as rape or incest has been approved by the Food and Drug Administration. The treatment involves taking 250 mg. of diethylstilbestrol (DES) over a period of five days. Many persons question the safety of the morning-after pill because DES has been linked to vaginal and cervical cancer.

---

[26] Zero Population Growth, "Teenage Pregnancy: A Major Problem for Minors," August 1977.

[27] Quoted in *McCall's*, July 1978, p. 46.

[28] Andrew Cherlin, "Carter Half Sees the Problem," *The Nation*, June 17, 1978, p. 729.

Sex Education for Adolescents

THE KEY to reducing pregnancies among adolescents, most family planning specialists agree, is to provide them the information they need to make responsible decisions relating to their sexuality. One way to do this is through sex education classes in the schools. But only 29 states and the District of Columbia require health education courses in public schools. Of these only six states[29] and the District mandate some form of family life or sex education, according to the Alan Guttmacher Institute. One state, Louisiana, forbids such courses.

Even when sex education is provided in schools, contraception often is not discussed. According to a 1976 survey of high school teachers who teach population-related subjects, only three in ten taught anything about birth-control methods. Only about one-third taught anything about human reproduction or abortion. An earlier study found that of every five school districts offering sex education courses, only two taught anything about birth control. Venereal disease, "changes in adolescence" and human reproduction were the most popular topics. According to the Alan Guttmacher Institute, "There is little evidence that such limited sex education programs have had any effect on prevention of early pregnancy."

The failure of schools to provide adequate sex education contrasts sharply with widespread public support for such programs. According to a survey conducted by the Gallup polling organization in December 1977,[30] nearly eight of every ten persons questioned (77 percent) favored sex education instruction in the schools. When those who approved were asked if they would still approve if these classes included discussions of birth control, only one in ten said no. Over half of those surveyed (56 percent) favored making contraceptive devices available to teenagers.

Several organizations have been working to improve sex education classes. The National Parent-Teachers Association has been testing ways to develop community support for health education, including sex education. Affiliates of the Planned Parenthood Federation last year recommended that the national organization produce a policy statement on sex education, serve as a clearinghouse for resources, and develop training programs and educational materials. The American Association of Sex Educators, Counselors and Therapists has helped create over 30

---

[29] Hawaii, Kentucky, Maryland, Michigan, Missouri and North Dakota.
[30] Results published in *The Gallup Opinion Index*, July 1978, pp. 27-30.

sex education programs nationwide. They encourage an interdisciplinary approach. Rather than having a special sex education class, they incorporate information about sex into existing classes or projects.

Promoting Contraception Through Radio

Some family planning experts are skeptical about the success of school-based sex education classes. So many young people are turned off by school, they argue, that the programs are not taken seriously. Many are equally skeptical about attracting teenagers to special family-planning clinics. "The key to reducing the teen birth rate," wrote Michael Castleman, "is to develop programs that touch teens directly, as opposed to clinic-type programs which force them to step out of their lives and into the unfamiliar world of family-planning professionals."[31]

One thing most kids can relate to is the mass media. Teenagers tend to spend as much time watching television or listening to the radio as they do in school. The Population Institute of San Francisco is trying to promote teenage contraception through radio. It has been recruiting popular rock stars to deliver public service messages about birth control while their hit songs play in the background. These "Rock Spots," as they are called, are syndicated to about 500 radio stations. "The stars talk about their own personal experiences," said project director Kathi Kamen. "The spots come across more real than the typical celebrity public service announcement."

Laws Affecting Access to Birth Control

In recent years there has been a liberalization of public laws and policies affecting access of teenagers to birth control services and devices. At least 26 states and the District of Columbia have passed laws affirming the right of minors to contraceptive care. In July 1976 the Supreme Court overturned a Missouri law which required girls under age 18 to have parental consent before obtaining an abortion.[32] Two months earlier the court ruled that family planning programs receiving federal funds may not require parental permission as a condition of service. The right of minors to purchase non-prescription contraceptives was upheld in June 1977 when the court ruled invalidated a New York law that banned such sales.

Despite this liberalizing trend, and despite the fact that no doctor has been held liable for providing contraceptive services to minors of any age, many hospitals, health agencies and physicians still refuse birth control services to teenagers. Aside from legal questions, many physicians are afraid that by giving

---

[31] Michael Castleman, "Why Teenagers Get Pregnant," *The Nation*, Nov. 26, 1977.
[32] *Planned Parenthood of Central Missouri v. Danforth*, 428 U.S. 152.

contraception to teenagers they will appear to be encouraging or condoning sexual activity among young people.

But the American Medical Association has adopted a pro-access policy. "The teenage girl whose sexual behavior exposes her to possible conception," the association stated, should "have access to medical consultation and the most effective contraceptive advice and methods ... and the physician so consulted should be free to prescribe or withhold contraceptive advice in accordance with his best medical judgment in the best interests of his patient."

Criticism of a Contraceptive Orientation

The emphasis on providing adolescents with birth control devices and information has been attacked by some individuals and organizations. Testifying before the House Select Committee on Population on June 16, 1978, Regis Wallis, director of

> "At the very least, teenagers should have as much knowledge of sex, as many and as good services available, and as many choices open to them, as do adults."

Pregnancy Services of Michigan, criticized existing sex education courses for "encouraging" teenagers to be sexually active and, once active, to use only chemical methods of contraception. Jeannette M. Reinecker of Pregnancy Aid Centers Inc. told the committee that current methods of sex education have been a failure "not because of the absence of contraceptive techniques, but because of an absence of basic values and the assumption that most kids engage in sex, and the grosser assumption that the adult practice of sex and birth control can be handled by the children." Rather than teaching contraceptive techniques, she suggested programs that relied on "virtue and self-control."

The Carter administration has indicated that it is sympathetic to this position. "We want to add a moral dimension to sex education," Peter Schuck of the Department of Health, Education and Welfare said last spring. "Kids hunger for moral guidance, and the purely clinical approach is not very effective."[33]

Many family planning organizations also are trying to help kids abstain from sex. The Planned Parenthood Federation has

---

[33] Quoted in *The New York Times*, June 18, 1978.

published a pamphlet called "Teensex: It's Okay to Say No Way." The pamphlet points out that individuals develop at different rates and that it is important that they know their own feelings and not base their actions on what others are doing. Teenagers are urged to put their own feelings first rather than worry about hurting the one making sexual demands.

For millions of teenagers who already are sexually active, such advice is not enough. These youngsters must be encouraged to take precautions to avoid the harsh realities of teenage pregnancy. "At the very least, teenagers should have as much knowledge of sex, as many and as good services available, and as many choices open to them, as do adults," said Daniel Callahan, director of the Institute of Society, Ethics and the Life Sciences. "Adults hardly have all the knowledge they should have, or all the services they need. But whatever they have at least should be shared equally with teenagers."[34]

---

[34] Writing in "11 Million Teenagers," *op. cit.*, p. 59.

▼▼▼

Selected Bibliography

Books

Bowerman, Charles E., *Unwed Motherhood: Personal and Social Consequences*, University of North Carolina Press, 1966.
Furstenberg, Frank F. Jr., *Unplanned Parenthood*, The Free Press, 1976.
Hartley, Shirley, *Illegitimacy*, University of California Press, 1975.
Klerman, Lorraine V. and James F. Jekel, *School-Age Mothers: Problems, Programs and Policy*, Linnet Books, 1973.
Osofsky, Howard J., *The Pregnant Teenager*, Charles C. Thomas, 1968.
Zackler, Jack and Wayne Brandstadt, eds., *The Teenage Pregnant Girl*, Charles C. Thomas, 1975.

Articles

Castleman, Michael, "Why Teenagers Get Pregnant," *The Nation*, Nov. 26, 1977.
Cherlin, Andrew, "Carter Half Sees the Problem," *The Nation*, June 17, 1978.
Fielding, Jonathan E., "Trends in Births to Adolescents," *New England Journal of Medicine*, Oct. 19, 1978.
Fosburgh, Lacey, "The Make-Believe World of Teenage Maternity," *The New York Times Magazine*, Aug. 7, 1977.
Peterson, Anne C., "Can Puberty Come Any Earlier?" *Psychology Today*, February 1979.
Schwartz, Toney, "Pregnant Teens," *Newsweek*, May 30, 1977.
"The Teenage Pregnancy Epidemic," *McCall's*, July 1978.
Willson, Peters D. and Stacy Duncan, "What Carter Would Do For Teens," *ZPG National Reporter*, May 1978.
Weiss, Laura B., "Interest Groups Are Seeking Modifications in Pregnancy Prevention and Care Bill," *CQ Weekly Report*, Aug. 26, 1978.

Reports and Studies

Alan Guttmacher Institute, "11 Million Teenagers: What Can Be Done About the Epidemic of Adolescent Pregnancies in the United States," 1976.
Editorial Research Reports, "Contraceptives and Society," 1972 Vol. I, p. 415; "Sexual Revolution: Myth or Reality," 1970 Vol. I, p. 241; "Venereal Disease: Continuing Problem," 1979 Vol. I, p. 45.
Moore, Kristin A., et al., "Teenage Motherhood: Social and Economic Consequences," The Urban Institute, January 1979.
"Planned Parenthood-World Population Washington Memo," selected issues.
Population Reference Bureau, "Adolescent Pregnancy and Childbearing — Growing Concerns for Americans," *Population Bulletin*, May 1977.
U.S. Department of Health, Education and Welfare, "Teenage Childbearing: United States, 1966-75," *Monthly Vital Statistics Report from the National Center for Health Statistics*, Sept. 8, 1977.
Zero Population Growth Inc., "Teenage Pregnancy: A Major Problem for Minors," August 1977.

SINGLE-PARENT FAMILIES

by

Sandra Stencel

	page
INCREASE IN ONE-PARENT HOMES	63
Impact of Rising Divorce Rate on Family Units	63
Increased Child Adoptions by Single Persons	65
Money Problems of Families Headed by Women	66
Emotional and Social Issues in Single Parenting	68
AMERICAN FAMILIES IN TRANSITION	69
Trend of Later Marriages and Fewer Children	69
Government Support of Traditional Family Life	71
Concern for Children in Family Disorganization	72
THE PUBLIC POLICY IMPLICATIONS	73
Stricter Enforcement of Child-Support Decrees	74
Child-Care Programs; Debate Over Federal Role	75
Laws on Discrimination Against Single Persons	77
Arrangements for the Joint Custody of Children	78

**Sept. 10
1 9 7 6**

SINGLE-PARENT FAMILIES

THE PROBLEMS of the American family and what the government can do toward solving them have become a popular theme in this year's presidential campaign. Typical of his comments about home and family, Democratic candidate Jimmy Carter told a group of supporters in Manchester, N.H., on Aug. 3: "There can be no more urgent priority for the next administration than to see that every decision our government makes is designed to honor and support and strengthen the American family." The Republican Party Platform, adopted in Kansas City two weeks later, expressed similar sentiments. "It is imperative," the Republicans stated, "that our government's programs, actions, officials and social welfare institutions never be allowed to jeopardize the family."

Policies of the federal government relating to the family traditionally have been geared to the needs of the two-parent or nuclear family, with a working father, a homemaking mother and dependent children. Only recently has the government begun to respond to the actual and growing variety of American family lives, including the tremendous growth in the number of families headed by women who work. One of the most significant changes in family structure in recent years has been the increase in the number of children living with only one parent. Over 11 million children—more than one out of every six children under age 18—live in single-parent homes. Since 1960 the number of such families has grown seven times as fast as the number of two-parent families. By 1975, there were 4.9 million one parent families in the United States—up from 3.26 million in 1970.[1]

Most Americans raising their children alone are women. Of the 4.9 million single-parent families, 4.4 million were headed by women.[2] The number of children living in homes where the father was absent more than doubled from 1960 to 1975. Today, approximately 15 per cent of all families with children under 18 are headed by single mothers. This trend has been particularly

---

[1] U.S. Bureau of the Census, "Household and Family Characteristics: March 1975," *Current Population Reports*, Series P-20, No. 291, February 1976, p. 7.

[2] The tendency to use figures on families headed by women as indicators of characteristics of families headed by single mothers can be somewhat misleading since not all households headed by women have children living at home. Of the seven million households headed by women in 1975, approximately two-thirds had children under 18.

pronounced among black families—more than 40 per cent of all black children live in homes where the father is absent. Behind this growth in one-parent families is the explosive rise in the divorce rate, which doubled in the past decade. There were over one million divorces in the United States in 1975—a record high. If the current divorce rate continues, three out of every five couples who marry this year will not remain together.

The rapid growth in the number of single-parent families is a source of concern among some social scientists, child psychologists and public officials. Many view the trend as evidence of the breakup of the American family. "Profound changes are taking place in the lives of America's children and young people," writes Urie Bronfenbrenner, professor of human development and family studies at Cornell University. "The institution which is at the center of these changes and that itself shows the most rapid and radical transformation is the American family...."[3]

Another expert troubled by the increase in one-parent families is Dr. Herbert Hendin, director of psychosocial studies at the Center for Policy Research and a professor at Columbia University. "As a culture we encourage the forces that are pulling the family apart...," he wrote recently in *The New York Times*. "A well-functioning culture can tolerate many individual alternatives to family life. But our effort should not be to institutionalize such alternatives; rather, we should help men and women to make their families work."[4]

Not everyone views the increase in single-parent families with alarm. Carole Klein, author of *The Single Parent Experience* (1973), suggests that the United States is in the midst of a significant change in child-rearing patterns. "The story of the single parent is the story of a growing, if grudging, acceptance of variations on our most treasured theme. Like every other aspect of our culture, the family as we knew it is in transition. We are rethinking assumptions on which generations of people have lived, and finding that they were after all only assumptions. For some people, this is terribly exciting. It opens up a tremendous range of possibilities for behavior."

Other social scientists contend that the growth of single-parent families should not be viewed as a rejection of marriage or family living. They cite statistics indicating that half of these one-parent families are likely to evolve into new nuclear families within five years. "We need to recognize that single parenting is not a static category but rather a state of transition," said Martin Rein, a sociologist at the Massachusetts Institute of

---

[3] Urie Bronfenbrenner, *The Origins of Alienation* (1975).
[4] *The New York Times*, Aug. 26, 1976.

15% of all families with children are headed by women

4.4 million of the 4.9 million single-parent families in U.S. are headed by women

11% of all white children live in homes where the father is absent

41% of all black children live in homes where the father is absent

Technology in a research paper on single-parent families prepared for the U.S. Office of Child Development in 1974.[5] This transitory theme is echoed in a recent report on the growth of families headed by women prepared by Urban Institute economists Heather L. Ross and Isabel V. Sawhill. For most people, they write, "single parenthood is a 'time of transition' between living in one nuclear family and another."[6]

Increased Child Adoptions by Single Persons

In recent years, those men and women who become single parents through death or divorce have been joined by a small but growing number who have freely chosen this role. Some single persons decided to adopt children. Some unmarried

---

[5] Hugh Helco, Lee Rainwater, Martin Rein and Robert Weiss, "Single Parent Families: Issues and Policies," unpublished manuscript, 1974.
[6] Heather L. Ross and Isabel V. Sawhill, "Time of Transition: The Growth of Families Headed by Women," The Urban Institute, 1975, p. 159.

women deliberately became pregnant, often without ever letting the man know he was the father. Others accidentally conceived and decided to go through with the pregnancy even though marriage with the baby's father was not likely. According to Carole Klein, well over half of the single pregnant women who contact social service agencies are deciding to keep their babies rather than give them up for adoption. "If this cannot yet be called a trend," she wrote, "it certainly indicates a shift in some of our most entrenched social attitudes."

Statistics on the number of single persons who have become adoptive parents are vague, but according to Betsy Cole, director of the North American Center for Adoption of the Child Welfare League of America, "there are more single parents today than in the entire history of adoption." In the past, single parents were chosen only for youngsters no one else wanted. Today, however, single adults are actually sought out for many children. "In many cases, particularly with older children, there may be a better emotional relationship with just one parent," said Lenore K. Campbell, director of Los Angeles Adoptions.[7] Nevertheless, some professionals continue to oppose single-parent adoptions. Dr. Lee Salk, a leading child psychologist, wrote recently: "I always wonder if people who deliberately choose to be single parents are thinking of the child or are trying to satisfy some hidden self-interest."[8]

Money Problems of Families Headed by Women

As the number of single-parent families has increased, Americans have become increasingly aware of the multitude of legal, financial, emotional and social problems that confront this growing minority. The great majority of one-parent families face severe economic handicaps. Often single parents start off with sizable debts, the result of costly divorce proceedings or medical treatment for a now-deceased spouse. Divorced couples quickly discover that two cannot live as cheaply as one. As a result, both households are forced to reduce their living standard.

Generally, economic problems are greatest for single mothers. The income of single-parent families headed by women is much lower than of those headed by men *(see box, p. 74)*. In 1974, over half (51.5 per cent) of all children living in families headed by women were living below the official poverty level.[9] For black children living with single mothers, this figure was even higher—almost two-thirds (65.7 per cent) were living in poverty.

One factor contributing to the poverty of families headed by

---

[7] Cole and Campbell were quoted in *The Christian Science Monitor*, Dec. 22, 1975.
[8] Dr. Lee Salk, "Guilt and the Single Parent," *Harper's Bazaar*, March 1976, p. 89.
[9] In 1974 the official federal poverty line for a non-farm family of four was $5,038; for a family of five, $5,950; for a family of six, $6,699.

American Families*, 1975
(in thousands)

Total
(55,712)

Husband-Wife	Male-Headed	Female-Headed
(46,971)	(1,499)	(7,242)

With Children	Without Children	With Children	Without Children	With Children	Without Children
(25,169)	(21,802)	(484)	(1,015)	(4,404)	(2,838)

*Families are defined for census purposes as consisting of two persons or more who are related by blood, marriage or adoption and who reside together.

SOURCE: U.S. Bureau of the Census

---

single mothers is the number of fathers who default on their child-support payments. On the basis of a much-cited study conducted by the University of Wisconsin in the 1950s, it is estimated that four of every ten divorced fathers are not paying any child support one year after the divorce. After ten years, eight of the ten make no support payments. Non-support is as prevalent among affluent and middle-class fathers as among low-income men, according to a research paper published by the Rand Corporation in 1974.[10]

Data collected by the General Accounting Office in 1974 also indicate that there is little relationship between a father's ability to pay and either the amount of the payment agreed to or his compliance with the law. While some low-income men are paying substantial portions of their income to support their children, many who are more affluent have failed to comply at all.[11] A study by Robert Hampton of the University of Michigan's Institute for Social Research portrays ex-wives as being worse off financially than ex-husbands. Of all the married couples in his survey who separated between 1968 and 1973, 35 per cent of the women but only 19 per cent of the men fell into the botton 30 per cent of the nation's income brackets after being divorced.[12]

The federal government has opened a campaign to track down negligent fathers and make them pay for their children's support *(see p. 74)*. The government hopes that better enforcement of child-support orders will reduce the number of single-parent families on welfare. The number of single mothers who are dependent on public largesse is smaller than is commonly

---

[10] Marian P. Winston and Trude Forsher, "Nonsupport of Legitimate Children by Affluent Fathers as a Cause of Poverty and Welfare Dependence," the Rand Corporation, April 1974.

[11] *Congressional Record,* Dec. 4, 1974.

[12] These figures took into account family size and any child support or alimony obligations. See *Five Thousand Families—Patterns of Economic Progress,* Vols. 1-3, Institute for Social Research, University of Michigan, 1973-1975.

believed. According to the U.S. Office of Child Development research paper, only 35 per cent of all families headed by mothers receive welfare aid; no more than 20 per cent receive half of their income from welfare; and no more than 10 per cent get as much as three-quarters of their income from welfare.

Most single mothers support themselves and their families with their earnings. The Women's Bureau of the Department of Labor reported that in 1975 some 62 per cent of these mothers held paying jobs; among other mothers, only 43 per cent were employed.[13] Many of these women enter the job market untrained or after a long absence, and are forced to take low-paying jobs as office workers, waitresses or sales clerks. The median income of single working mothers in 1975 was $6,575—substantially below the $13,675 median income of two-parent families in which the husband worked but the wife did not.

A major expense for most single parents—men and women—is day care for their children. This is particularly true for single-parent families that fail to qualify for federally subsized care for their children *(see p. 75)*. Private day-care centers often charge from $20 to $50 a week per child. Even if a parent has the money, day-care facilities are hard to find. According to the latest government estimates, care in licensed centers is available for only slightly more than one million children. It is estimated that more than six million pre-school children and several million school-age children need this service. Some children of working mothers are cared for by friends or relatives. Some stay with babysitters. Others—"latchkey children"—care for themselves.

Emotional and Social Issues in Single Parenting

Many of the problems single parents face initially are related to the event which led to their new social status—divorce, separation or the death of a spouse. "The end of a marriage, especially if children are involved, is for most people a traumatic experience," said George B. Williams, executive director of Parents Without Partners. "Even if problems are anticipated, nobody ever expects them to be so critical. The frequent responses are demoralization and despair."[14] Many single parents suffer from loneliness. They find that they no longer fit in with their married friends and they learn that it is sometimes difficult to meet members of the opposite sex. Single parents "don't seem to fit any of the normal social patterns," Professor Benjamin Schlesinger of the University of Toronto has observed. "They are the self-styled fifth wheels of society."[15]

---

[13] U.S. Department of Labor, "1975 Handbook on Women Workers," p. 25.

[14] Quoted in "Rising Problems of 'Single Parents,'" *U.S. News & World Report,* July 16, 1973, p. 32.

[15] Benjamin Schlesinger, *The One-Parent Family* (1975), p. 9.

Single-Parent Families

In the case of divorce or separation, problems are apt to arise with the former or absent spouse. Financial arrangements between the couple frequently cause intense conflict. Most often the problems center on the children. A frequent complaint of divorced fathers is that their ex-wives prevent them from seeing their children as often as they would like. On the other hand, the parent with custody often feels burdened by the full responsibility for the children and resents the apparent freedom of the other parent.

Child-care problems do not end once a suitable babysitter is found or the child is enrolled in day care. There are vacations to contend with, school conferences to attend, days when the child is sick, the race to get home before the day-care center closes, the question of what to do with older children before and after school. These problems confront all working parents. But they can be doubly hard on single parents who have no one else to share responsibility for decision making and discipline, no one else to help with the household chores, no one else to give the children the love and attention they need. Under such pressures many single parents develop ambivalent feelings about their children. They may feel their children are a burden to them, interfering with their jobs, their social lives and even their chances of remarriage.

One of the more startling developments in recent years has been the growing number of broken families in which neither parent wants custody. "It's a critical problem," according to Judge John R. Evans of Denver, "and it's definitely increasing."[16] The dread of getting stuck with the children may even be holding some marriages together, *Newsweek* has commented. The magazine said a Chicago divorce lawyer told of a couple who had entered into a written agreement which stipulated that the first one to ask for a divorce had to take the kids. Despite the many difficulties, family counselors stress, most single parents still manage to raise their children successfully.

American Families in Transition

THE SHARP INCREASE in one-parent families parallels other changes in the structure of American families. Marriages have been occurring later and less often. The age at which young couples get married has been rising since the 1950s. Many single persons are delaying marriage in favor of additional

---

[16] Quoted in "The Broken Family: Divorce U.S. Style," *Newsweek*, March 12, 1973, p. 51.

Living Arrangements of Children Under 18

Living With	1975 Total	1975 White	1975 Black	1970 Total	1970 White	1970 Black
Both parents	80.3%	85.4%	49.4%	84.9%	89.2%	58.1%
Mother only	15.5	11.3	40.9	10.7	7.8	29.3
Father only	1.5	1.5	1.8	1.1	0.9	2.2
Neither parent	2.7	1.7	7.9	3.3	2.2	10.4

SOURCE: U.S. Bureau of the Census

schooling and a period of living away from home prior to marriage. Others are living together without the benefit of marriage. In 1975 the average age at marriage—23.5 for males and 21.1 for women—was close to a year higher than it had been in the mid-1950s. Since 1960 the proportion of women who remained single until their early twenties had increased by one-third.[17]

The postponement of marriage, along with the availability of contraceptives and legal abortions, has contributed to a marked decline in childbearing. Young couples today are not having their first child as soon after marriage as their parents did, are spacing the children farther apart and are sharply reducing the number of large families. The total fertility rate[18] among American women in 1975 has been estimated at 1.9, almost half the 1960 figure (3.7) and well below the 1970 figure (2.5). If the estimate proves to be correct, and the rate does not rise again, the national population growth will cease and then decline—unless immigration fills the gap.[19]

The single most important factor contributing to the growth in one-parent families is the rising divorce rate. Social scientists anticipate even higher rates in the future. Dr. Richard A. Gardner, assistant clinical professor of child psychiatry at Columbia University and author of *The Boys and Girls Book About Divorce* (1970), has said: "Today, easier divorce laws and having the economic capacity for an independent existence make it easier for couples to contemplate divorce. The lessening of religion's influence is a factor, too. Furthermore, a kind of cycle develops in these things. Having divorced parents makes it easier for youngsters to get divorces because it's in their scheme of things."[20]

---

[17] U.S. Bureau of the Census, "Some Recent Changes in American Families," *Current Population Reports*, Series P-23, No. 52, 1975.
[18] The average number of births expected during a woman's childbearing life span, arbitrarily determined for statistical purposes as ages 15-44. The *general* fertility rate, in contrast, is the number of babies born per year relative to the number of women aged 15-44. The *birth rate* is the number of children born each year per 1,000 general population.
[19] See "Zero Population Growth," *E.R.R.*, 1971 Vol. II, pp. 903-924.
[20] Quoted in *U.S. News & World Report*, Oct. 27, 1975.

Single-Parent Families

Children are no longer the deterrent to divorce that they used to be. As divorce has become a more common and increasingly acceptable event, the pressure to stay together for the sake of the children has lessened considerably. All of this has produced a shift in the living arrangements of children. Census figures indicate that during the 1960s the number of children living with only one parent increased 12 times as rapidly as children living with both parents. During that decade, the absolute increase in numbers of children in single-parent homes exceeded the increase in children in two-parent homes. Furthermore, this increase occurred among whites as well as blacks.

Government Support of Traditional Family Life

The government was slow to respond to these changes in the American family. Well into the 1970s, according to Louise Kapp Howe, the white, middle-class family with a male breadwinner and female homemaker remained the model against which all who lived differently were judged deviant. Despite the huge numbers of working mothers, of single-parent homes, of youth in communes, and unemployed fathers, she wrote, the government, in practically all its policies related to the family, continued to act as if there were one and only one worthy way to run a household.[21]

In this vein, a report issued by the Department of Labor's Office of Policy Planning and Research in 1965 argued that the black family was "deteriorating" because about a fourth of the black families did not have a male at the head. The report noted:

> Nearly a quarter of urban Negro marriages are dissolved; nearly one-quarter of Negro births are now illegitimate; as a consequence, almost one-fourth of Negro families are headed by females, and this breakdown of the Negro family has led to a startling increase in welfare dependency.

The report, "The Negro Family: The Case for National Action," prepared under the direction of Daniel Patrick Moynihan, the sociologist and author who has held high posts in the Johnson, Nixon and Ford administrations, concluded that only concerted planning and action directed to a new kind of national goal—establishment of a stable black family structure—could forestall "a new crisis in race relations."[22]

Six years later, on Dec. 9, 1971, President Richard Nixon vetoed a bill that would have expanded the government's role in

---

[21] Louise Kapp Howe, ed., *The Future of the Family* (1972), pp. 11-13.

[22] The report was issued in March 1965, intended solely as an internal policy paper. It was made public in August 1965 after some of its contents had been leaked to newsmen. Its release to the public generated a storm of controversy. A detailed account of the genesis of the report and ensuing controversy were the subject of a book published in the spring of 1967, *The Moynihan Report and the Politics of Controversy* (Massachusetts Institute of Technology Press) by sociologists Lee Rainwater and William L. Yancey.

providing child care because of its "family weakening implications." Nixon said the bill "would commit the vast moral authority of the national government to the side of communal approaches to child rearing against the family-centered approach." Furthermore, he said, the bill would impede the government's most important task: "to cement the family in its rightful role as the keystone of our civilization." The persistence of the traditional view of the family was addressed in a discussion of child care alternatives in a 1972 Brookings Institution study of federal budget priorities.

> Decisions about day care and early childhood programs are likely to provoke a heated national debate over the next few years [the Brookings authors wrote], not only because the budgetary consequences might be large, but because sensitive emotional issues are involved. How should the responsibility for children be divided between the family and society? Should mothers of small children work? The spectrum of views is wide....
>
> Traditionally in the United States, the responsibility for the care and supervision of children has rested squarely with parents. Only when a child reached age six did society at large take a major stand by insisting that he attend school.... What happens to the child the rest of the time is his parents' business. Society intervenes only if he is severely abused or neglected or runs afoul of the law.[23]

Public prejudice has been particularly strong against single-parent families. "On the whole, in our society, the one-parent family has been viewed as a form of un-family or sick family," wrote Elizabeth Herzog and Cecilia E. Sudia. "For a number of reasons it would be wiser to recognize the one-parent family as a form that exists and functions...such families can be cohesive, warm, supportive and favorable to...[child] development."[24]

Concern for Children in Family Disorganization

The possibility that the single parent-child arrangement could conceivably be another legitimate form of the family is something the government has been reluctant to admit. This reluctance is linked to the traditional view that children are more likely to grow up to be law-abiding, healthy and happy adults if they spend their entire childhood with both parents than if the family unit is broken by death or divorce. "It has long and widely been thought that [the one-parent family] is damaging to children—not only when they are young but also later in their adult life—and that this, in turn, hurts society, which must cope with the damaged childrens' anti-social behavior or impaired abilities to achieve."[25]

---

[23] Charles L. Schultze, et al., "Child Care," *Setting National Priorities: The 1973 Federal Budget* (1972), pp. 252-290.

[24] Elizabeth Herzog and Cecilia E. Sudia, "Boys in Fatherless Families," Department of Health, Education, and Welfare reprint, 1972.

[25] Ross and Sawhill, *op. cit.*, p. 132.

Single-Parent Families

Sociologists have traditionally linked broken homes with juvenile delinquency. Their thinking is this: Children from broken homes, boiling with anger and resentment over the loss of a parent—usually the father, thus leaving them without a father's guidance and discipline—can succumb to anti-social behavior such as bullying, truancy, vandalism or worse.[26]

Other experts maintain that delinquency cannot be blamed solely on the lack of a second parent in a home. One study concluded that the onset of delinquency in children from broken homes cannot be attributed to the absence of a parent, but rather to "certain parental characteristics—intense conflict, rejection, and deviance—which occur more commonly in broken families."[27] Many studies have found that children living with unhappily married parents are more likely to get into trouble than children whose parents have little conflict or children in single-parent families.

The emotional impact of divorce on children is a major concern of many single parents. Psychiatrists tend to agree that divorce itself does not necessarily cause psychiatric problems to develop in children. One recent study found that children from one-parent families were under the greatest stress when (1) relations between the parents continued to be turbulent following the divorce, or (2) relations with the parent not in the home were forbidden the child. The authors speculate that children in a family headed by a woman suffer not from the father's absence but from maternal deprivation; women who become single parents are forced to spread their energies beyond their prior childrearing tasks.[28]

The Public Policy Implications

THE CHANGES occurring in children's living arrangements present a challenge to public-policy makers. But exactly what policy response is called for is not clear, according to economists Heather L. Ross and Isabel V. Sawhill.

> Should efforts at keeping families together be undertaken; efforts to make female-headed family life less isolated and deprived; or efforts to facilitate remarriage and the formation of new husband-wife families? What acceptable, effective policy devices are there to promote any of these objectives?

---

[26] See Sheldon and Eleanor Glueck's *Unraveling Juvenile Delinquency* (1951).

[27] Joan McCord, William McCord and Emily Thurber, "Some Effects of Paternal Absence on Male Children," *Journal of Abnormal and Social Psychology,* March 1962, pp. 361-369.

[28] Ruth A. Brandwein et al., "Women and Children Last: The Social Situation of Divorced Mothers and Their Families," *Journal of Marriage and Family,* August 1974, pp. 498-514.

Mean Family Income, 1974

Age of Head	Husband-Wife Families	Single-Parent Families Male-Headed	Female-Headed
Under 25	$ 9,931	$10,351	$3,600
25-44	16,118	12,093	6,481
45-64	18,244	13,045	8,438

SOURCE: U.S. Bureau of the Census

The most pressing policy need, they conclude, is to make life less difficult for female-headed families. Furthermore, they say, "some of the policy options in this area—for example, improved day care, social services, and child-support arrangements—are better defined and more within the range of accepted public policy than are devices to influence private decisions on marriage and family."

The biggest problem facing single-mother households is inadequate income. The traditional response to low-family incomes has been welfare, specifically Aid to Families with Dependent Children. This program is federally aided but administered by the individual states which set eligibility requirements and benefit levels. The average monthly payment in 1975 was $212.90, ranging from $50 in Mississippi to $360 in Massachusetts. Total federal, state and local spending for the program reached $8.5-billion in fiscal year 1975. About three-quarters of the recipient families were headed by women.

Many divorced, separated and deserted mothers end up on welfare because their absent husbands fail to make alimony and child-support payments. In an effort to reduce welfare costs, Congress in December 1974 passed a law requiring states and localities to make a vigorous effort to track down absentee fathers of children on public assistance and make them pay.

The law requires each state to set up special offices responsible for searching for the missing parent, establishing paternity of children born out of wedlock, and bringing action to collect support payments. States must have these services in full operation by Jan. 1, 1977, or face the loss of 5 per cent of their federal welfare funds under the Aid to Families with Dependent Children program.[29]

---

[29] The 1974 act authorized the federal government to pay 75 per cent of the cost of state child-support-enforcement programs. However, the following year Congress reduced this share to 50 per cent for states that had begun setting up their own programs by Aug. 1, 1975.

Single-Parent Families

To help the states locate missing parents, the law provided for a central parent-locator service within the U.S. Department of Health, Education, and Welfare. Through the central unit, the states have access to information in federal files, including Social Security, Civil Service, Treasury and Defense Department records. Currently 14 states[30] are linked to the central unit by computers; the rest send in their requests by mail. The government reports that it has found addresses for almost 90 per cent of the persons for whom the states sought information.

Once the recalcitrant parent is found, the states are permitted under the law to use the federal courts to collect support payments. If the parent fails to comply with a court order mandating payment, the Internal Revenue Service is authorized to collect the money in the same way it collects back taxes. Government employees and members of the military forces are subject to paycheck deductions for child support. Families not on welfare may use these collection services for a fee set by the states. The rationale for allowing this use of the service is that it could help reduce future claims on welfare funds.

A welfare mother who cooperates in locating the absentee father receives up to $20 each month the support is collected. The rest of the money is kept by the government to offset welfare payments made that month to the family or to compensate for past welfare payments to the family. Originally, a mother who failed to help locate the absent father was cut off from welfare payments. But Congress in 1975 exempted the mother from this requirement if a state agency determined that the missing father might subject the children to physical harm or harassment.

Child-Care Programs: Debate Over Federal Role

The U.S. Office of Child Development research paper *(see p. 65)* concluded that federal policies aimed at helping single-parent families have been directed almost exclusively toward those on welfare. Day care is an example. This year the federal government is expected to spend $1.2-billion on child-care services. The bulk of the money will be spent on day care for welfare children whose mothers work or receive job training and on the Head Start program which provides pre-school education for children in poverty.

Federal child-care support available to middle and upper-income families is usually indirect—allowing working parents to deduct some child-care expenses from income subject to federal taxation. The Revenue Act of 1971 greatly liberalized child-care deductions. Under that law, persons working full-time and earn-

---

[30] California, Iowa, Massachusetts, Michigan, Minnesota, Nebraska, New Jersey, New York, Pennsylvania, Tennessee, Texas, Washington, New Mexico, North Carolina.

> ### Bachelor Fathers
>
> Men are raising their children alone, either by choice or circumstance, in increasing numbers. By 1975 there were 500,000 bachelor fathers, twice as many as a decade earlier, in the United States. They were caring for nearly one million children under age 18.
>
> Although adoption by single males has contributed to the increase, the main reason is the liberalized attitude of the courts about awarding custody of the children to the father in divorce cases. In the past, fathers had almost no chance of being awarded custody unless they could prove that their wives were unfit mothers. Women still wind up with the children in 90 per cent of the divorce cases, but this percentage is slowly decreasing.
>
> New York, California and Illinois are among those states which have abandoned the "tender years" doctrine—which holds that children generally are better off with their mothers—and amended their laws to specify that either parent can be awarded custody.

ing $18,000 a year or less could deduct up to $200 a month for the care of one child under age 15; up to $300 a month for two children; and up to $400 a month for three or more children. If the adjusted gross income of the couple or individual exceeded $18,000, the deduction was reduced on a sliding scale. After reaching $27,600 no child-care deduction was allowed. The Tax Reduction Act of 1975 raised the income limits for the child-care deduction from $18,000 to $35,000 and from $27,600 to $44,600.

The deduction is a tremendous help to many single parents. But there is one catch. In order to qualify the parent must (1) have custody of the child and (2) be entitled to claim the child as a tax deduction. The parent who has custody of the child for the greater part of the year normally will be entitled to the dependency exemption. However, the non-custodial parent may claim the exemption if (1) he or she contributes at least $600 a year in child support and the separation agreement or divorce decree gives the exemption to the non-custodial parent; or (2) if he or she contributes $1,200 or more a year in child support and the custodial parent cannot clearly show that he or she contributed a greater amount of support.

If the non-custodial parent does claim the child as a tax deduction, neither parent can deduct day-care or babysitting expenses incurred for the child. To remedy this situation, many single parents advocate changes in tax laws to allow divorced or separated parents to split exemptions and child-care deductions, or allow the parent with custody to claim the deduction whether or not he or she claimed the child as a tax exemption. Single parents also support proposals that would make child-care deductions available to part-time workers and to full-time

Single-Parent Families

students. Single parents also argue that child-care expenses should be treated as a legitimate business expense rather than a personal expense. The point is often made that if a company or self-employed person can claim a secretary's salary as a business expense, why cannot an employee claim child-care expenses.

Another special concern of single parents is the lack of day-care facilities for school-age children. Nearly 18 million children from ages 6 to 14 need some form of supervision after school hours, according to the National Council of Organizations for Children and Youth.[31] Dr. Edward Zigler of Yale University told the Senate Subcommittee on Children and Youth in September 1973: "Because of our slowness in developing day-care models for school-age children and inducing schools and other institutions to employ such models, we are now witnessing the national tragedy of over one million latchkey children, cared for by no one, with probably an equal number being cared for by siblings who are themselves too young to assume such responsibilities."

A few corporations have set up supervised day-care centers on their premises. Single-parent groups are trying to encourage more employers to take advantage of section 162 (a) of the Internal Revenue Code. The provision allows a company to claim as a business expense whatever it spends to establish and operate day-care programs for the children of employees if it can show that this is done to increase employee morale and productivity.

"It is not inconceivable," said Dr. Ruby Takanishi, assistant professor of early childhood development at the University of California at Los Angeles, "that child care services can join the range of employee benefits now provided, including health and disability insurance, maternity and military leaves, credit unions, retirement plans and recreational facilities."[32] Dr. Urie Bronfenbrenner of Cornell University advocates extending tax incentives to businesses and industries that modify their work schedules so that parents can be home when their children return from school. Most working parents would welcome the flexible work schedules.

Laws on Discrimination Against Single Parents

In the past, single parents—particularly women—frequently complained of discrimination in trying to obtain housing, credit and insurance. "When I got divorced," said Mrs. Diane Meyers, a Houston secretary, "I discovered that I didn't have any credit. I didn't have a car and couldn't get a loan to buy one. I even had

---

[31] National Council of Organizations for Children and Youth, "America's Children 1976," p. 74.

[32] Quoted in *The Single Parent News*, Vol. 1, No. 2, 1976. The publication is issued bimonthly in Santa Monica, Calif.

trouble finding a place to live because apartment owners feared that a divorced woman could not give proper supervision to the children."[33]

In recent years Congress has taken action to correct these ills. In October 1974, it amended the Consumer Credit Protection Act by adding an "Equal Credit Opportunity" provision. This provision, which went into effect Oct. 28, 1975, makes it illegal to consider sex or marital status in determining credit worthiness. The law applies to all credit transactions, including mortgage applications. Title I of the Housing and Community Development Act of 1974 amended the Fair Housing Act of 1968[34] to prohibit sex discrimination in the financing, sale or rental of housing.

In Denver, Colo., a low-income housing development designed specifically for single parents and their children opened in February 1974. Besides low rent, it offers other advantages to the single parent: day-care facilities for pre-school and school-age youngsters; financial counseling by qualified members of the staff; a group therapy program run by the Denver Mental Health Clinic; educational counseling and adult education programs provided by three colleges in the area.[35]

Arrangements for the Joint Custody of Children

One way to ease the burdens of single parenthood—both financial and emotional—is to encourage more shared responsibility by both parents, according to Dr. Lee Salk. "Women have been reluctant to give up the responsibility for fear they'd be looked down upon," he writes. "I think we ought to move to a point where women will be freer to relinquish some responsibilities to males without feeling stigmatized or guilty. This guilt is all part of the motherhood myth. And children are not benefitting by it."[36]

Although women still retain custody of the children in most divorces, a small but growing number of divorced parents are experimenting with a new kind of arrangement—joint custody. The child spends equal time with both parents. In practice the idea takes many forms. Usually both parents live in the same community so that the child's school life and friendships will not be disrupted. In some joint custody arrangements, each parent maintains a home in which the children have their own space and some of their own things. "This way they are not visitors," Emily Jane Goodman writes.[37]

---

[33] Quoted in *U.S. News & World Report*, July 16, 1973, p. 34.

[34] Title VIII of the 1968 Civil Rights Act.

[35] See Ann O'Shea, "Housing for the Single Parent," *McCall's*, June 1975, p. 36.

[36] Dr. Lee Salk, "Problems and Pleasures of the Single Parent," *Harper's Bazaar*, March 1975, p. 77.

[37] Emily Jane Goodman, "Joint Custody," *McCall's*, August 1975, p. 34.

Single-Parent Families

Some parents avoid the constant moving back and forth by alternating custody every six months or so. Still another variation is for the children to remain in the family home and the parents to take turns living there. Joint custody is also construed to mean that the children live with one parent but the other lives very close by and spends considerable time with them every day. So far the courts have not looked too favorably upon joint custody arrangements. Ms. Goodman said: "Judges tend to follow precedent and are likely to regard joint custody as putting the needs of the parents above those of the children." Consequently, most joint custody agreements are arranged privately between the parents.

How do such arrangements affect the children? It's still too early to tell, but according to Marcia Holly, a free-lance writer who has shared custody of her daughter for four years, children living in joint custody arrangements are less likely to feel that they may be abandoned—a common fear among children of divorce. "Abandonment seems less likely to children where there are two parents and two homes that welcome them," she said. "Their dual homes force them to develop more ways of interacting with a variety of people. Most of these children seem to feel pleasurable anticipation about alternating homes rather than resentment or sadness at leaving one house for the other."[38]

Those parents who do retain full custody of their children are looking for other solutions to the problems of single parenthood. In some areas, single parents are forming small collectives that allow them to pool their financial and emotional resources. This arrangement also allows them to share babysitting and housekeeping chores. Other single parents are finding emotional support in informal, extended family arrangements, a concept pioneered by the Unitarian-Universalist Church. Many single parents find that other single parents are their best source of support. Over 80,000 single parents belong to Parents Without Partners, a nationwide organization offering counseling, seminars and social activities for members and their children.

Momma, an organization for single mothers with headquarters in Los Angeles, has about 50 chapters across the country. Its goals are to stimulate research on single motherhood and its impact on the general society, to provide a clearinghouse for resources and information relevant to single mothers, and to assist single mothers in achieving economic self-sufficiency, education and child-rearing guidance. These goals will be easier to achieve as the government becomes more responsive to the needs of this growing minority.

---

[38] Marcia Holly, "Joint Custody: The New Haven Plan," *Ms.*, September 1976, pp. 70-71. See also Elizabeth Dancy, "Who Gets the Kids?" *Ms.*, September 1976, p. 70.

Selected Bibliography

Books

Gardner, Richard A., *The Boys and Girls Book About Divorce,* Bantam Books, 1970.
Howe, Louise Kapp, ed., *The Future of the Family,* Simon & Schuster, 1972.
Kay, F. George, *The Family in Transition,* John Wiley & Sons, 1972.
Ross, Heather L. and Isabel V. Sawhill, *Time of Transition: The Growth of Families Headed By Women,* The Urban Institute, 1975.
Schlesinger, Benjamin, *The One-Parent Family,* University of Toronto Press, 1975.
Yorburg, Betty, *The Changing Family,* Columbia University Press, 1973.

Articles

Dancey, Elizabeth, "Who Gets Custody?" *Ms.,* September 1976.
Holly, Marcia, "Joint Custody: The New Haven Plan," *Ms.,* September 1976.
MacDonald, Steve, "The Alimony Blues," *The New York Times Magazine,* March 16, 1975.
McEaddy, Beverly Johnson, "Women Who Head Families: A Socioeconomic Analysis," *Monthly Labor Review,* June 1976.
Salk, Lee, "Guilt and the Single Parent," *Harper's Bazaar,* March 1976.
———"Problems and Pleasures of the Single Parent," *Harper's Bazaar,* March 1975.
"Rising Problems of 'Single Parents,'" *U.S. News & World Report,* July 16, 1973.
"The Broken Family: Divorce U.S. Style," *Newsweek,* March 12, 1973.

Reports and Studies

"America's Children 1976," National Council of Organizations for Children and Youth, 1976.
Editorial Research Reports, "Marriage: Changing Institution," 1971 Vol. II, p. 759; "Child Care," 1972 Vol. II, p. 439; "Child Support," 1974 Vol. I, p. 61; "No-Fault Divorce," 1973 Vol. II, p. 777.
Helco, Hugh, et al., "Single-Parent Families: Issues and Policies," unpublished draft manuscript, 1974.
Senate Subcommittee on Children and Youth, "American Families: Trends and Pressures 1973," hearings Sept. 24-26, 1973.
U.S. Bureau of the Census, "Female Family Heads," *Current Population Reports,* Series P-23, No. 50, July 1974.
———"Household and Family Characteristics, March 1975," *Current Population Reports,* Series P-20, No. 291, February 1976.
———"Marital Status and Living Arrangements, March 1975," *Current Population Reports,* Series P-20, No. 287, December 1975.
———"Some Recent Changes in American Families," Series P-23, No. 52, 1975.
Winston, Marian P. and Trude Forsher, "Nonsupport of Legitimate Children By Affluent Fathers as a Cause of Poverty and Welfare Dependence," the Rand Corporation, April 1974.

WOMEN IN THE WORK FORCE

by

Sandra Stencel

	page
WORK PATTERNS OF THE SEVENTIES	83
Women's Big Entry Into U.S. Job Market	83
Economic and Social Factors in the Upsurge	84
Widening Pay Gap Between Men and Women	86
Shift to Professional and Blue-Collar Jobs	89
HISTORY OF WORKING WOMEN IN U.S.A.	90
Place in Economic Life of the Early Republic	90
Civil War, Immigration and Labor Activity	91
Job Gains Coinciding With Push for Suffrage	92
Breakthrough in the World War II Job Market	94
Laws Banning Discrimination in Employment	95
CONTINUING FIGHT FOR JOB EQUALITY	98
Criticism of Equal Employment Commission	98
Attempt to Nullify Court Ruling on Pregnancy Pay	99
Psychic Barriers to Women's Advancement	100
Child Care Problems for Working Mothers	101

**Feb. 18
1977**

Editor's Note: Since this report was published, the number of women either working or actively looking for work has risen to over 50 percent. Women now constitute about 41 percent of the nation's work force. The wage gap between male and female employees, discussed on pp. 86-87, has persisted. According to a survey released by the U.S. Bureau of Labor Statistics in September 1978, women working full-time in 1975 earned an average of $5,000 less than men. The national median income was $12,700 for men and $7,531 for women. For those with college educations the gap was even wider, with men earning $17,891 and women $10,861.

Complaints against the Equal Employment Opportunity Commission, discussed on pp. 98-99, have decreased in recent years. Eleanor Holmes Norton, the former human rights commissioner for New York City, who became head of EEOC in 1977, has been credited for introducing competent management to the agency, for reducing its tremendous case backlog and for focusing the agency's enforcment efforts on broad "patterns and practices" of discrimination in particular companies or industries rather than isolated instances. When President Carter appointed Norton to the EEOC in 1977, the backlog of discrimination complaints had reached nearly 130,000. The current backlog stands at about 119,000 cases.

WOMEN IN THE WORK FORCE

RESPONDING TO changing views of their role in society and inflationary pressures on family budgets, women are surging into the U.S. labor force at an unprecedented rate. Not even in the World War II days of Rosie the Riveter did so many women work outside the home. Nearly half—47 per cent—of the American women 16 and older held jobs or were actively looking for work last year. Among women aged 20 to 64, the prime working year, the percentage was even higher. Over 56 per cent of the women in this group were employed.[1]

The number of American women who work has been rising steadily since 1947 *(see box, p. 85)*. But during the last few years and especially in 1976, women entered the job market at a pace called "extraordinary" by Alan Greenspan, chairman of President Ford's Council of Economic Advisers.[2] Last year 1.6 million women entered the work force. Over the past 25 years the number of American working women more than doubled, rising to nearly 39 million in 1976 from just 19 million in 1951. The Bureau of Labor Statistics estimates that nearly 12 million more women will be added to the work force by 1990.[3] According to the same projection, the number of men in the labor force will grow by less than 10 million during that period. Although men are expected to continue to make up the larger part of the labor force, their participation is expected to continue its slow, long-term decline.

The Department of Labor, in its "1975 Handbook on Women Workers," labeled this increase in the number and proportion of women who work as "one of the most spectacular changes in the American economy in the past quarter-century." Eli Ginzberg, a Columbia University economist and chairman of the National Commission for Manpower Policy, called it "the single most outstanding phenomenon of our century," and he went on to say that "its long-range implications are absolutely unchartable."[4]

Some economists say that the influx of women—and also teenagers—into the labor force accounts for the nation's con-

---

[1] Statistics from U.S. Department of Labor, Bureau of Labor Statistics, "Employment and Earnings," Vol. 23, No. 5, November 1976, pp. 21-22.
[2] White House press conference, Sept. 3, 1976.
[3] *Monthly Labor Review*, October 1976, p. 2. The *Monthly Labor Review* is published by the Department of Labor.
[4] Quoted in *The New York Times*, Sept. 12, 1976.

tinued high unemployment rate. In 1976, the nation's unemployment rate fluctuated between 7.3 and 8.1. For both adult men and women, the rate was lower, but for teenagers it was far higher, as the following table illustrates:

Period	Overall Rate	Adult Women*	Adult Men*	Teen-agers
1976	7.7%	7.4%	5.9%	19.0%
1975	8.5	8.0	6.7	19.9
1974	5.6	5.5	3.8	16.0

* 20 and older

The primary cause of the current unemployment rate has not been people losing their jobs, John O'Riley of *The Wall Street Journal* wrote, but rather "the unprecedented number of new job seekers scrambling to get on the paycheck bandwagon." *Time* magazine commented that "the profound consequence" of women and teenagers entering the job market in large numbers "is that the number of people looking for work is leaping faster than the economy can provide jobs...."[5]

Feminists contend that such arguments ignore the economic reasons which force most women to seek work. "The only justification for those who, for political advantage, try to blame our high unemployment rate primarily on the spectacular influx of women into the labor force is that at least they have pinpointed a profound change in the labor force," wrote financial columnist Sylvia Porter last September. "Their argument is viciously sexist. Their explanation shrugs off the vital importance of the woman's paycheck to prosperity and to the standard of living of millions of households."[6]

Economic and Social Factors in the Upsurge

Like all complex social changes, the back-to-work movement has been shaped by many economic and cultural forces. Economic need is clearly one of them. "Women now work because they have to," said Arlene Kaplan Daniels, a Northwestern University sociologist. This was especially true for the 8.5 million single women in the labor force in 1975 and for the nearly seven million women workers who were divorced or separated from their husbands. Of all women in the work force, about one out of eight (12.3 per cent) was either divorced or separated, according to a recent report by Allyson Sherman Grossman, an economist with the Bureau of Labor Statistics.[7]

---

[5] *The Wall Street Journal*, Jan. 17, 1977, and *Time*, Nov. 1, 1976, p. 25.

[6] Sylvia Porter, writing in *The Washington Star*, Sept. 20, 1976.

[7] Allyson Sherman Grossman, "The Labor Force Patterns of Divorced and Separated Women," *Monthly Labor Review*, January 1977, pp. 48-53. Daniels was quoted in *Newsweek*, Dec. 6, 1976, p. 69.

Women in the Work Force

Year	Number (add 000)	Percentage of Adult Female Population*
1947	16,683	31.8
1951	19,054	34.7
1956	21,495	36.9
1961	23,838	38.1
1966	27,333	40.3
1971	32,132	43.4
1972	33,320	43.9
1973	34,561	44.7
1974	35,892	45.7
1975	37,087	46.4
1976	38,520	47.4

*Ages 16 and older

Source: U.S. Department of Labor

Economic need was also behind the sharp rise in the labor force participation of married women in recent years. Of the more than 21 million married women who were in the labor force in March 1975, approximately 26 per cent were married to men earning less than $10,000 a year. Nearly three million working women had husbands who were unemployed or unable to work.[8] As inflation has eroded real disposable income, many middle-class families have come to rely on wives' earnings to maintain their standard of living. Without a second paycheck, they would find it difficult—if not impossible—to buy a house or send their children to college.

A number of factors other than economic need and the rising divorce rate have contributed to the increased number of working women. These include: (1) more effective means of birth control and the trend toward fewer children; (2) the increased life expectancy of women; (3) the greater number of college-educated women; and (4) the widespread use of labor-saving devices in the home. Other factors are the expansion of the white-collar job market in which most women are employed, the increase in part-time employment opportunities, and legal action prohibiting job discrimination based on sex.

There has been a tremendous change in attitude toward working women in recent years, primarily as a result of publicity given to the woman's movement. "As recently as 10 years ago, a woman had to defend her position if she wanted to work," said Beatrice Buckley, editor of a new monthly magazine called

---

[8] U.S. Department of Labor, "Why Women Work," July 1976.

Working Woman. "Now you have only to go out and ask the nearest housewife what she does and she'll answer, 'Just a housewife.'"[9] A recent survey of teenage girls and young women conducted for the American Council of Life Insurance found that only one in four wanted to be a housewife.[10]

A Roper Poll for *Fortune* in 1936 indicated that only 15 per cent of the population believed "married women should have a full-time job outside the house." Another Roper Poll for the magazine 10 years later found that by a 5-3 ratio Americans thought that housewives had more interesting lives than women who held full-time jobs. By 1969 the national temper had changed, according to a Gallup Poll. By a 5-4 majority, the poll's respondents said there was nothing wrong with married women earning money in business and industry.

A Gallup Poll in March 1976 found that 68 per cent of those interviewed approved of working wives. A study conducted later in the year by *The Washington Post* and the Harvard University Center for International Affairs indicated that men favored careers for women by a 2-1 ratio, women by 4 to 3. However, a nationwide poll conducted by Research Analysis Corp. of Boston for *Newsday* found that nearly half of those it surveyed agreed with the statement, "If a man doesn't want his wife to take a job, she should respect his wishes."[11]

Widening Pay Gap Between Men and Women

Women's pay has increased significantly in recent years but not as fast as men's *(see graph, p. 87)*. Consequently the difference between men's and women's pay is wider today than it was 20 years ago, according to a report issued last October by the Women's Bureau of the Department of Labor titled "The Earnings Gap Between Women and Men." It also noted that women earned substantially less than men at the same level of education. In fact, the average woman college graduate earned less than the average male high school drop-out. The study found that women were overrepresented at the lower end of the pay scale as the following table illustrates:

Earning Group	Male	Female
$ 3,000-$4,999	36.6%	63.4%
5,000-6,999	41.9	58.1
7,000-9,999	59.3	40.7
10,000-14,999	83.1	16.9
15,000 and over	94.7	5.3

---

[9] Quoted in *Newsweek,* Dec. 6, 1976, p. 69.
[10] American Council of Life Insurance, "The Family Economist," Nov. 3, 1976.
[11] *Post*-Harvard poll appeared in *The Washington Post,* Sept. 28, 1976, and the Research Analysis Corp. poll in *Newsday,* June 15, 1976.

MEDIAN EARNINGS
Thousands

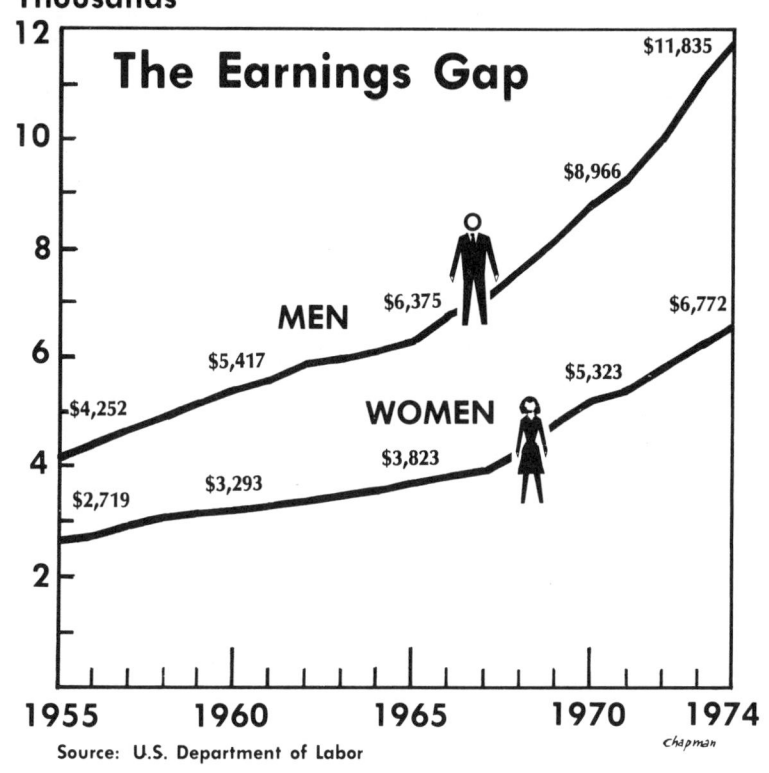

The Earnings Gap

MEN: $4,252 — $5,417 — $6,375 — $8,966 — $11,835
WOMEN: $2,719 — $3,293 — $3,823 — $5,323 — $6,772

1955   1960   1965   1970   1974

Source: U.S. Department of Labor   Chapman

    The widening wage gap between the sexes reflects the continued concentration of women in relatively low-skilled, low-paying jobs. According to the Department of Labor's "1975 Handbook on Women Workers," more than two-fifths of all women workers were employed in just 10 job categories in 1973: secretary, retail sales worker, bookkeeper, private household worker, elementary school teacher, waitress, typist, cashier, sewer and sticher, and registered nurse. Salaries were relatively low, averaging $4,700 for sales clerks and $6,400 for clerical workers. More than one-third of all women workers were employed in clerical jobs.

    Helping to fill the clerical ranks are many college-educated women who cannot find other work. The Equal Employment Opportunity Commission estimates that 20 per cent of the college graduates who work are in clerical, semi-clerical or unskilled jobs. Economists say this is partly because many women major in the liberal arts and enter the job market with few marketable skills and partly because of discrimination. Businesses still tend to groom male college graduates for management jobs and women graduates for the secretarial pool.

Occupational segregation stems from many sources—discrimination, cultural conditioning, and the personal desires of women themselves. The jobs women traditionally have held are frequently related to the work they performed in the home—teaching children and young adults, nursing the sick, preparing food, assisting their husbands and other men. According to Dr. Nancy Smith Barret, an economics professor at American University in Washington, D.C., women have been conditioned to believe that these are the only "proper" jobs.[12]

During the period in which women were entering the job market in large numbers, jobs in the service industries, including health care and teaching, were opening up faster than in other occupations. Between 1964 and 1974, employment in the service industry nearly doubled. Another factor contributing to the concentration of women in the service industries is that part-time employment is more obtainable there than elsewhere.[13] In 1974, according to the Department of Labor, about 28 per cent of all working women held part-time jobs.

Despite the plethora of statistics indicating that the majority of women work because of economic need, many employers still hold to the traditional view that men ought to be paid more than women. Employers reason that men merit higher salaries or preference in hiring because they will not withdraw for marriage and childbearing; that men can give more time and effort to the job because they have no domestic responsibilities; that they are more valuable as employees because of their greater mobility; or that they need more money to support their families. Because they see women as temporary fixtures in the labor force many employers tend to shuttle women into jobs where the skills are quickly learned and there is little opportunity for advancement.

"The threat of discontinuity in a woman's worklife is perhaps the greatest single barrier to higher wages for young women," the new Secretary of Commerce, Juanita Kreps, wrote in her book *Sex in the Marketplace: American Women at Work* (1971). She added:

> The period of heaviest domestic responsibility occurs fairly early in a woman's worklife, when she is likely to be forced to make some quite long-range decisions: whether to acquire further job training, or additional formal education; how many children she will have; whether to continue working, at least part-time, during the childbearing period.... Her immediate job choice is dictated in large measure by the time constraint imposed in the short-run, and this choice in turn directs her subsequent career development.

---

[12] Quoted in *Redbook*, March 1975, p. 88.
[13] See article by Elizabeth Waldman and Beverly J. McEaddy, "Where Women Work—An Analysis by Industry and Occupation," *Monthly Labor Review*, May 1974, p. 3.

Women in the Work Force

Because of their family responsibilities, many women prefer jobs that require little or no overtime work or traveling. One of the attractions of elementary school teaching for women is that they can coordinate their work with their children's schedules.

Shift to Professional and Blue-Collar Jobs

The pay gap does not disappear when women go into the professions. The median income for women college professors is 91 per cent that of their male colleagues. The average salary for women high school teachers is 81 per cent that of men. Female scientists earn 76 per cent as much as male scientists, and female engineers 85 per cent as much as their male counterparts. In some professions the situation for women is getting worse, not better. The latest figures from the National Center for Education Statistics in the Department of Health, Education and Welfare show that during the 1975-76 school year, the average salary for male faculty members rose faster than for females.

Almost 16 per cent of all women in the U.S. labor force are in the professions, mostly nursing and teaching. But growing numbers are seeking fuller access to such traditionally male-dominated professions as law, medicine, architecture, business and engineering. Today about 23 per cent of all law students in the United States are women, up from 8.5 per cent in 1971. The number of first-year women medical students has more than doubled since 1972.[14] About 25 per cent of all entering medical students are women, up from 11.3 per cent in 1970 and 8.9 per cent in 1965.

Among the nation's 1,300 biggest companies, *Business Week* reported Jan. 10, 1977, there are about 400 women directors versus about 20 just five years ago. However, these 400 represent only 2.7 per cent of the 15,000 board members of major corporations. More and more women are becoming junior executives and sales representatives, positions that often lead to the top. International Business Machines, which employed 400 women sales representatives in 1973, now has 1,400. At Xerox the percentage of women in the sales force has grown to 14.9, up from 1.7 in 1971. In other fields, too, women are starting to move up through the ranks. A recent report on commercial banking by the New York-based Council on Economic Priorities showed women making significant gains in managerial, professional, technical and sales posts.[15]

---

[14] See Mary Lynn M. Luy, "Status Report on Women in Medical Education: Up and Coming," *Modern Medicine,* Nov. 1, 1976, p. 33. The American Bar Association figure of 23 per cent is limited to women enrolled in ABA-approved law schools.

[15] The council found that between 1971 and 1975 the percentage of all bank managers and officials who were women jumped from 16 to 26. The number of women in professional, technical and sales categories climbed from 22 to 35 per cent. However, only 13 per cent of the bank officers and 1.8 per cent of the senior executives were women.

Women have made some inroads into blue-collar jobs that up until recently have been largely male enclaves. The signs of change are everywhere. From 1962 to 1975 the ratio of men to women changed from 70-1 to 20-1 among garage workers and gas station attendants, from 35-1 to 11-1 among mail carriers, and from 27-1 to 11-1 among taxicab drivers.[16] In Seattle, an organization called Mechanica has placed women as carpenters, machinists, diesel mechanics, laborers and truck drivers. Over 3,000 women were employed on the Trans-Alaska Oil Pipeline as craftsmen, clerks and cooks. Approximately 11,000 women make their living as carpenters and 700 women as coal miners.[17]

Despite these gains, the number of women who have cracked the sex barriers is relatively small, and the sight of women at the bottom of mines, at the top of telephone poles, and in the ranks of the police, firefighters and the military academies still draws the attention of the public and the news media. The Department of Labor, in its latest report on the subject, said that only 18 per cent of the total number of blue-collar workers were women at the end of 1975, about five million women in all.

History of Working Women in U.S.A.

VERY FEW PEOPLE know that the official version of the Declaration of Independence, the one that was circulated to all the colonies, was printed by a woman—Mary Katherine Goddard of Baltimore. "The job of printing the Declaration went to a woman," author Caroline Bird wrote, "because as publisher of the leading newspaper in town, she had the facilities to do it."[18] In addition to being a successful newspaper publisher and printer, Mary Katherine Goddard was the new nation's first, and for many years the only, woman postmaster.

Although Mary Goddard was not typical of the women of her time, she was not unique either. Many colonial women were employed in the trades. Since most work was done at or near home, wives often assisted their husbands and frequently carried on the business if they were widowed. Many had come to the colonies as indentured servants and worked as domestic servants during their bondage. Other colonial women (especially

---

[16] Figures from Peter A. Morrison and Judith A. Wheeler, "Working Women and 'Woman's Work': A Demographic Perspective on the Breakdown of Sex Roles," The Rand Corporation, June 1976, p. 2.

[17] The Kentucky Commission on Human Rights has ordered a number of coal companies in the state to hire more women and wants women eventually to fill 20 per cent of the mining jobs in Kentucky. See *United Mine Workers Journal*, January 1977, p. 13.

[18] Caroline Bird, *Enterprising Women* (1976), p. 6.

widows) kept inns and taverns, managed retail businesses, and became seamstresses and milliners. The most important occupations for women during this period were spinning and weaving. At first most of this work was done at home. But as the demand for textiles increased, the factory system developed. By 1850, the textile mills of New England employed some 92,000 workers, two-thirds of them women.[19]

The earliest female mill operators were primarily the unmarried daughters of native Yankee farmers. Most of them worked in the mills only a few years before moving to marriage and occasionally school teaching. "Mill work was generally regarded as a desirable way to preserve young women from the moral perils of idleness," wrote Robert W. Smuts in his classic work *Women and Work in America* (1959). Between 1840 and 1860, Irish and French-Canadian immigrant women, many of them married, took over many of the mill jobs. Other immigrant women helped produce boots, shoes and cigars; toiled in printing plants and paper mills; or worked as housekeepers, chambermaids, charwomen, laundresses and cooks.

Civil War, Immigration and Labor Activity

The Civil War expanded the job opportunities for women, especially in office work, government service and retailing. Yet, in 1870, 70 per cent of the women who worked were still domestics. The average age of those employed was 23, and nearly 85 per cent were single and most contributed to the support of their families and lived with their parents. Their wages averaged $5.25 a week.

As immigrant women took over more of the industrial jobs, middle-class women began entering new occupations, such as teaching and social work. Mainly as a result of the Civil War, large numbers of women went into nursing and many stayed in the profession after the war. Despite these new opportunities, it was still rare for married women to work, especially in the middle classes, and even rarer for mothers to work. Among the four million working girls and women counted by the 1890 census, only half a million were married. A Bureau of Labor study of 17,000 women factory workers in 1887 found that only 4 per cent of them were married. Only one woman teacher out of 25 was married in 1890, partly because many communities would not hire married women. "Should a female teacher marry," declared the bylaws of New York City, "her place shall thereupon become vacant."[20]

By and large, married women worked only if their husbands

---

[19] Heidi I. Hartmann, "Women's Work in the United States" *Current History,* May 1976, p. 216.

[20] Cited in Robert W. Smuts' *Women and Work in America* (1959), p. 19.

were permanently or temporarily unable to support their families. Around the turn of the century, Smuts wrote, "When a married woman worked it was usually a sign that something had gone wrong." Only among blacks and the immigrant populations of New England textile towns was a large minority of wives employed outside the home. Among the blacks, according to the 1890 census, nearly one-fourth of the wives and nearly two-thirds of the widows were employed.

Partly because their options were so limited, many 19th century women eagerly embraced womanhood as a vocation in itself. The ideology of "True Womanhood," popularized through women's magazines such as *Godey's Lady's Book*, revolved around the notion that women's rightful place was in the home. However, this ideal was not readily attainable by most working-class women, who were more concerned with improving their working conditions.

Women industrial workers had formed local workingwomen's societies as early as the 1830s. "In the 1840s, women workers were in the leadership of labor militancy in the United States."[21] Women participated in attempts to form national unions in the 1860s and 1870s and in the Knights of Labor in the 1880s. At its height, the Knights of Labor had 50,000 women members—most of them organized into "separate but equal" locals. In 1886, the Knights hired the first woman investigator of female working conditions, Leonora Barry. But for the most part, women were discouraged from joining unions. "Keeping women out of the union was a way...to keep women out of the trade or to limit their participation."[22]

Nevertheless, women were active in the New England textile mill strikes conducted by the Industrial Workers of the World ("Wobblies") in 1912, and the AFL's International Ladies' Garment Workers Union began to organize vast numbers of women, many of them immigrants, in the needles trade in New York City in 1909. The tragic Triangle Fire in New York City in 1911, which killed 146 young women shirtmakers because the fire exits were locked, was a tremendous spur to organization. By 1920, the garment workers union had nearly 100,000 members.

Job Gains Coinciding With Push for Suffrage

World War I created new job opportunities for women, and thousands moved into jobs formerly held by men. Feminist leaders in the campaign for woman's suffrage were convinced that a new era of feminine equality was dawning. "Wonderful as

---

[21] Rosalynn Baxandall, Linda Gordon and Susan Reverby, eds., *America's Working Women* (1976), p. 66.
[22] *Ibid.*, pp. 83-84.

Women's Share of the U.S. Labor Force

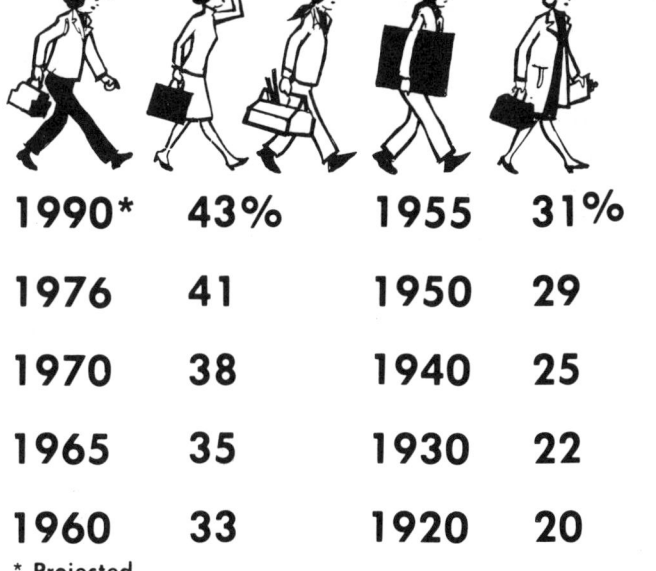

1990*	43%	1955	31%
1976	41	1950	29
1970	38	1940	25
1965	35	1930	22
1960	33	1920	20

* Projected

Source: U.S. Department of Labor

---

this hour is for democracy and labor," Margaret Drier Robbins told the Women's Trade Union League in 1917, "it is the first hour in history for the women of the world.... At last, after centuries of disabilities and discrimination, women are coming into the labor and festival of life on equal terms with men."[23]

But it was not to be. After the war both employers and male employees assumed that women would happily relinquish the new jobs and skills that they had acquired. The male-dominated AFL unions led the fight for legislation to exclude women from such jobs they had held during the war as meter reading, streetcar conducting, taxi driving and elevator operating; they were also excluded from night work and overtime, which effectively eliminated them from fields like printing.

Despite these restrictions, more women were working than ever before. During the 1920s the female labor force grew to 10.7 million from 8.4 million, a 26 per cent increase. Single women of the middle classes were entering clerical and sales work in in-

---

[23] Quoted in William Henry Chafe, *The American Working Woman: Her Changing Social, Economic and Political Roles, 1920-1970* (1972), p. 49.

creasing numbers. "Even the girls who knew that they were going to be married pretended to be considering important business positions," Sinclair Lewis wrote in his 1920 novel, *Main Street*. Frederick Lewis Allen noted in *Only Yesterday* (1931), his account of the 1920s, that after passage of the suffrage amendment in 1919 middle-class girls "poured out of schools and colleges into all manner of occupations," But according to William Henry Chafe, historians have overstated the amount of economic change which occurred in the decade.

> There is no evidence that a revolution took place in women's economic role after World War I, nor can it be said that the 1920s represented a watershed in the history of women at work.... Aspiring career women were still limited to positions traditionally set aside for females; the overwhelming majority of American working women continued to toil at menial occupations for inadequate pay; and the drive to abolish economic discrimination enlisted little popular support.[24]

The number of married women entering the labor force steadily increased. By 1940, 17 per cent of all women who worked were married. Still many people continued to oppose married women working, particularly during the Depression. The Gallup Poll in 1936 found that 82 per cent of the population objected. In the late 1930s bills were introduced in 26 state legislatures to keep married women from holding jobs. Only one of these passed. This was in Louisiana, and it was later repealed.

Breakthrough in the World War II Job Market

World War II had profound effects on the U.S. economy, and particularly on women workers. As millions of men went into uniform, women went into industry as never before, accounting for 36 per cent of the nation's labor force in 1945, up from 25 per cent in 1940. Wages rose, the number of wives holding jobs doubled and unionization of women quadrupled. Employers' attitudes toward women remained skeptical, but since women were the only available labor, they were hired.

Black women found jobs in manufacturing for the first time. Previous bans on the employment of married women were discarded; by 1944, married women comprised almost half of the female labor force. The war gave women access to more skilled and higher-paying jobs. Although the war made rapid changes in women's economic status, it did not make a lasting or profound difference in the public attitude toward working women, nor did it lead to greater equality between the sexes. Women continued to receive less pay than men (65 per cent less in manufacturing), to be denied opportunities for training and advancement, and to work in separate job categories. During the

---

[24] Chafe, *op. cit*, p. 51.

war, concluded William Henry Chafe, "traditional attitudes toward women's place remained largely unchanged."[25]

After the war, women were expected to return to their traditional role of homemaker. Behind the efforts of employers, educators, social workers and the media to persuade women to leave the work force were two important economic considerations, said the editors of *America's Working Women:* "On the one hand, the system could not provide full employment; on the other hand, continued industrial profits required, with the diminution of military spending, an expansion in the consumption of household durable goods. An emphasis on 'homemaking' encouraged women to buy."[26]

This view overlooked the fact that the majority of women were working for economic reasons. A Department of Labor survey in 1945 found that 96 per cent of all single women, 98 per cent of the widowed and divorced women, and 57 per cent of the married women seriously needed to continue working after the war. Many women were laid off in the heavy industries. But for the most part, these women did not return to their kitchens. Instead, they found work in the traditional areas still available to them. These were the only options open to many women until the 1960s, when anti-discrimination legislation opened up new opportunities.

Laws Banning Discrimination in Employment

Laws dealing with sex discrimination in employment have been enacted on both the federal and state levels in the past 15 years, beginning with the federal Equal Pay Act of 1963. It required all employers subject to the Fair Labor Standards Act[27] to provide equal pay for men and women performing similar work. In 1972, coverage of this act was extended to executives, administrators and professionals, including all employees of private and public educational institutions.

The courts have held that jobs do not have to be identical, only "substantially equal," for the Equal Pay Act to apply. In a well-publicized case involving the Corning Glass Works, the Supreme Court ruled in 1974 that shift differences (with men working at night and women working during the day) did not make the working conditions of the men and women dissimilar and thus would not justify a higher wage for the men.[28]

---

[25] Chafe, *op. cit.*, p. 188. See also Lyn Goldfarb, "Separated & Unequal: Discrimination Against Women Workers After World War II (The U.A.W. 1944-54)," The Women's Work Project, 1976.
[26] Rosalyn Baxandall, et al., *op. cit.*, pp. 282-283.
[27] The Fair Labor Standards Act of 1938 established a minimum wage for individuals engaged in interstate commerce or the production of goods for commerce. The law has been amended from time to time to increase the minimum rate and to extend coverage to new groups of employees.
[28] *Corning Glass Works v. Brennan,* 417 U.S. 188 (1974).

A milestone in equal employment opportunity for women was reached with the passage of the Civil Rights Act of 1964. Title VII of that act prohibited discrimination based on sex—as well as race, religion and national origin—in hiring or firing, wages and salaries, promotions or any terms, conditions or privileges of employment. Exceptions were permitted only when sex was a bona fide occupational qualification, as in the case of an actor or a wet nurse. Title VII is administered by the Equal Employment Opportunity Commission, whose five members are appointed by the President. Initially, the powers of the EEOC were limited largely to investigation and conciliation, but Congress amended the act in 1972 to let the agency go directly to court to enforce the law. The 1972 amendments also provided that discrimination charges could be filed by organizations on behalf of aggrieved individuals, as well as by employees and job applicants themselves.

Because sex discrimination sometimes took forms different from race discrimination, the EEOC issued sex-discrimination guidelines. They stated that the refusal to hire an individual cannot be based on assumed employment characteristics of women in general, and that the preferences of customers or existing employees should not be the basis for refusing to hire an individual. The guidelines also prohibited hiring based on classification or labeling of "men's jobs" and "women's jobs," or advertising under male and female headings.

The EEOC guidelines declared that state laws that prohibited or limited the employment of women—in certain occupations, in jobs requiring the lifting or carrying of specified weights, for more than a specified number of hours, during certain hours of the night, and immediately before and after childbirth—discriminate on the basis of sex because they do not take into account individual capacities and preferences. A series of court cases upheld this guideline, and according to the Bureau of Labor's "1975 Handbook on Women Workers," the conflict between state and federal laws on this point "was for the most part resolved in the early 1970s." In a case involving the guidelines, the Supreme Court ruled in 1971[29] that discrimination need not be intentional to be unlawful.

In October 1967, President Johnson issued an executive order barring sex discrimination and other forms of bias in hiring by federal contractors. Executive Order 11246 required federal contractors to take "affirmative action to ensure that applicants are employed and that they are treated during employment without regard to their race, color, religion, sex or national origin."[30]

---

[29] *Griggs et al. v. Duke Power Co.*, 401 U.S. 424 (1971).
[30] See "Reverse Discrimination," *E.R.R.*, 1976, Vol. II, pp. 561-580. See also *Affirmative Action For Women* (1975), by Dorothy Jongeward and Dru Scott.

> ## Working Wives
>
> The age of the two paycheck family has arrived. Since 1960, the number of families in which both husband and wife work has jumped to 42 per cent from 29 per cent. In 1976 alone an additional one million wives joined their husbands in the work force, according to the Department of Labor. The prime reason for their working was to help keep up with family bills.
>
> During the 1950s the largest increase in labor force participation was among married women beyond the usual childbearing years (20 to 34). In recent years, however, there has been a sharp upturn in labor force participation of young married women, especially among married women with small children. Of the 21.1 million wives in the work force in March 1975, over half—11.4 million—had children under 18 years of age.
>
> Why the dramatic upturn in working mothers? Perhaps one reason is that economists now estimate that it costs between $70,000 and $100,000 to raise a child for the first 18 years of his or her life.*
>
> *Reported by the Association of American Colleges in "Project on the Status and Education of Women," October 1976.

Other federal laws, orders and regulations have prohibited employment discrimination in special occupations or industries. For example, Title IX of the Education Amendments of 1972[31] specifically prohibited sex discrimination in education. Other laws and rules required affirmative action for minorities and women in construction and maintenance of the Alaska Pipeline.

The campaign to wipe out sex discrimination has resulted in court decisions and out-of-court settlements costing employers hundreds of millions of dollars in back pay and other benefits. Perhaps the most significant settlements were the two that the EEOC arranged with American Telephone & Telegraph Co. The first, signed January 1973, applied mostly to women and also to minority-group males who had been denied equal pay and promotion opportunities in non-management jobs. The agency ordered AT&T to award them $15-million in back pay and up to $23-million in pay increases. The second settlement, filed in May 1974, provided similar awards to management employees who were victims of illegal sex discrimination in pay. "The AT&T decision was important for symbolic reasons...," said Isabel Sawhill, a labor-market economist at the Urban Institute in Washington. "It established that companies have to look at their patterns of employment."[32]

---

[31] Amendments to the Higher Education Act of 1965, the Vocational Education Act of 1963, the General Education Provisions Act, and the Elementary and Secondary Education Act of 1965.

[32] Quoted in *Newsweek*, Dec. 16, 1976, p. 69. Other big cases subsequently have involved the Bank of America and the brokerage firm of Merrill Lynch.

Continuing Fight for Job Equality

DESPITE THESE VICTORIES, there still is widespread discrimination against women in the workplace. Many feminists say the problem lies not with the anti-discrimination laws and regulations, but with the enforcement efforts of the Equal Employment Opportunity Commission. The General Accounting Office, an investigative arm of Congress, reported recently: "Although the EEOC has had some success in obtaining relief for victims of discrimination in specific instances, it does not appear to have yet made the substantial advances against employment discrimination which will be necessary to make a real difference in the employment status of minorities and women."[33]

The backlog of discrimination complaints has risen to nearly 130,000, according to *The Washington Post,* Feb. 6, 1977. Workers who file complaints frequently wait years even to be told whether their charges have merit. By then, the worker may have given up and found other employment. The General Accounting Office said that nearly half (47.7 per cent) of the cases completed by the EEOC between July 1, 1972, and March 31, 1975, were "administrative closures," meaning that the worker could no longer be found or had lost interest in pursuing the charge. Only 11 per cent of the cases resolved during that period involved successfully negotiated settlements. According to the General Accounting Office, an individual has only one chance in 33 of having the charge settled successfully in the year it is filed. The average case takes nearly two years to settle.

In its 11-year history, the agency has had six successive chairmen and 10 executive directors. Not one chairman has completed his full five-year term. The position has been vacant since May 1976, when Lowell W. Perry resigned after one year in office. The agency's acting director, Ethel Bent Walsh, an EEOC commissioner since 1971, counts it as a sign of progress that the commissioners now meet and discuss problems. "When I first came here we didn't even talk to each other unless we met in the hall," she told the *Post*.

Dissension among the five commissioners may be inherent in the structure of the commission, according to Eleanor Holmes Norton, head of the New York City Commission on Equal Opportunity. "A commission structure involving five highly paid

---
[33] "The Equal Employment Opportunity Commission Has Made Limited Progress in Eliminating Employment Discrimination," Report to the Congress by the Comptroller General of the United States, Sept. 28, 1976.

Women in the Work Force

presidential appointees, as EEOC now has, assumes that *policy* as opposed to *operational questions* will predominate," she said recently. "Administering an already unwieldy ship with what at times are five captains must be especially difficult in a period when operational problems are out of hand."[34] Her suggestion for improving EEOC operations—abolish the commission and appoint a single boss.

Other criticism has been directed toward the EEOC staff. In a recent article in *Fortune* magazine, Dorothy Rabinowitz accused the agency of being biased toward blacks at the expense of women and other minorities.[35] One reason for the agency's possible bias in favor of blacks, said Robert Ellis Smith, a former civil rights executive at the Department of Health, Education and Welfare, is that many of the senior positions are filled with alumni of the southern civil rights battles.[36] Acting Director Walsh told a House subcommittee in 1975 that many of the complaint investigators were "not of the caliber we required and have insufficient training." The National Commission on the Observance of International Women's Year in 1976 recommended that the EEOC "make a substantial effort to upgrade the quality of training of its personnel.[37]

Most criticism of the EEOC has focused on the backlog of cases. Initially it was thought that no more than 2,000 complaints a year would be filed, but in fiscal 1976 alone 75,173 were filed. Contributing to the agency's inability to cope with the growing number of complaints was a policy change in 1968. That year the agency began shifting much of its staff away from processing individual complaints in order to undertake broad investigations into widespread discriminatory patterns of certain corporations and industries. Some say the EEOC should abandon the case-by-case approach altogether. But many feminists oppose this idea. "The whole purpose of Title VII," said Judith Lichtman of the Women's Legal Defense Fund, "was to remove the burden from individual employees and make the government investigate complaints." Perry, the former commissioner, wonders whether the EEOC ought not to be abolished entirely and its responsibilities turned over to the Justice Department. But the agency's supporters credit it with fostering an atmosphere that encourages job equity.

---

[34] Quoted by Robert Ellis Smith in "The EEOC and How to Make it Work," *Ms.* February 1977, p. 64. See also "A Look at What is Happening in Fight on Job Discrimination," *U.S. News & World Report,* Dec. 13, 1976, pp. 35-36.

[35] Dorothy Rabinowitz, "The Bias in the Government's Anti-Bias Agency," *Fortune,* December 1976, p. 138.

[36] Smith, *op. cit.,* p. 103.

[37] "To Form a More Perfect Union: Justice for American Women," Report of the National Commission on the Observance of International Women's Year, June 1976, p. 192. Walsh made her comments before the House Appropriations Subcommittee on State, Justice, Commerce, the Judiciary and Related Agencies on May 6, 1975.

[38] Also dissenting were Justices Thurgood Marshall and John Paul Stevens in the case, *General Electric v. Gilbert,* 429 U.S. 1976.

Attempt to Nullify Court Ruling on Pregnancy Pay

Women's rights groups and organized labor plan to lobby this year for legislation to ensure sick pay for working women on leave because of pregnancy and thus counteract a recent Supreme Court ruling. The court held, on Dec. 7, 1976, that General Electric could exclude pregnancy from its employee disability insurance benefits without violating the 1964 Civil Rights Act. Writing for the court's 6-3 majority, Justice William H. Rehnquist said the exclusion was not discriminatory because "there is no risk from which men are protected and women are not...." In dissent, Justice William J. Brennan Jr.[38] wrote: "Surely it offends common sense to suggest...that a classification revolving around pregnancy is not, at the minimum, strongly 'sex related.' "

The business community generally applauded the decision. It saved American business $1.6-billion, the American Society for Personnel Administration estimated. In contrast, Karen DeCrow, president of the National Organization for Women, called the ruling a "slap in the face to motherhood," and added, "If people are paid sick leave when they're out for nose jobs, hair transplants and vasectomies, why not for childbirth?"[39] In addition to lobbying for legislative remedies, union representatives plan to push for collective bargaining agreements with large employers that would ensure disability pay for women during pregnancy. It is estimated that 40 per cent of all U.S. companies have disability plans, and approximately 40 per cent of those include some maternity benefits.

Psychic Barriers to Women's Advancement

In many instances the barriers to women are not overt discrimination. Psychologists say working women are frequently handicapped by a weak self-image and lack of confidence. In a classic study in 1968, psychologist Matina Horner, now president of Radcliffe College, concluded that as a result of their childhood training and various social pressures of home and family, many women are hobbled by a "fear of success"—an acquired fear that the risks of succeeding are "loss of femininity."

The reasons for the absence of women in top management positions go beyond the "fear of success" syndrome, according to Margaret Hennig and Anne Jardim, co-directors of the Simmons College graduate program in management. They found that women's attitudes toward work are totally different from men's and that this impedes women's progress in the male-dominated corporate world. Men, they said, tend to have long-term career goals, while women are likelier to focus on short-

---

[39] Quoted in *The New York Times*, Dec. 16, 1976.

> ### The Secretary Trap
>
> An experiment conducted recently at the University of Maryland demonstrated the tendency of employers to shunt women into secretarial jobs. Male and female students, all white so that racial bias would not enter the picture, and all equally qualified, applied for jobs at 39 employment agencies.
>
> Seventy-seven per cent of the men and 59 per cent of the women received job offers. Among the men, nine of ten job offers were for administrative or managerial positions and the rest were clerical. For the women, 82 per cent were clerical and 17 per cent were managerial. All of the women applicants were asked to take typing tests. The men were interviewed about their interests, ambitions and favorite sports.

term planning, largely because they have been brought up to think of careers conditionally—as an alternative to marriage. This ambiguity causes women to make their career decisions late, about the age of 30 to 33, while men generally build the foundations of their careers while they are still in their twenties.

Women are further hindered, according to Hennig and Jardim, by their lack of exposure to the informal factors that govern a man's world—contacts built up through clubs and golf games, or "old boy" relationships often started in college. "In the competition for career advancement...men have a clear advantage over women."[40] To help women overcome some of these disadvantages, some employers are encouraging their female employees to attend assertiveness training courses and other programs designed to enhance their self-image.

Changing women's attitudes may take some time. But there are other factors hindering women's participation in the labor force. One-third of the working women have children to care for. There are 6.5 million children under the age of 6, and 18 million others 6 to 14, whose mothers work. Yet according to the latest government estimates, care in licensed day-care centers is available for only slightly more than one million children.[41]

The burdens of child care for working mothers are compounded by other household responsibilities. Although men are doing more of the child rearing and housework these days, the women still bear the brunt of it. Despite all the difficulties, working women show no signs of abandoning their new roles in the work force. However, more and more working women are demanding that society and their families adjust to the new realities of women's lives.

---

[40] Margaret Hennig and Anne Jardim, "Women Executives in the Old-Boy Network," *Psychology Today*, January 1977, p. 81.
[41] See "Child Care," *E.R.R.*, 1972 Vol. I, pp. 441-460, and "Single-Parent Families," *E.R.R.*, 1976 Vol. II, pp. 661-680.

Selected Bibliography

Books

Baxandall, Rosalyn, Linda Gordon and Susan Reverby, *America's Working Women,* Vintage Books, 1976.
Bird, Caroline, *Born Female: The High Cost of Keeping Women Down,* Pocket Books, 1971.
—— *Enterprising Women,* New American Library, 1976.
Chafe, William Henry, *The American Woman: Her Changing Social, Economic and Political Roles, 1920-1970,* Oxford University Press, 1972.
Jongeward, Dorothy and Dru Scott, *Affirmative Action for Women,* Addison-Wesley, 1975.
Kreps, Juanita, *Sex in the Marketplace: American Women at Work,* The Johns Hopkins Press, 1971.
Smuts, Robert W., *Women and Work in America,* Schocken, 1959.

Articles

"A Powerful New Role in the Work Force," *U.S. News & World Report,* Dec. 8, 1975.
Cowley, Susan Cheever, "Women at Work," *Newsweek,* Dec. 6, 1976.
Hartmann, Heidi I., "Women's Work in the United States," *Current History,* May 1976.
Hennig, Margaret and Anne Jardim, "Women Executives in the Old-Boy Network," *Psychology Today,* January 1977.
Kron, Joan, "The Dual Career Dilemma," *New York,* Oct. 25, 1976.
Rabinowitz, Dorothy, "The Bias in the Government's Anti-Bias Agency," *Fortune,* December 1976.
Smith, Robert Ellis, "The Equal Employment Opportunity Commission and How to Make It Work," *Ms,* February 1977.
"Women of the Year: Great Changes, New Chances, Tough Choices," *Time,* Jan. 5, 1976.

Reports and Studies

Editorial Research Reports, "Child Care," 1972 Vol. II, p. 439; "Single-Parent Families," 1976 Vol. II, p. 661; "Status of Women," 1970 Vol. II, p. 565.
Goldfarb, Lyn, "Separated and Unequal: Discrimination Against Women Workers After World War II (The U.A.W. 1944-1954)," The Women's Work Project, 1976.
Morrison, Peter A. and Judith P. Wheeler, "Working Women and 'Woman's Work': A Demographic Perspective on the Breakdown of Sex Roles," The Rand Corporation, June 1976.
"The Equal Employment Opportunity Commission Has Made Limited Progress in Eliminating Employment Discrimination," General Accounting Office, Sept. 28, 1976.
U.S. Department of Labor, "The Earnings Gap Between Women and Men," October 1976.
—— "U.S. Working Women: A Chartbook," 1975.
—— "Why Women Work," July 1976.
—— "Women Workers Today," October 1976.
—— "1975 Handbook on Women Workers," 1975.

YOUTH UNEMPLOYMENT

by

Sandra Stencel

	page
EXPANDING SIZE OF THE PROBLEM	105
Concentration of Joblessness Among Youth	105
Consequences and Causes of Unemployment	105
Federal Work Programs for Young People	106
Special Difficulties Facing Black Youngsters	108
Disdain for Work Ethic Among Teenagers	111
FEDERAL ROLE IN JOB CREATION	112
Unemployment in the Depression Thirties	112
Civilian Conservation Corps and NYA	113
Availability of Jobs During and After War	115
Controversy About the Job Corps in 1960s	116
IMPLICATIONS FOR THE FUTURE	117
Debate Over Effects of Minimum Wage Bill	117
Different Views as to Problem's Severity	119
Projected Decline in Teenage Population	120

Oct. 14
1977

> **Editor's Note:** The rate of joblessness among black teenagers in 1978 was 36.3 percent, slightly under the 1977 level. The unemployment rate for white teenagers in 1978 was 13.9 percent.

YOUTH UNEMPLOYMENT

THIS MONTH the Department of Labor will begin recruiting unemployed youths for a wide variety of jobs in public parks, forests and recreation areas. By the end of the year nearly 8,000 young people are expected to be enrolled in the program. Thousands of other jobless youths will be put to work in community improvement projects ranging from rehabilitation of public buildings to insulation and repair of low-cost housing. These young people will be the first hired under a $1-billion youth employment and training program approved by Congress last summer. By next September 200,000 young people are expected to be working in jobs or enrolled in training programs authorized by the Youth Employment and Demonstration Projects Act of 1977. An additional 250,000 teenagers and young adults could be enrolled if Congress appropriates an additional $500-million which President Carter has requested for the program.

Community leaders, government officials and social scientists generally applauded the new program, but many caution that it will not be a cure-all for persistent high rates of joblessness among the nation's 23 million young workers (ages 16 to 24). The Bureau of Labor Statistics reports that more than three million of them are unemployed. This age group makes up only a quarter of the nation's labor force but accounts for nearly half of the unemployed. The overall unemployment rate in the United States during September was 6.9 per cent, but far higher among the nation's teenagers (18.1 per cent) and especially among black teenagers (37.4 per cent).

Some say such statistics understate the scope of the problem. For one thing the figures do not include the scores of youngsters who become discouraged and quit looking for work. Also excluded are those who want full-time jobs but find only part-time work, and the tens of thousands of college graduates who must take jobs outside their chosen fields *(see p. 118)*.

Consequences and Causes of Unemployment

The consequences of high rates of unemployment among youth were spelled out by President Carter upon signing the 1977 Youth Employment Bill at a ceremony in the White House Rose Garden on Aug. 5. "If a young person...cannot get a job in the formative years of life," Carter said, "there is a feeling of despair, discouragement, a loss of self-esteem, an alienation from the structure of society, a lashing out against the authorities who are responsible...." Sometimes this "lashing out" takes a violent form. More than half of all serious crimes[1] in the United States are committed by youths under the age of 18. Though offenders come from every ethnic group and environment, the majority are non-white kids from urban slums. Until America solves the problem of youth unemployment, said Sen. Hubert H. Humphrey (D Minn.), "there is absolutely no way" to stop crime.[2]

Today's job situation can be attributed partly to the high birth rates in the 1950s and early 1960s. According to the Census Bureau, there are now four million more Americans of ages 16-24 than when this decade began. But there are other factors, as noted in a recent study by economist Anne McDougall Young. She reported that while the number of youths increased by one-third between 1966 and 1976, their representation in the work force rose by one-half.[3] The winding down of the war in Vietnam and the elimination of the draft put more young men in the civilian job market. From 1969 to 1975, according to Donald Eberly, a senior policy analyst for the government agency Action, the number of 18-to-24-year-olds in the armed forces dropped by 1.26 million.[4] Not only were fewer young men in uniform but apparently many left school to seek work when the draft ended.

Many of these youths hit the job market at the very time the United States was hit by recession in 1974-75. In addition, there was increased competition from the growing number of women entering or reentering the labor force.[5] Even during times of greater prosperity youth unemployment has been much greater than the national average. Between 1965 and 1973, viewed as economic "boom" years, youth unemployment remained at about 15 per cent, while the national unemployment rate fluctuated between 3 and 5 per cent.

Federal Work Programs for Young People

The federal government already spends billions of dollars each year on job and training programs for unemployed youths. During fiscal year 1976 some two million young people took part in programs under the Comprehensive Employment and Train-

---

[1] Murder, rape, aggravated assault, robbery, burglary, larceny, motor vehicle theft.
[2] Quoted in *The Christian Science Monitor*, March 7, 1977. See also "Crime Reduction: Reality or Illusion," *E.R.R.*, 1977 Vol. II, pp. 537-556.
[3] Anne McDougall Young, "Students, Graduates and Dropouts in the Labor Market, October 1976," *Monthly Labor Review* (Department of Labor publication), July 1977, p. 40.
[4] Donald Eberly, "National Service: Alternative Strategies," *Armed Forces and Society*, May 1977, p. 448. Action is the federal agency that directs a number of volunteer programs, including the Peace Corps.
[5] See "Women in the Work Force," *E.R.R.*, 1977 Vol. I, pp. 121-142.

Youth Unemployment Rates

	All Youths 16-19	Black and Minority Youths 16-19	All Youths 20-24
1950	12.2%	—	7.7%
1955	11.0	15.6%	7.0
1960	14.7	24.3	8.7
1965	14.8	26.5	6.7
1970	15.2	29.1	8.2
1972	16.2	33.5	9.3
1974	16.0	32.9	9.0
1975	19.9	36.8	13.6
1976	19.0	37.1	12.0
1977 (Sept.)	18.1	37.4	10.7

SOURCE: Bureau of Labor Statistics

ing Act of 1973 (CETA). These included 160,000 in public service jobs, 500,000 in work experience programs, 200,000 in on-the-job and classroom training programs, 40,000 in the Job Corps *(see p. 94)*, and 1,135,000 in the Summer Neighborhood Youth Corps programs.[6] Responding to an administration request, Congress on May 5 added $68-million to the fiscal 1978 Job Corps budget,[7] thereby increasing the number of trainees to 30,000 from 22,700.

In July Congress passed the 1977 Youth Employment Act, incorporating many of the features of a youth employment package that President Carter had proposed in March to complement his economic stimulus plan.[8] The bill added new provisions—Title VIII—to the Comprehensive Employment and Training Act to authorize a year-round program of conservation-related work modeled after the Depression-era Civilian Conservation Corps *(see p. 113)*. A total of 22,000 unemployed youths, 16-23, are expected to be enrolled in the Young Adult Conservation Corps by September 1978. The

---

[6] Congress in June 1977 enacted a law providing for a simple extension through fiscal 1978 for existing programs under the Comprehensive Employment and Training Act.

[7] Included in a $20-billion supplemental fiscal 1977 appropriations bill containing funding for job programs and other elements of President Carter's economic stimulus plan.

[8] See *Congressional Quarterly Weekly Report*, May 28, 1977, pp. 1072-1073, and July 30, 1977, pp. 1595-1596.

enrollees will be paid the minimum wage for work on a variety of conservation projects. Most corps members will continue to live at home during the first year of operation; only about a quarter of the enrollees will be housed at residential projects. The Department of Labor, which administers the corps, hopes to open more residential camps in 1980 and 1981.

Some critics of the young Adult Conservation Corps believe that the long-range benefits to the participants might be negligible, since the skills that will be learned might not be transferable to jobs in urban areas. They further say that urban youths may benefit more from two experimental one-year projects created under Title III of CETA: the Youth Community Conservation and Improvement Projects and the Youth Employment and Training Programs. Both give preference to the economically disadvantaged, especially minority youths who have a hard time finding jobs. Both stress the role of neighborhood and community-based organizations and encourage the involvement of local labor organizations.

It is estimated that the Youth Community Conservation and Improvement Projects will employ 17,000 youths aged 16-19 in supervised projects of obvious benefit to the local community, such as rehabilitation of low-income housing. Some 112,000 low-income youths aged 16-21 are expected to benefit from a variety of projects authorized by the Youth Employment and Training Programs. In addition to work experience, participants will be provided with job counseling, on-the-job training and placement services.

The Youth Employment and Training Programs are intended to help youths overcome some of the most obvious obstacles to their employment—lack of marketable skills, lack of job experience, poor work habits, problems coordinating school and work. Another barrier to employment is the high dropout rate among disadvantaged and minority youths. The 1977 Youth Employment Act sets aside $115-million to test the feasibility of guaranteeing low-income students, 16-19, year-round jobs as an incentive to finish high school. The experimental, 18-month program—known as Youth Incentive Entitlement Pilot Projects—will begin in January 1978 and provide jobs for about 20,-000 students and dropouts who are willing to return to school. The jobs will pay the minimum wage and will average 20 hours a week during the school year and 40 hours a week during the summer.

Special Difficulties Facing Black Youngsters

About 60 per cent of the participants in the new youth employment programs will be blacks and other minorities, according to Secretary of Labor F. Ray Marshall. Unemployment

> ## Youth Unemployment in Europe
>
> Youth unemployment is also a serious problem in Europe. When the leaders of Britain, France, West Germany, Italy, Canada, Japan and the United States met at an economic summit conference in London last May, youth unemployment emerged as one of the principal topics of discussion. The seven leaders pledged to exchange ideas on providing the young with job opportunities.
>
> Currently more than one-third of all unemployed persons in Europe are under 25 years of age. In Britain more than half a million young people are out of work, equal to 35 per cent of all the unemployed. French youths account for more than one-third of the jobless in that country. French President Valery Giscard d'Estaing said finding jobs for young people was the "No. 1 national priority."
>
> Joblessness among the young in Italy is considered a threat to the political and social order. It is estimated that of the 132,000 Italians who will graduate from college next year, only 75,000 will be able to find jobs. As a result, Italian universities have become hotbeds of violence and extremism.

among non-white youths is the highest of any single component in the U.S. labor force. On Sept. 7, President Carter told the black members of Congress—the Congressional Black Caucus—that he regarded the plight of jobless black teenagers his "most important domestic issue right now." Carter was responding to recent criticism from black leaders that his administration has ignored the problems of blacks and other poor people. Adding to Carter's difficulties with the black community was the release Aug. 31 of a Department of Labor survey of summertime employment trends among youth.

The overall unemployment situation among youths aged 16-21 had improved slightly—falling to 15.3 per cent in July 1977 from 15.9 per cent in July 1976, the survey showed. But the improvement took place almost entirely among white youths, whose jobless rate fell to 12.6 per cent from 13.8 per cent a year earlier. Among blacks, however, there were 100,000 more jobless youths this past summer than the previous summer. The unemployment rate among black youths reached 34.8 per cent, the highest for any July on record.

The situation was even worse in some of the nation's largest cities. In New York 86 per cent of the non-white teenagers did not have jobs in July. Herbert Bienstock, a regional commissioner of the Bureau of Labor Statistics, characterized New York as "the non-working teenage capital in the country."[9] The high rate of joblessness among teenagers was said to have con-

---

[9] Quoted by Sen. Jacob Javits (R N.Y.) in a press release issued Aug. 4, 1977.

tributed to the outbreak of looting during the city's power blackout in July.

Despite the billions of dollars already spent on work programs aimed at minority youth, young blacks are relatively worse off now than they were 20 years ago. Herbert Hill, formerly the national labor director of the National Association for the Advancement of Colored People (NAACP) and now a professor at the University of Wisconsin, has said that if the situation does not improve soon "a large part of a generation of urban black youths will never enter the work force." Dr. Robert S. Browne, director of the Black Economic Research Center, pointed out that many of these youths come from families that have been without jobs for three generations or more. "What's developing is an entrenched social and economic underclass...," he said. "It's going to be awfully hard to get at."[10]

Persons trying to account for high rates of joblessness among black youths point to the effects of the ghetto environment, continuing racial discrimination and the lack of stable, job-oriented family patterns. Many black leaders blame inner-city schools, which, they say, produce graduates who are scarcely able to read or write. In recent years several factors have intensified the employment problems of black youths. These include (1) the flow of jobs from central cities to neighboring suburbs, and from the North and upper Midwest to the South and Southwest; (2) fewer low-paying, low-skill jobs; and (3) the effects of the recession. Industries in which blacks traditionally have been employed in large numbers, such as steel and textiles, were among the hardest hit by the recession.

Compounding the problem has been the high black birth rate, which is about triple that for whites. Arnold Packer, an Assistant Secretary of Labor, noted Sept. 7 in a report to President Carter on black unemployment that the black teenage population had increased by 43 per cent during the past 10 years. For white teenagers the increase was only 17.6 per cent.

Deprived of jobs, many young blacks become alienated from society and develop hostile attitudes toward it. Many spend their days "hanging out" on the streets, where they often turn to crime. The high unemployment rate among ghetto youth is generally blamed for the new rash of gang activity in the nation's cities. According to a study in 1976 by Walter B. Miller of the Harvard Center for Criminal Justice, "violence perpetuated by members of youth gangs in major cities is at present more lethal than at any time in history."[11] Some observers

---

[10] Hill and Browne were quoted in *The New York Times;* Hill on Sept. 11 and Browne on Sept. 21, 1977.

[11] "Violence by Youth Gangs and Youth Groups in Major American Cities," summary report, April 1976, p. 8. See also "Violence in the Schools," *E.R.R.*, 1977 Vol. II, pp. 581-600.

say that resentment among black youths has been intensified by the knowledge that growing numbers of blacks are escaping the poverty of the ghetto and moving into the middle class. "The awareness that many blacks have been successful," explained Harvard sociologist David Riesman, "means that the underclass is more resentful and more defiant because its alibi isn't there."[12]

Disdain for Work Ethic Among Teenagers

In a controversial article in the September 1977 issue of *Commentary,* Midge Decter declared that even if there were jobs for everybody, sizable numbers of black youths still would not be working.

> For large numbers of those young men on street corners [Decter wrote] it does not pay to take a job. Not only because there is nothing much they are qualified to do; and not only because welfare payments are at least adequate to keep them housed and fed; and not only because they have increasingly been brought up in, and seem content to perpetuate, a system of being kept by women; but because so many of them have access, or the occasional promise of access to a different kind of money—money sometimes dangerously, but always easily, come by.[13]

These youngsters, like those described in Claude Brown's book about his growing up in Harlem, *Manchild in the Promised Land* (1965), would not be caught dead holding down a regular job. They prefer to scratch out a living on the streets as con-artists, muggers, thieves, drug pushers, pimps and prostitutes. "This list of employments is not very pretty..." Decter wrote, "but one pays those young men less than proper respect to imagine that President Carter can so easily afford the means to buy them away from their present life."

Many people would dispute Decter's arguments,[14] but others contend that the disdain for work is pandemic among teenagers—white and black. School guidance counselors report that teenagers are more demanding about the hours they work, the money they earn and the kind of work they do. Alan Ribnick, vocational counselor at Yates High School in Houston, declared: "The work ethic is dead. Somewhere along the line, people have lost sight of pride in what they do. Kids no longer realize that whatever job they have it has some dignity."[15]

Young workers are also hampered by poor work habits. Many do not know what it means to come to work on time or how to cooperate with fellow workers, take supervision or separate per-

---

[12] Quoted in *Time,* Aug. 29, 1977, p. 15.
[13] Midge Decter, "Looting and Liberal Racism," *Commentary,* September 1977, p. 52.
[14] See, for example, Leonard Goodwin, *Do the Poor Want to Work: A Social-Psychological Study of Work Orientations* (1972), a study sponsored by the Brookings Institution which concluded that the poor value work as much as others in society, and that they lose interest in work only when they discover that their efforts do not lead to success.
[15] Quoted in *U.S. News & World Report,* May 9, 1977, p. 95.

Editorial Research Reports   *Oct. 14, 1977*

sonal problems from the job. "The first time there is a hassle on the job, they just quit," said Ribnick. "This general lack of respect for anyone in authority is an attitude developed at home, passed to school and then to an employer."

This disdain for work and authority was one factor cited by apple growers in nine northeastern and mid-Atlantic states[16] in asking the Department of Labor to approve the importation of about 5,000 foreign workers, mainly Jamaicans, to harvest this fall's crop. The growers said they could not recruit enough American workers to do the job. A federal district court judge in Virginia agreed and, on Aug. 24, he ordered the department to admit the foreign workers. Some Labor officials, including Secretary Marshall, said the growers did not try hard enough to find domestic workers.

Federal Role in Job Creation

IT WAS NOT until the Depression years of the 1930s that the federal government assumed the burden of providing jobs for the nation's unemployed. Government concern was previously directed toward supplying employers with needed workers rather than assuring workers a sufficiency of jobs. Such measures as the establishment of land grant colleges[17] and provision of funds for vocational education reflected government interest in improving the skills of the nation's youth to meet the demands of technologically advancing agriculture and industry.

With the massive unemployment that followed the stock market crash of October 1929, the government's attention was forcibly turned to the problem of what to do with an idled labor force of unprecedented dimensions. When President Roosevelt took office on March 4, 1933, nearly 13 million persons—about one-fourth of the labor force—were out of work and looking for jobs. Because of the high level of adult unemployment, thousands of young people who normally would have gotten jobs on farms or in factories, stores and offices found most doors closed. "By 1933, 200,000 'wandering boys' were riding the freight trains in search of work or simply escape from a society that had no place for them."[18] They slept in shanty towns, in haystacks, on the floors of missions or jails. Robert Carter was one of the young men wandering around the country during the

[16] Virginia, West Virginia, New York, Vermont, Massachusetts, New Hampshire, Connecticut, Rhode Island and Maine.
[17] By the Morrill Act of 1862.
[18] *Life Magazine Special Report: The New Youth*, fall 1977, p. 45.

Youth Unemployment

Depression, and he managed to put down some of what he did and saw in an article published in *The New Republic* on March 8, 1933.

> Leaving Macon I am the only one on the freight to Atlanta [Carter wrote]. Perhaps there are others, for this line has a bad name and we may be hiding from each other.... Forty miles from Atlanta the train stopped for water and the railroad detective found me and said I could ride no further—that I would be arrested in Atlanta anyway. I must have been a strange sight. My hair was long and billowed like rank vegetation beneath the dirty, once white, cap I wore....
>
> Leaving Atlanta with three other boys, youngsters going deeper South, we were rounded up in the railroad yards by five detectives carrying pistols and shotguns. They caught 18 or 20 of us after beating the bushes about the yards. They herded us to a bank beside the railroad, all of us young, none over 25 except a middle-aged man looking for a place by some river to jungle-up for the winter.... They herded us to the highways, took our names and told us if they caught us again it would be six months on the chain gangs....
>
> Was walking up a road when I met a new recruit to our ranks. He was a young farmer boy just leaving home, and he had a wild, vague look of pride and uneasiness at his venture. With his bundle and his unkempt clothes he was on his way to Texas, where he said he had heard they were paying three dollars a day for farmhands. We wished each other good luck and went on our way.[19]

Civilian Conservation Corps and NYA

To deal with the problems of unemployed youths, the Roosevelt administration devised two programs, the Civilian Conservation Corps and the National Youth Administration. The CCC put young[20] single men from families on public relief to work in forestry, flood control and similar projects. Roosevelt outlined the goals of the program in a message to Congress delivered March 21, 1933:

> The CCC [Roosevelt said] will conserve our precious natural resources. It will pay dividends to the present and future generations. More important, however...will be the moral and spiritual value of such work. The overwhelming majority of unemployed Americans...would infinitely prefer work. We can take a vast army of these unemployed out into healthful surroundings. We can eliminate to some extent at least the threat that enforced idleness brings to spiritual and moral stability. It is not a panacea for all unemployment but it is an essential step....

Reaction to Roosevelt's proposal was mixed. Some Cabinet members said that it might be dangerous to collect large groups

---
[19] Reprinted in *The Strenuous Decade: A Social and Intellectual Record of the Nineteen-Thirties*, edited by Daniel Aaron and Robert Bendiner (1970), pp. 45-52.
[20] Between the ages of 18 and 25, extended in 1935 to 17-28.

of jobless, and presumably resentful, young men in the woods. The labor movement said the plan would mean the militarization of labor and the reduction of wages to a subsistence level.

Despite the opposition, Congress approved the CCC legislation on March 31, 1933. By the middle of June, 1,300 CCC camps were established; by the end of July, more than 300,000 boys were enrolled. Over the next nine years, more than 2.5 million youths would spend from six months to a year in the program. Approximately 10 per cent of the CCC recruits were black, serving usually in segregated camps. In addition to food, shelter and military clothing, each person received $30 a month, most of which—$22 to $25—he was required to send home to his parents or other dependents. In exchange, the young men planted millions of trees; constructed roads, reservoirs and fish ponds; built terraces in eroded areas; restored historic battlefields; built bridges and fire towers; cleared beaches and camping grounds; and in a multitude of ways protected and improved parks, forests, watersheds and recreational areas. The value of the land improvements carried out by the CCC was estimated at $1.75-billion.[21]

The CCC program is believed to have had a tremendously beneficial effect on the participants, some of whom had never before been out of the city. Historian Arthur M. Schlesinger Jr. described the impact of the program: "The CCC participants [Schlesinger wrote] did more...than reclaim and develop natural resources. They reclaimed and developed themselves.... Their muscles hardened, their bodies filled out, their self-respect returned. They learned trades; more important, they learned about America, and they learned about other Americans."[22]

Although the work of the CCC is better remembered than that of the National Youth Administration, the latter at times employed larger numbers of people. Roosevelt created the NYA by executive order on June 26, 1935, to give public service jobs to out-of-school youngsters who could find no place in the shrunken job market. At the time the NYA was established, there were 2,827,000 young people, 16-24, out of work and out of school. By 1938, the NYA had 481,000 youngsters on its rolls, about evenly divided between boys and girls. The agency set up a special office of minority affairs, with a leading black educator, Mary McLeod Bethune, as director. In Texas, a local administrator was Lyndon B. Johnson.

NYA enrollees worked about 40 hours a month and received a

---

[21] Senate Labor Committee, "Report on Youth Conservation Act of 1959," p. 13.
[22] Schlesinger, *The Age of Roosevelt: The Coming of the New Deal* (1939), pp. 338-339.

Youth Unemployment

monthly salary of $6 to $40. Most of them lived at home and, unlike CCC boys, had no distinctive uniform or insignia. They repaired highways, streets and public buildings; did clerical jobs; worked in libraries; constructed and landscaped parks; made maps and distributed health materials. In fact, their range of activities was immensely broad.[23] Between 1935 and 1943, some 2,667,000 young people participated in the NYA out-of-school work program. Close to 750,000 students in 1,700 colleges and universities and over 28,000 high schools received benefits through NYA student jobs.

Availability of Jobs During and After War

World War II brought an end to the lingering unemployment problems which the New Deal had been unable to solve. Both the Civilian Conservation Corps and the National Youth Administration were phased out during the war. More than 16,000,000 Americans—more than 10 per cent of the U.S. population—served in the armed forces during the war years, 1941-45.

American youths entering the job market during the 1940s and early 1950s had a relatively easy time finding work. The great economic expansion of the war and postwar years provided ample employment opportunities, except in brief periods of recession. Competition for jobs was reduced by the manpower demands of the military during the Korean War and by the opening of educational opportunities to veterans under the GI Bill. The job situation for youth changed in the late 1950s and early 1960s. The GI education program tapered off and the number of enlisted men fell from about three million in 1953, when the Korean War ended, to around two million in mid-1961.

Several other trends affected youth employment in the early 1960s.[24] Automation and other technological changes in industry led to the curtailment of some traditional entry-level jobs for young workers. At the same time employers began to tighten skill and education requirements. A high school diploma generally was required, and more employers looked for a college background. Opportunities for work on farms or in unskilled industrial jobs—areas in which one-fifth of all workers under 25 were employed in 1957—were declining. By May 1961, the unemployment rate for workers aged 16-20 was 17 per cent—two and a half times higher than the national average.

As is the situation today, the unemployment rate was highest among young blacks living in urban slums. Special surveys conducted for a 1961 conference on the problems of unemployed

---

[23] See Betty and Ernest K. Lindley, *A New Deal for Youth* (1938).
[24] See "Jobs for Young People," E.R.R., 1961 Vol. II, pp. 499-517.

urban youth[25] showed that in one slum section, 59 per cent of the males between the ages of 16 and 21 were out of school, unemployed and "roaming the streets." In another ghetto area, 70 per cent of the boys and girls in that age group were neither in school nor at work. In an address to the conference, James B. Conant, president emeritus of Harvard University, described the consequences of these high unemployment rates. "The building up of a mass of unemployed and frustrated Negro youth in congested areas of a city," Conant said, "is a social phenomenon that may be compared to the piling up of inflammable material in an empty building.... Potentialities for trouble—indeed, possibilities of disaster—are surely there."

Controversy Over the Job Corps in 1960s

Conant's warning did not go unheeded. President Johnson made finding jobs for disadvantaged youths an important part of his war on poverty. At the center of Johnson's plan for improving the employment prospects of urban youths was the Job Corps, created as part of the Economic Opportunity Act of 1964. "Its avowed purpose was to take poor youths aged 16 to 21 years, to remove them from their debilitating poverty environments to distant residential centers, and there provide them with educational and vocational training needed to improve their employability."[26] By mid-1967, the Job Corps had 42,000 trainees enrolled in 123 centers around the country. A total of $989-million was allocated to the program during its first four years of operation.

From the first the Job Corps was controversial. Many questioned the basic premise of the program—that disadvantaged youngsters must be removed from their homes before they could be rehabilitated through training and education. Many of the centers were too big and were plagued by social tensions, partly because none of them was coeducational and many were placed in small towns and rural areas. There were a number of fights and shootings, which led to bad publicity. Critics said the training was costlier than a year at Harvard; it ran as high as $9,500 per trainee. Others questioned the program's effectiveness, pointing to the high dropout rate and the number of graduates who were unable to find jobs. According to Sar A. Levitan, "The Job Corps could have avoided a great deal of criticism and unfavorable publicity if the administration had decided to attract the 'cream' of the disadvantaged youth."[27]

---

[25] Conference on Unemployed, Out-of-School Youths in Urban Areas sponsored by the National Committee for Children and Youth in Washington, D.C., on May 24, 1961.
[26] Sar A. Levitan and Benjamin H. Johnston, *The Job Corps: A Social Experiment That Works* (1975), p. 1.
[27] Sar A. Levitan and Garth L. Mangum, *Federal Training and Work Programs in the Sixties* (1969), p. 166.

Instead the Job Corps concentrated on the most poorly educated, those who were least able to obtain jobs on their own.

Adding to the Job Corps' problems and its negative image was the continued increase in the proportion of black and other non-white enrollees—a factor which, according to Levitan, "contributed to the tensions experienced in the centers and to the early departure of some enrollees." During the first year of the program, whites constituted a majority of the Job Corps trainees. By July 1967, the ethnic distribution of Job Corps enrollment was 32.3 per cent Caucasian, 58.5 per cent black, and 9.2 per cent other minorities. Another continuing operational difficulty was the declining age of enrollees. By mid-1967 over half of the participants were 16 and 17 years old. Some local communities began to lobby for the closing of nearby local centers and in April 1969 President Nixon complied. He closed 59 centers around the country and cut the Job Corps budget from $280.5-million to $180.5-million, a level that prevailed until this year despite inflation *(see p. 107).*

Implications for the Future

CONTINUED HIGH LEVELS of youth unemployment have produced renewed interest in proposals to establish a separate, lower minimum wage for teenage workers. Supporters argue that a low wage is an incentive for employers to hire young, inexperienced workers. Without such an incentive, they say, employers are less willing to invest time and effort in training young workers. Opponents of a subminimum wage for teenagers fear that employers would be tempted to substitute lower-paid youths for adult workers. The House, on Sept. 15, narrowly defeated an amendment to the Minimum Wage Bill that would have permitted employers to pay teenage workers (below age 19) 85 per cent of the minimum wage for the first six months on the job. A similar proposal was defeated by the Senate on Oct. 7, but public debate on the issue is expected to continue.

Proponents of a separate youth wage point to several recent studies showing that past increases in the minimum wage have been followed by increases in teenage unemployment. Professor James F. Ragan Jr. of Kansas State University wrote in the May 1977 issue of Harvard's *Review of Economics and Statistics* that about 225,000 teenage jobs—equal to about 17 per cent of the teenage employment total—were lost after Congress voted in 1966 to raise the minimum wage by 28 per cent and expand its coverage. In a 1976 study prepared for the Brookings Institution,

> ## Underemployment of College Graduates
>
> Unskilled high school dropouts are not the only young people having trouble finding a job. Great numbers of college graduates are either unemployed or have taken jobs outside their chosen fields. This is especially true for liberal arts majors. Many are underemployed—working at jobs which traditionally did not require a college degree. Ivar Berg, a Columbia University economist, estimates that 80 per cent of the college graduates today are taking jobs that were once held by the less-educated. The spillover of college graduates into low-skilled jobs is pushing people without a degree further down the employment ladder.
>
> Government statistics indicate that the situation will get worse before it gets better. The Bureau of Labor Statistics, in its most recent "Occupational Outlook for College Graduates," estimated that during the 1974-1985 period there would be 950,000 more college graduates than jobs that have traditionally required degrees. This surplus of college graduates "does not necessarily mean that college graduates will experience significant levels of unemployment," the bureau concluded. "Instead, problems for college graduates will center on underemployment and job dissatisfaction...."
>
> The psychological impact of the current job crunch was described by Joel Kotkin, a Los Angeles writer: "In the past a man with training and an education knew that sooner or later his skills would be marketable. Today our growing surplus population, many with Ph.D.'s, wonder if they'll ever get a job. This feeling of being surplus, no longer necessary, plagues the generation of the '70s. They are bitter, anxious and harshly aware of the Darwinian economic struggle."*
>
> *Human Behavior, May 1977.

economist Edward M. Gramlich of the University of Michigan estimated that there was a 13 per cent rise in teenage unemployment because of the 25 per cent boost in the minimum wage in 1974.[28]

Walter E. Williams, a well-known black economist from Temple University in Philadelphia, argues that the minimum wage should be abolished because it perpetuates discrimination against blacks and other minority youths.[29] Williams contends that they should have the right to enhance their employment prospects by charging less for their services. Rep. Parren J. Mitchell, chairman of the Congressional Black Caucus, disagrees. Noting the potential for displacement of adult workers by lower-paid youth, Mitchell told the House during debate on

---

[28] Edward M. Gramlich, "Impact of Minimum Wages on Other Wages, Employment and Family Incomes," *Brookings Papers on Economic Activity,* 1976, pp. 409-451.

[29] Walter E. Williams, "Government Sanctioned Restraints that Reduce Economic Opportunities for Minorities," *Policy Review,* fall 1977, preprint 2, p. 9.

the minimum wage bill: "Unemployment is chronic and endemic and deep across-the-board in the black community, and it does not make any sense to play one group of workers off against another."

Organized labor attacked the idea of a youth differential in the minimum wage as a thinly disguised way of assuring cheap labor. "Lowering wages does not create jobs, but it does create poverty," AFL-CIO President George Meany testified before the House Education and Labor Committee in August. Kenneth Young, the federation's associate director of legislation, argued that employers might be tempted to fire young workers after six months when the differential expired. Labor Secretary Marshall said at a press conference Aug. 31 that a subminimum wage for youth would have "catastrophic" effects on employment generally by substituting "white middle-class kids" for older workers, especially blacks. More effective in helping young blacks find employment, Marshall said, would be legislation to curb the flow of illegal aliens into this country, since illegal aliens compete most directly with young blacks for jobs.[30]

Some foes of the subminimum wage say the best solution to the teenage unemployment problem is a more vigorous economy that would create more jobs. They advocate enactment of the Humphrey-Hawkins bill,[31] requiring the federal government to reduce joblessness to 4 per cent within four years, through public service jobs if necessary. The measure also calls for comprehensive youth job programs and grants to local and state governments for job generation. First introduced in 1974, the bill has undergone numerous modifications. President Carter on Sept. 25 told a fund-raising dinner sponsored by the Congressional Black Caucus that he would try to work out differences with Congress and seek an acceptable draft version of the bill.

Different Views as to Problem's Severity

Experts disagree on the severity of the youth unemployment problem. Economist Richard B. Freeman of Harvard University said recently, "Teenage unemployment may be mainly a transitional problem without long-term consequences."[32] Those who think the problem has been overstated point to the special character of teenage unemployment. Teenagers tend to remain unemployed for shorter periods than adults and to change jobs more frequently. Many remain dependent on their families and are not seeking permanent or full-time employment. Others are experimenting with different kinds of jobs before they settle

---

[30] See "Illegal Immigration," *E.R.R.*, 1976 Vol. II, pp. 907-926.
[31] Named for its chief sponsors, Sen. Hubert H. Humphrey (D Minn.) and Rep. Augustus F. Hawkins (D Calif.).
[32] Quoted in *Business Week*, Oct. 10, 1977, p. 68.

down. "A youngster who is looking for a part-time job to earn enough to buy a stereo may be upset if he can't find work readily, and he certainly adds to the unemployment statistics," Freeman said. "But he is hardly going to suffer long-term damage."

A recent report on youth unemployment by the National Advisory Council on Vocational Education[33] declared that "the severity of the problem varies from mild to extreme." The council went on to say: "Many youths classified as 'unemployed' are sampling the labor market, and may be temporarily idle between jobs. Some youths who are out of work longer are from middle-income families, live at home, and do not suffer immediate economic hardship. For others, especially minorities, lack of employment can mean severe economic hardship and is often a matter of survival for themselves and their families."

Projected Decline in Teenage Population

Some experts say that time alone is needed to cure the problem. They point out that the last of the "baby boom" generation is entering adulthood and, consequently, the number of teenagers is starting to decline. The latest population projections by the Census Bureau[34] indicate a decline in the 14-17 age group in the years ahead, and, starting in 1980, in the 18-24 category as well, as is shown in the following table:

Years	Ages 14-17	Ages 18-24
1975-80	−7 %	+6.7%
1980-85	−8.7	−5.5

By 1990 the youth labor force is likely to total 21 million, about 1.3 million less than in 1975, according to Department of Labor projections. "By the end of the century, youth unemployment may not be an issue at all," the National Advisory Council on Vocational Education has concluded. "The issue may be, instead, the retraining of adult and retired persons to fill vacant job slots." George Iden, an economist with the Congressional Budget Office, has said that the teenage population decline could bring their jobless rate down by as much as 3.3 per cent by 1985.[35] But Iden went on to say that government youth employment programs may still be necessary because geography rather than demography is the key factor in minority-youth unemployment.

---

[33] "Youth Unemployment: The Need for a Comprehensive Approach," a report by the National Advisory Council on Vocational Education, March 1977, p. 1.
[34] U.S. Bureau of the Census, "Projections of the Population of the United States: 1977 to 2050," *Current Population Reports*, Series P-25, No. 704, 1977, p. 10.
[35] Quoted in *The New York Times*, Aug. 30, 1977.

Youth Unemployment

Donald Eberly thinks it is "unlikely" that population changes will solve the youth job problem. "The decline in the youth population," he wrote, "may easily be more than compensated for by the continuing entry of women into the labor force." And, he went on to say, "It seems almost certain that many older people will extend their stay in the labor force." A bill that would raise the mandatory retirement age in private industry from 65 to 70 was approved Sept. 23 by the House but has encountered opposition in the Senate.

Even if population changes improve the job prospects of future generations of teenagers, the effects of the current job crunch are likely to be felt for a long time. For one thing, many young people have had to settle for low-level positions that are needed by the next wave of job seekers. As these "underemployed" workers pile up, said Princeton University sociologist Charles F. Westoff, more and more Americans will find career ladders blocked by a glut of senior employees. At that point, "our view of America as the land of opportunity is going to fade." Philip M. Hauser, director of the Population Research Center at the University of Chicago, has said that the fierce competition for jobs could lead to pressure for a welfare state. "What this all adds up to," he said, "is that you're going to have a huge generation for whom the American system has not worked."[36]

Whether current youth employment problems will have such consequences is unknown. What is certain is that there are no instant answers. But until the United States solves the youth unemployment problem the nation will continue to pay the price, in terms of higher welfare costs, a higher crime rate, and a growing number of embittered, alienated youths who may never find productive roles in society.

---

[36] Westoff and Hauser are quoted in *U.S. News & World Report*, Oct. 3, 1977, p. 55.

Selected Bibliography

Books

Goodwin, Leonard, *Do the Poor Want to Work? A Social-Psychological Study of Work Orientations,* the Brookings Institution, 1972.

Levitan, Sar A. and Benjamin H. Johnston, *The Job Corps: A Social Experiment That Works,* Johns Hopkins University Press, 1975.

____ and Garth L. Mangum, *Federal Training and Work Programs in the Sixties,* Institute of Labor and Industrial Relations, 1969.

Articles

"A Bitter New Generation of Jobless Young Blacks," *U.S. News & World Report,* Sept. 27, 1976.

Decter, Midge, "Looting and Liberal Racism," *Commentary,* September 1977.

Eccles, Mary Eisner, "Lower Minimum Wage Urged for Teenage Workers," *Congressional Quarterly Weekly Report,* Sept. 10, 1977.

____ "Congress Mounts Attack on Youth Unemployment," *Congressional Quarterly Weekly Report,* May 28, 1977.

"The Explosive Issue of Youth Unemployment," *Business Week,* Oct. 10, 1977.

"Why It's Hard to Cut Teenage Unemployment," *U.S. News & World Report,* May 17, 1976.

Williams, Walter E., "Government Sanctioned Restraints That Reduce Economic Opportunities for Minorities," *Policy Review,* fall 1977.

"Would the 'Teenwage' Cut Unemployment?" *Business Week,* Sept. 19, 1977.

Young, Anne McDougall, "Students, Graduates, and Dropouts in the Labor Market, October 1976," *Monthly Labor Review,* July 1977.

"Young People Without Jobs—How Real a Problem?" *U.S. News & World Report,* May 9, 1977.

Reports and Studies

American Enterprise Institute, "Minimum Wage Legislation," June 27, 1977.

Bureau of Labor Statistics, "Occupational Outlook for College Graduates, 1976-1977 Edition," 1977.

Editorial Research Reports, "Government Youth Corps," 1961 Vol. I, p. 1; "Jobs for Young People," 1961 Vol. II, p. 499; "Underemployment in America," 1975 Vol. II, p. 503.

National Advisory Council on Vocational Education, "Youth Unemployment: The Need for a Comprehensive Approach," March 1977.

National Child Labor Committee, "Rite of Passage: The Crisis of Youth's Transition from School to Work," 1976.

"The Job Crisis for Black Youth: Report of the Twentieth Century Fund Task Force on Employment Problems of Black Youth," Praeger, 1971.

U.S. Bureau of the Census, "Projections of the Population of the United States: 1977 to 2050," *Current Population Reports,* Series P-25, No. 704, 1977.

COLLEGE TUITION COSTS

by

William V. Thomas

	page
DEMANDS FOR TUITION RELIEF	125
Congressional Reaction to Rising Costs	125
Debate Over Packwood-Moynihan Bill	126
Economic Opposition to Tax Credit Plan	128
Carter Program for Student Assistance	130
FEDERAL AID FOR HIGHER EDUCATION	132
Morrill Land-Grant College Act of 1862	132
Tuition Assistance for U.S. Veterans	133
Government Aid to College Since 1950s	134
Past Action on Tuition Relief Proposals	136
NEW APPROACHES TO COST-CONTROL	136
Effort to Set Up Education Department	136
High Rate of Default on Student Loans	138
Carter vs. Congress on Education Policy	139

Feb. 24
1978

Editor's Note: The tuition tax-credit legislation discussed in this report suffered defeat in the Senate in December 1978. The Senate had passed a bill applying the tax credit to college tuition only. The House, in passing the bill, extended the credit to tuitions for private elementary and secondary schools. The Senate refused to accept the House version of the legislation.

On another matter discussed in this report, the Census Bureau in March 1978 contradicted the contention that rising tuition costs are keeping students from middle-income families out of college. The study, "School Enrollment: Social and Economic Characteristics of Students," found that "the trend of declining enrollment among middle-income students had reversed and returned to higher levels." Between 1967 and 1974, it stated the percentage of students from families with incomes in the $10,000-$15,000 range dropped from 51.9 to 41.4. But this pattern reversed in 1975 and the percentage rose in 1976 to 47.5 per cent.

COLLEGE TUITION COSTS

THE AMERICAN MIDDLE-CLASS got some bad news last year. The shock came in the form of a study published by the Population Reference Bureau, a private statistical information organization. It calculated that the average family will spend $64,215 to rear a child from birth to age 21. That amount represents an increase of nearly 50 per cent over a 1969 forecast of child-rearing costs, according to economist Thomas J. Espenshade, who wrote the study.[1]

College tuition still is the biggest single expense parents have to meet. Average four-year costs—including room and board—at a state university amount to $10,000; four years at a private college average $25,000. Current college fees are up 4 per cent over the 1976-77 school year. By 1995, when today's babies are old enough to be freshmen, it is estimated that the cost will have risen to $47,330 at a public university and to $82,830 at a private one.[2]

Between 1969 and 1976, according to the Congressional Budget Office,[3] college enrollment of students from families earning $15,000 or more dropped by 5.5 per cent; enrollment of students from families with incomes between $10,000 and $15,000 fell by 6.4 per cent. The decline in middle-class college enrollment, some observers believe, is an indication that a growing number of families cannot afford to support their children's postsecondary education.

This belief has produced what Rep. Al Ullman (D Ore.), chairman of the House Ways and Means Committee, called "one of the hottest political issues" of the current Congress—tuition relief. So far, 87 bills have been introduced in the House and Senate to provide some form of tax credit or tax deduction[4] for families sending children to college. "Tuition

---

[1] Thomas J. Espanshade, "The Value and Cost of Children," Population Reference Bureau, April 1977, p. 25.

[2] Estimates by the Oakland Financial Group, Inc. of Charlottesville, Va., an independent financial consulting organization. Projected costs are based on a yearly inflation rate of 6 per cent.

[3] See "Report on Hearings before the Task Force on Tax Expenditures, Government Organization and Regulation on College Tuition Tax Credits," House Budget Committee, April 28 and May 12, 1977, p. 16.

[4] A tax deduction lowers the income base on which tax is paid; a tax credit lowers the amount of the tax itself.

relief is an idea whose time has come," said Sen. William V. Roth Jr. (R Del.), author of a measure that would allow heads of families a yearly tax credit of up to $500 for each family member attending college full-time. Roth's proposal has passed the Senate three times in the last three years, but each time House leaders have prevented it from reaching the floor for a vote.

Critics of tax-related tuition relief complain that it constitutes an outright subsidy to the middle class. But according to Roth, such support is necessary. "There are millions of families today who are neither affluent enough to afford the high cost of college nor considered poor enough to qualify for the government assistance programs which their taxes make possible," Roth said. "We are rapidly approaching a situation in this country where only the very rich and the very poor will be able to attend college, and I am convinced that action must be taken to ease the financial plight of middle-income families."[5]

Despite broad support in Congress for tax-related tuition relief, the Carter administration has opposed the concept, calling it too expensive. A $500 tax credit, for example, could cost the federal government as much as $5 billion annually in lost revenue. In an effort to head off congressional action, the administration has proposed to increase the education assistance budget for fiscal 1979 by some $1.5 billion and at the same time expand scholarship grants and loans to students from middle-income families. Nevertheless, Congress in this election year appears determined to put its stamp of approval on legislation to reduce taxes for families with children in college. The question is how much the U.S. Treasury can afford to lose for the sake of cutting the cost of higher education and how far any of the proposed measures will go to cover ever-rising college fees.

Debate Over Packwood-Moynihan Bill

The most comprehensive tuition relief plan now before Congress is the Packwood-Moynihan bill, introduced jointly by Sens. Robert Packwood (R Ore.) and Daniel P. Moynihan (D N.Y.). The bill, which has 47 Senate co-sponsors, would provide a tax credit of up to $500 not only for parents with children in college but also for those paying tuition at private elementary or secondary schools. In addition, the bill would authorize comparable payments to lower-income families with children in non-public schools but who have little or no income tax to pay. This provision "guarantees that benefits will be evenly distributed among the various economic classes," said a spokesman for Packwood.

Private education groups generally favor the Packwood-Moynihan proposal. During three days of hearings before the

---

[5] *Congressional Record*, Dec. 15, 1977, p. 19847.

Family Income and College Enrollment
(families with at least one dependent in college)

Per cent of households

Family income	Percent
UNDER $5,000	17.2
$5,000 To $9,999	26.7
$10,000 To $14,999	34.1
$15,000 To $19,999	44.8
$20,000 To $24,999	46.5
ABOVE $25,000	63.7

SOURCE: U.S. Bureau of the Census, 1975 figures.

Senate Finance Committee in January, witnesses argued that a tax credit would promote diversity in education and help both low- and moderate-income families meet the cost of private schooling. It was pointed out that parents who send their children to non-public schools must pay twice for a single education—once through their taxes for public schools and again in tuition for the private ones. John E. Tirell, vice president for governmental affairs of the American Association of Community and Junior Colleges, also voiced support for tuition tax credits, saying that they would open educational opportunities to many students who could not otherwise afford to attend college. A $500 tax credit would pay nearly the entire cost at many two-year colleges and thus attract more students to those institutions.

Some educators believe tax credits will draw students away from public education by making private schools more affordable. But Victor Solomon, director of educational affairs for the Congress of Racial Equality (CORE), told the Senate Finance Committee Jan. 19 that a tax write-off was needed to increase the "educational choices" of poor parents by enabling them to send their children "to better, non-public schools when the public schools have failed them." He added that "perhaps tax credits will even provide a competitive stimulus to the public schools to improve."

One of the most controversial aspects of the Packwood-Moynihan bill is that it would give direct financial aid to parents with children in parochial schools. During the 1976 presidential campaign, candidate Jimmy Carter declared his commitment to finding "a constitutionally acceptable method"[6] of providing such aid. However, because of the administration's strong opposition to tuition tax credits, Sen. Moynihan charged the President with "reneging"[7] on his campaign promise and predicted that Carter's stand will cost Democrats votes in this year's congressional elections. "I have invited the administration to devise other means of assisting parents of parochial school children, if it disagrees with our bill. But nothing of this sort is being done, or, as I understand, is even under consideration," Moynihan said.

Opponents of an education tax break concede that support for the idea is substantial. Nevertheless, they vow to fight it because of what they consider the serious constitutional implications of using the tax system as a vehicle to aid non-public schools. Andrew L. Gunn, president of Americans United for the Separation of Church and State, a group opposed to federal assistance to religious education, said the Packwood-Moynihan bill clearly violates the Constitution's principle of church-state separation. At recent hearings, Gunn told the Senate Finance Committee Jan. 19 that the measure was "an effort to get public funding for parochial schools to teach religion."

In other testimony, Leo Pfeffer, professor of constitutional law at Long Island University in New York, said "as the proposed law relates to tuition at elementary and secondary schools, it is irremediably unconstitutional." But Pfeffer noted that the Supreme Court has made a distinction between federal aid to parochial elementary and secondary schools and aid to colleges which, though church-related, perform essentially secular educational functions *(see box p. 129)*.

Economic Opposition to Tax Credit Plan

Although college costs have risen sharply in the last decade, in many cases the increases have been offset by the upward trend in gross family incomes.[8] From 1967 to 1975, average family earnings rose by 72.9 per cent compared to an increase in

---

[6] In a letter to the Rev. Russell M. Bleich, president of the Chief Administrators of Catholic Education, Oct. 19, 1976.
[7] Quoted in *The Washington Post*, Jan. 20, 1978.
[8] See Congressional Budget Office, "Tax Allowances for Post-Secondary Education Expenses," July 1977, pp. 14-15.

> **Some Supreme Court Decisions on School Financing**
>
> **Tilton v. Richardson,** 403 U.S. 672 (1971), validated federal construction grants to church-related colleges, provided buildings would be used for secular purposes. The court's majority opinion distinguished between lower and higher institutions of learning primarily on the ground that "college students are less susceptible to religious instruction."
>
> **Committee for Public Education and Religious Liberty v. Nyquist,** 413 U.S. 756 (1973), overturned a New York law that extended tuition reimbursements and special tax benefits to low-income parents of parochial school children.
>
> **Essex v. Wolman,** 409 U.S. 808 (1973), affirmed a lower court decision (342 F. Supp. 399) ruling unconstitutional an Ohio tuition grant law.
>
> **Sloan v. Lemon,** 413 U.S. 825 (1973), struck down a Pennsylvania plan to reimburse parents for a portion of tuition expenses incurred in sending their children to non-public schools.
>
> **Grit v. Wolman,** 413 U.S. 901 (1973), upheld a lower court decision (353 F. Supp. 744) invalidating an Ohio law to provide tax credits for parents of children attending non-public schools.
>
> **Roemer v. Maryland Board of Public Works,** 426 U.S. 736 (1976), found constitutional general state aid to church-related colleges and universities, provided recipient institutions performed essentially secular functions.

college costs of about 65 per cent. "Because of this growth in family income," the Senate Budget Committee concluded, college costs in 1975 actually made up a "significantly smaller portion of income than in 1967."[9] Student charges at public institutions decreased from 13.4 to 12.7 per cent of median family income, while student charges at private institutions fell from 27.8 per cent of median family income to 26.7 per cent. Increases in college fees also have been met by increases in federal aid to students, which, according to the committee, grew by 281 per cent between 1967 and 1975.

Armed with these statistics, some have expressed doubts about the argument that middle-class families need a special education tax break. Appearing before the House Budget Committee last May, Laurence N. Woodworth, a former Assistant Treasury Secretary, and Mary F. Berry, Assistant Secretary of Health, Education and Welfare, both questioned the advisability of universal tax relief that would extend tuition aid to families that don't need it along with those that do. Woodworth predicted that if the proposed tax credit plan were to take effect

---

[9] Senate Budget Committee, "The College Tuition Tax Credit: An Analysis and Possible Alternatives," Dec. 19, 1977, p. 9.

there would be immediate consumer pressure to raise it. "When your bill is $4,000," he reasoned, "$500 isn't much."[10] Once a system of credits was adopted, Woodworth added, nothing would prevent colleges from raising their fees, thus eliminating the advantage of a tax adjustment.

Instead of tax credits or deductions, the Carter administration wants to expand access to existing tuition subsidy programs by readjusting family income requirements so as to make more middle-income students eligible to receive educational aid funds. Current federal policy provides financial assistance to students based on family need. Families with annual incomes above $16,000 do not qualify for basic education grants, except in cases where they have more than one child in college.

Carter Program for Student Assistance

Earlier this month, President Carter asked Congress to raise the 1979 student assistance budget from $3.8 billion to a record $5.25 billion. Included in the plan is a $1.5 billion expansion of existing scholarship and loan programs that would make some 60 per cent of the nation's college students eligible for federal aid. Carter said that he intends "to work" for passage of the proposal and would use his veto powers, if necessary, to prevent enactment of a tax credit bill.[11] He added that the country cannot afford both increased student scholarships and loans and a tax reduction.

The Carter plan for student aid contains the following major elements:

1. The basic educational opportunity grant program (BEOG), which provides tuition scholarships to students based on family income and the cost of college attendance, would be increased by $1 billion over the $2.1 billion appropriated in 1978. By the administration's calculations, this would make basic grants available to 3.1 million additional students, raising the total from 2.2 to 5.3 million.

2. College students from families with incomes in the $16,000 to $25,000 range, previously not eligible for the BEOG program, would receive annual grants of $250. Grants for students from families that earn $8,000 to $16,000 would be raised from the present $850 to $1,050, while maximum awards for students whose families earn under $8,000 would increase from $1,600 to $1,800.

3. The college work-study program, which provides 80 per cent of the salary payments for student campus employment, would receive an added $165 million over the current $435 million allotment. That amount, according to the administration, will open part-time work opportunities to as many as 380,000 new

---

[10] Quoted in *The National Observer*, May 5, 1977.
[11] Speaking at a White House press conference, Feb. 8, 1978.

> **Federal Student Assistance Programs**
>
> **Basic educational opportunity grants (BEOG)** provide tuition aid to needy students. The size of an individual grant—up to $1,600 in 1977—is determined on the basis of family and student contribution. Last year, awards to deserving students averaged $847.
>
> **Supplemental educational opportunity grants** offer additional aid for exceptionally needy students. In 1977, grants ranged from $200 to $1,500; they averaged $525 per recipient.
>
> **Direct student loan program** supplies funds to colleges and universities for low-interest, long-term loans to needy students. The average loan last year was $690.
>
> **Guaranteed student loan program** enables students to borrow up to $2,500 per year from private lending institutions. Loans are guaranteed either by state or federal agencies, and borrowers have up to 10 years to repay them. The average loan in 1977 was $1,245.
>
> **Work-study program** provides part-time campus employment to students. Last year, nearly 800,000 earned an average of $545.

students from families making over $16,000.

4. The guaranteed student loan program, which assures repayment of low-interest student loans, would get an additional $327 million over the $540 million appropriated in fiscal year 1978. This change, it is anticipated, would support 260,000 new loans to students from families with incomes above $16,000. In fiscal 1978, about 1 million students will receive federally guaranteed loans.

Should Congress go along with these proposals, the White House predicts that the number of awards in federal student assistance programs will more than double from approximately 3.2 million in 1978 to more than 7 million in fiscal 1979. "Because some students receive awards under more than one program," a spokesman for the Department of Health, Education and Welfare said, "we estimate that more than 5 million college students nationwide will receive financial assistance from the federal government in fiscal 1979, an increase of 2 million students over last year."

Rep. Ullman has indicated that he favors the President's package. In the past, Ullman has repeatedly blocked House action on Senate-approved education tax credit bills. The Ways and Means Committee, however, was almost evenly divided on the issue the last time it came up for a vote in 1977. Advocates of the credit have said they hope to line up enough support this year to bring the measure through the committee. Sen. Roth, a leader of this group, labeled Carter's proposal "just an effort to derail" the credit legislation.[12] Spokesmen for organizations seeking "parochiaid" also said they would continue the fight for a tax break. They oppose Carter's plan because it includes no provisions to give financial assistance to parents of children in non-public elementary and secondary schools.

Federal Aid for Higher Education

THOMAS JEFFERSON believed that an educated electorate was the best assurance of the survival of democracy in America. For this reason, Jefferson and other Founding Fathers advocated the establishment of free public schooling. Public school systems were set up in most states in the early part of the 19th century. The movement to promote public colleges and universities did not gain headway until the Civil War period. The Land-Grant College Act of 1862, also known as the Morrill Act, was the federal government's first, and perhaps its most significant, investment in higher education. Under the terms of the act, over 11 million acres of public land were transferred to the states for the endowment of agricultural and mechanical colleges.

The Morrill Act was intended "to promote the liberal and practical education of the industrial classes in the general pursuits and professions of life." But it did not require the institutions that benefited from it to be state-run. Private schools such as Cornell University and the Massachusetts Institute of Technology have received funds under the original legislation and its subsequent amendments. While the Morrill Act originally emphasized agriculture and science, its provisions were flexible enough to allow for expansion into many fields.

In this century, federal support for higher education grew as colleges and universities increasingly came to be viewed as tools for solving national problems. The government subsidized "research, specialized services, and—through student aid—instruction," wrote Earl F. Cheit, dean of the School of Business at the University of California at Berkeley. "But unlike governments in some countries and unlike other supporters of education in this country..., the federal government showed little inclination to control the colleges...its investments helped to fund."[13]

Unlike federal grants to colleges and universities, government aid to students was largely a post-World War II development. During the 1930s, a federally supported student work program

---

[12] Quoted in *The Washington Post*, Feb. 9, 1978.
[13] Earl F. Cheit, "Benefits and Burdens of Federal Financial Assistance to Higher Education," *The College Board Review*, spring 1977, p. 14.

was provided as an emergency relief measure, and during World War II students in disciplines where manpower was scarce received loans to help them complete their training.

Tuition Assistance for U.S. Veterans

The Servicemen's Readjustment Act of 1944, the famous "GI Bill," opened a new era of federal support for higher education. Under the measure, the federal government provided veterans enrolled as full-time students with a monthly living allowance and made direct payments of up to $500 per year to institutions for tuition, fees and other school costs. The educational provisions of the original act have been revised several times to increase the benefits and broaden the types of training covered. One study, completed in the early 1950s, reached the conclusion that 20 to 25 per cent of the World War II veterans who took advantage of the GI Bill would not have attended college without it.[14]

The Korean War (1950-1953) made far less of an impact on college enrollment than World War II did since full-time students in good standing generally were able to get military deferments. Vietnam veterans, like Korean War vets before them, receive a fixed stipend, from which they must pay all their college expenses, including books and tuition. The current basic monthly education benefit paid by the Veterans Administration is $311. However, the rapidly rising cost of higher education in recent years has made it difficult for many Vietnam-era veterans to meet college expenses.[15]

There are wide disparities in tuition charges in different regions of the country. Tuitions generally are lower in the southern and western states than in the eastern and midwestern states. Since all veterans, regardless of where they attend school or how much tuition they must pay, receive the standard education allotment, those in the East and Midwest often find it harder to cover their college expenses. For instance, a veteran choosing to attend Long Beach State College in California, where resident fees are $200 a year,[16] would use only 7 per cent of his $2,799 nine-month education allotment to pay tuition. A veteran at Indiana University, a state-run institution costing residents $722 a year, would spend 25.8 per cent of his benefits on tuition. At Dartmouth, a private college costing $4,230, a veteran would need to supplement his VA payments by $1,431 in order to meet tuition charges alone.

---

[14] Norman Fredricks and W. B. Schraeder, *Adjustment to College: A Study of 10,000 Veteran and Non-Veteran Students in Sixteen American Colleges* (1951), p. 34.

[15] See "Vietnam Veterans: Continuing Readjustment," *E.R.R.*, 1977 Vol. II, pp. 785-804.

[16] Costs for 1976-77, excluding room and board, according to the Life Insurance Marketing and Research Association, an independent actuarial organization.

The education provisions in the G.I. Bill Improvement Act of 1977, passed last November, may help to eliminate some of the problems veterans have faced in the past. It called for:

1. Increasing educational benefits by 6.6 per cent.

2. Increasing the maximum annual amount of VA direct education loans from $1,500 to $2,500.

3. Removing the requirement that a veteran must first be turned down by a private lender before he can apply for a VA loan.

4. Setting up joint federal-state programs to provide special funds to assist veterans in paying off VA loans for tuition at more expensive schools.

The latest VA figures show that some 8.7 million Vietnam-era veterans have taken advantage of GI Bill education benefits—64.7 per cent of those eligible. That compares to a 50.5 per cent participation rate by World War II veterans and 43.4 per cent by Korean War vets.

Government Aid to Colleges Since 1950s

The launching of the Russian satellite Sputnik I in late 1957 provided impetus for a new wave of financial support for higher education. Reacting to charges that America was falling behind the Soviets in scientific know-how, Congress passed the National Defense Education Act of 1958. This law provided scholarships, loans and grants to improve teaching in science and foreign languages. It was followed in 1965 by the Higher Education Act which featured extensive aid for needy students.

As federal assistance to education increased, many educators began to worry that government aid would bring greater federal control over recipient institutions. Earl F. Cheit wrote: "Federal money has always carried with it regulations to assure that program purposes were followed, and that money was legally used. As a basis for regulation, both concepts have been extended to include nondiscrimination and affirmative action. The concept of program purpose has been enlarged to mean that federal financial assistance to one program...subjects any other...to regulation."[17]

Because of the fear of federal control, a few private institutions—Brigham Young University in Utah, Hillside College in Michigan and Wabash College in Indiana—have refused to accept federal aid, including student assistance. Other schools receiving government support have expressed the need to be free of what they consider the excessive federal "red tape" that goes along with it. According to John Gardner, Secretary of Health, Education and Welfare in the Johnson administration, most

---

[17] Earl F. Cheit, *op. cit.*, p. 15.

College Costs—1976-77

Private Colleges	Tuition and Fees	Room and Board	Total
Boston Univ.	$3,640	$1,850	$5,490
Brown	4,322	1,975	6,065
Bryn Mawr	4,190	1,875	5,490
Cornell	4,110	1,900	6,010
Univ. of Chicago	3,510	2,075	5,585
Dartmouth	4,230	2,025	6,255
Duke	3,250	1,420	4,670
Harvard	4,100	2,330	6,430
Notre Dame	3,030	1,260	4,290
Princeton	4,300	1,830	6,130

Public Colleges	Tuition and Fees*	Room and Board	Total
Univ. of California, at Los Angeles	$ 630	$1,500	$2,130
Univ. of Colorado	710	1,500	2,210
Grambling Univ.	414	910	1,324
Univ. of Houston	328	1,260	1,588
Indiana Univ.	722	1,229	1,951
Univ. of Massachusetts, Amherst	596	1,481	2,077
Michigan State Univ.	838	1,335	2,173
Univ. of Missouri	584	1,220	1,804
Ohio State Univ.	810	1,400	2,210
Purdue	750	1,390	2,140
San Francisco State Univ.	192	1,134	1,326
Texas Tech.	351	1,030	1,381

*Fees higher for non-state residents.

Source: Life Insurance Marketing and Research Association's 1976/1977 list of college costs, latest available figures.

college presidents prefer the "leave it on the stump" method of support—funding with no strings attached.

To increase or maintain enrollment without having to depend on government programs, many schools have adopted tuition deferral arrangements. Yale put such a plan into effect in 1971. First suggested by economist Milton Friedman in 1955, tuition deferral amounts to a long-term student loan. After graduating, the student-borrower has the option of extending loan repayment over a long period of time. At Yale, this method involves the graduate's paying the school four-tenths of one per cent of his or her yearly taxable income for each $1,000 borrowed. The obligation lasts until participants have either repaid their loans, which Yale expects to take about 27 years, or until 35 years have elapsed. Anyone can "buy out" of the plan at any time by paying Yale 150 per cent of the outstanding loan and interest. Although the deferred tuition concept has been praised by many economy-minded educators, some observers have criticized it as a way of masking tuition increases by raising the interest rates on loans.

Past Action on Tuition Relief Proposals

Congress has been debating the issue of college tuition assistance since the early 1950s. Most of the proposed plans have included some form of tax deduction or personal exemption to cover the costs of higher education. While every Congress since 1964 has considered tuition credit bills, none of them has managed to pass both houses. In 1965, lawmakers approved legislation creating the guaranteed student loan program. The measure was aimed at families with moderate incomes and was regarded at the time as an acceptable substitute for tax relief. A recent congressional study concluded: "Given the dual assumption that (1) there were substantial future income benefits to be derived from higher education and (2) that middle-income families suffered not from a deficiency in wealth but from a cash flow problem in paying the costs of higher education, a loan program was enacted as the most effective and least costly means to aid middle-income families."[18]

In 1967, Sen. Abraham Ribicoff (D Conn.) introduced the first Senate-passed tuition relief plan. That measure and subsequent ones like it offered in 1969, 1971 and 1973, went down to defeat in the House of Representatives after passing in the Senate. Senator Roth in 1976 submitted a tax credit proposal that differed from the previous bills in that it sought to award to low-, middle- and high-income families a fixed credit—$500 by 1980—not limited to a percentage of college expenses. Last December, Roth's plan, which has won Senate approval three times, was attached to the Social Security bill until House-Senate conferees voted to drop it when it threatened to hold up passage of that legislation.

New Approaches to Cost-Control

DURING the 1976 presidential campaign Jimmy Carter promised to improve the effectiveness of government by reorganizing the management and budgeting of more than 2,000

---

[18] "The College Tuition Tax Credit," *op. cit.*, p. 6.

federal agencies.[19] As part of his overall effort to restructure the bureaucracy, Carter has asked Congress to approve the establishment of a Cabinet-level Department of Education. At present, most federal education policies are implemented by the Office of Education in the Department of Health, Education and Welfare. In February 1976, Carter wrote that he supported the creation of an Education Department in order to "consolidate grant programs, job training...and other functions currently scattered thoughout the government."[20] He reiterated this argument in his January State of the Union address.

Sentiment favoring creation of a Cabinet-level education post has been building in Congress, although not as rapidly or as enthusiastically as the administration might have wished. The Senate Government Operations Committee has scheduled three days of hearings in mid-March on a bill authorizing a Department of Education. Sen. Abraham Ribicoff (D Conn.), who introduced the measure, has predicted swift action in both houses of Congress and probable passage before the end of the year. But pockets of opposition to the bill could delay or even defeat it.

"There are millions of families today who are neither affluent enough to afford the high cost of college nor considered poor enough to qualify for the government assistance programs which their taxes make possible."
Sen. William V. Roth (R Del.)

A number of educators have voiced misgivings about creating a separate department. According to *The Chronicle of Higher Education*, many are particularly concerned that education programs "would be more vulnerable to congressional attack if their appropriations were not part of a larger HEW package."[21] *The New York Times* editorialized that the establishment of an Education Department would "cheapen the Cabinet." "Even if the administration is willing to spend political capital generously," the Times concluded, "the legislative bargaining process is quite likely to erode the scope of a broad new department, leaving it no more than a new label for the old Office of Education."[22]

---

[19] See "Federal Reorganization and Budget Reform," *E.R.R.*, 1977 Vol. II, pp. 661-680.
[20] Jimmy Carter, "If I Am Elected," *Change*, February 1976, p. 11.
[21] *The Chronicle of Higher Education*, Dec. 12, 1977.
[22] *The New York Times*, Jan. 16, 1978.

Editorial Research Reports   *Feb. 24, 1978*

The federal government spends some $30 billion annually on education programs. About half of them are in HEW; the rest are spread throughout other bureaus and departments. That situation, Education Department proponents maintain, has led to costly rivalry among various agencies and needless work duplication. HEW Secretary Joseph A. Califano Jr. is on record opposing a Cabinet-level education office. Creation of a new agency could eliminate an estimated $15 billion from the HEW budget.[23] In place of a Department of Education, Califano, in a memo to President Carter last November, proposed creating three separately funded sub-agencies within HEW for health, education and welfare (modeled after the operation of the Department of Defense) with a Cabinet Secretary to coordinate their activities.

High Rate of Default on Student Loans

Since passage of The National Defense Education Act nearly 20 years ago, the government has dispensed about $17 billion in educational loans to some 15 million students. The Department of Health, Education and Welfare, which is responsible for overseeing most federal student aid programs, estimates that as many as 14 per cent of the loans have not been repaid. HEW officials say the high rate of default is the result of inefficient collection methods, sloppy bookkeeping and, in some cases, fraud on the part of recipients. In a separate educational loan program conducted by the Veterans Administration, records show that since 1975 ex-GIs have failed to repay 2,267 loans. In December, *The Chronicle of Higher Education* reported that between June and September in 1977 veterans defaulted on 1,005 loans.[24]

Leo Kornfeld, deputy commissioner of education, admitted that HEW bears a large part of the blame for the high rate of default. "The major point, as far as collections [are concerned], is the fact that students, for much longer than a year, even as many as four and five and six years, have not received a letter from the federal government telling them that they owe money," Kornfeld acknowledged on a recent CBS News broadcast.[25] An HEW survey taken last year found 205,000 errors in one master list of 50,000 student loans.

The Office of Education and the Veterans Administration have promised to crack down on defaulters and, they hope, recover close to $1 billion in outstanding debts. HEW Secretary Califano recently announced that his agency's "get-tough"

---

[23] The HEW budget in fiscal 1978 was $162 billion—the highest of any Cabinet department.
[24] See *The Chronicle of Higher Education,* Dec. 12, 1977.
[25] CBS Evening News, Feb. 7, 1978.

policy would include reorganizing computer files, bringing in more workers to handle the job of keeping track of student borrowers and contracting with an outside company to collect overdue payments. Meanwhile, the VA has put GI defaulters on notice that the names of veterans who refuse to pay their debts will be turned over to the Justice Department for prosecution.

If missing borrowers are located, HEW may have some legal difficulty in securing repayment. According to federal bank regulators, many of the original loan applications signed by students did not contain required truth-in-lending information, thus making them invalid. Critics of the federal student loan program argue that the government is responsible for most of the repayment problems. Consumer specialist Jean Carper wrote: "The uncontrolled release of federal funds for private vocational schools, starting in the late 1960s, created an atmosphere of deception and fraud, entrapping many students whom the Office of Education now wants to pay up. OE officials generally did little or nothing to protect students—they depended on self-serving accrediting agencies to approve the schools—and in many cases even collaborated in their entrapment."[26]

Maury Tansey, OE's debt collection chief, has said that students who have a valid defense may be excused from paying their loans. But according to Jean Carper "there is no firm policy [within the Office of Education] about how students can prove" their reasons for not repaying the loans are valid, and "no effort has been made by OE to identify or notify such students who may be paying unnecessarily."

Carter vs. Congress on Education Policy

It seems almost certain that a tuition relief bill will become law before the year is out. What is uncertain is whether relief will take the form of a tax credit allowance, which numerous members of Congress now are demanding, or an increase in existing scholarship and student loan programs, as proposed by President Carter. The ensuing legislative battle could provide a telling indication of the President's influence over Congress and, depending on the kind of measure finally adopted, a prediction of the administration's chances of achieving a balanced budget, as promised, by 1981.

Normally, a President's opposition to a tax reduction measure would be a formidable obstacle to passage, but feeling in Congress seems to be running strongly in favor of challenging the White House on this issue. "The voters are angry about rising education costs, and the pressure reached Capitol Hill

---

[26] Jean Carper, writing in *The Washington Post*, January 15, 1978.

Alternatives to College

"When the college gates start to close, nothing less is at stake than the future of an open, upwardly mobile, democratic society." This comment from a recent *New York Times* editorial reflects the traditional American faith in the value of a college education. But lately, it appears that a growing number of students—and their parents—are beginning to ask whether the time and money spent earning a college degree could be put to better use.

"However good or bad it might be for the individual students," wrote social critic Caroline Bird, "college is a place where young adults are set apart because they are superfluous people who are of no immediate use to the economy." In her book, *The Case Against College* (1975), Bird theorizes that college is not for everybody and cites estimates by teachers and administrators that only about 25 per cent of a given student body is interested in school. "For the other 75 per cent," she suggested, "college is at best a social center, a youth ghetto, an aging vat...or even a prison." Besides often failing to instill students with higher values, institutions of higher learning, Bird said, ultimately fail to provide most students with a degree that is worth anything in the job market.

Despite a slight improvement in job prospects for graduates, some college students are dropping out of school before graduation to pursue careers not requiring a degree. Others have taken to "stopping-out," leaving school for a period of time to work. Education specialist Gordon F. Sander has speculated that as many as two million college undergraduates—about 20 per cent of the national total—left school in 1976 "to spend some time in the outside world, or to try some other form of education" before returning to finish their degrees.

Educators still contend that college is the best preparation for a wide variety of later career possibilities. Nevertheless, many now encourage stopping-out. Stanford University has even established a stop-out counseling center to advise students on the educational and financial advantages of taking a leave of absence from school. "Our experience with stopping out has been a positive one," said Alean Clark, who works with the Stanford program. "We find that most students who stop out come back with a better perspective on things."

Americans over age 25—many far above—are filling what would otherwise be vacant seats in some college classrooms. Without the older students, enrollments would have sagged badly in recent years. Students 25 and older numbered 1.7 million and accounted for 22 per cent of the campus population in 1970. By 1975, these figures had jumped to 34 per cent and 3.7 million and, according to a Census Bureau estimate, four of every ten collegians may be 25 or older by 1985 if current enrollment rates by age continue at the prevailing pace.

before it reached the White House," said one congressional aide. "The people want the government to do something about two major expenses that have gotten far too high: hospitalization and college tuition."

If hospital care is a practical necessity, a college education is something sacred to most Americans, who regard the attainment of a degree as one way up the social and economic ladder. Speaking in Washington recently, the Rev. Ernest Bartell, director of the Fund for the Improvement of Postsecondary Education, said: "After losing its reputation as a healer of all social ills and faced with financial pressures to sustain enrollments, higher education will probably continue to find its principal entrée to the public purse strings through programs of financial assistance to students and institutions that link [it] to social goals of equality of opportunity. Access to educational opportunities endures as a principal vehicle, if not for guaranteed career success, at least for removing barriers to social and economic mobility."[27]

Although the job market value of a liberal arts degree recently has been called into question by some educators and economists, few disagree that rising tuition rates threaten to price many aspiring students out of a higher education. "One way or another," said Sen. Roth "the country will have to pay when children stop going to college." What Congress must decide is which of the many proposals now before it offers the best hope for holding down soaring college costs.

---

[27] Speech to the 64th annual meeting of the Association of American Colleges, Feb. 8, 1978, Washington, D.C.

Books

Bird, Caroline, *The Case Against College,* David McKay, 1975.
Brubacher, John S. and Willis Rudy, *Higher Education in Transition,* Harper & Row, revised edition, 1976.
Eidenberg, Eugene and Roy D. Morey, *An Act of Congress: The Legislative Process and the Making of Education Policy,* Norton, 1969.
Smith, Bardell L., et al., *The Tenure Debate,* Jossey-Bass Publishers, 1973.
Suchar, Elizabeth, et al., *Student Expenses at Postsecondary Institutions, 1977-78,* College Entrance Exam Board, 1977.
―― *Guide to Financial Aid for Students and Parents,* Simon & Schuster, 1975.

Articles

AAUP (American Association of University Professors) *Bulletin,* selected issues.
Cheit, Earl F., "Benefits and Burdens of Federal Financial Assistance to Higher Education," *The College Board Review,* spring 1977.
Carter, Alan M., "Faculty Needs and Resources in American Higher Education," *Annals of the American Academy of Political and Social Science,* November 1972.
Evans, M. Stanton, "The Tuition War," *National Review,* Jan. 20, 1978.
Gross, Theodore, "How to Kill a College: The Private Papers of a Campus Dean," *Saturday Review,* Feb. 4, 1978.
Gunn, Andrew L., "1978: Year of Crisis for Religious Liberty," *Church & State,* January 1978.
Higher Education Daily, selected issues.
Hoyt, Robert G., "Learning a Lesson from the Catholic Schools," *Saturday Review,* Sept. 12, 1977.
Leary, Mary Ellen, "Caught in the Purse Strings," *The Nation,* Jan. 28, 1978.
"Middle-Class Protest against College Costs," *U.S. News & World Report,* Jan. 30, 1978.
The Chronicle of Higher Education, selected issues.

Reports and Studies

Editorial Research Reports, "Future of Private Colleges," 1976 Vol. I, p. 305; "College Recruiting," 1974 Vol. II, p. 661; "Academic Tenure," 1974 Vol. I, p. 161.
Espenshade, Thomas J., "The Value and Cost of Children," Population Reference Bureau, April 1977.
The Carnegie Council on Policy Studies in Higher Education, "Low or No Tuition," Jossey-Bass Publishers, 1975.
Twentieth Century Fund Task Force on College and University Endowment Policy, "Funds for the Future," McGraw-Hill, 1975.
U.S. Senate, "Description of Bills Relating to Tuition Credits and Deductions Listed for Hearing by the Subcommittee on Taxation and Debt Management of the Committee on Finance," Jan. 17, 1978.

Housing Outlook

by
Suzanne de Lesseps

	page
CLIMBING COST OF HOME BUYING	145
Forecast for Record Construction in 1977	145
Effects of Various Factors on Housing Costs	146
Buyers' Resistance to 'No Frills' Housing	147
Restoration Through Urban Homesteading	148
'Do-It'Yourself' Housing; Mobile Homes	149
GOVERNMENT'S ROLE IN HOUSING	151
New Deal Laws to Stabilize the Market	151
Postwar Assistance to Overcome Shortages	152
Focus on the Urban Poor in the Late Sixties	153
Attempts to Alleviate 1973-74 Credit Crunch	155
INFLUENCES ON HOUSING TRENDS	157
Administration's Pledge of More Subsidies	157
Changes in Household Size, Demographics	158
Construction Techniques and Fuel Prices	160

**Apr. 22
1977**

Editor's Note: Price trends noted in this report have continued upward. From early 1977, when this report was issued, through the end of 1978, the average price of a new single family house rose from $51,600 to $66,400, an increase of almost 30 percent.

Kenneth Biederman, chief economist for the Federal Home Loan Bank Board in Washington, D.C., believes the housing demand will continue through the next decade and push home prices up by at least 10 percent a year.

HOUSING OUTLOOK

HOME BUILDING has often been characterized as a boom-or-bust industry, primarily because it is so sensitive to the availability and cost of mortgage credit. The housing industry is currently pulling out of its worst slump since World War II, and home builders have predicted that a near-record amount of new construction will begin this year.[1] But this optimism, though welcomed by the nation, does not necessarily extend to the various housing needs of the coming decade. Nor does the predicted increase in housing "starts" this year mean that more families will be able to buy new homes. Although the number of new homes may increase, so will the prices, and average-income families will continue to be squeezed out of the new single-family housing market.

According to a recent study on home ownership issued by the Joint Center for Urban Studies at Harvard University and the Massachusetts Institute of Technology, sales prices of new single-family homes have climbed twice as fast as family incomes over the past six years. And the monthly costs of home ownership, which includes utilities, taxes, insurance and maintenance, have increased even more rapidly than sales prices *(see graph, p. 156)*. "If the trends from 1971 to 1976 continue for another five years," say the authors of the study, "typical new homes in 1981 will sell for $78,000 and only the most affluent groups will be able to afford them."[2] The median sales price of a new single-family home currently is $47,500, the Bureau of the Census reported on April 8. Half of all new homes cost more and half less.

The Joint Center calculated that 46.6 per cent of American families could afford to buy a median-priced new house in 1970, but only 27 per cent could afford to in 1976 *(see p. 147)*. What is causing the price of newly built homes to increase at such a pace? One factor is demand arising from the increase in the number of households formed in this decade—from 63.6 million households in 1970 to 71.7 million in 1975. Young, single adults, the elderly, and those who are separated or divorced have all

---

[1] At the 1977 convention of the National Association of Home Builders at Dallas in January, some 1.8 million housing "starts" were forecast for the year, up from 1.5 million in 1976 and 1.1 million in 1975. During March, new housing units were started at an annual rate of 2.1 million, the highest rate since May 1973. Single-family homes were started at an annual rate of more than 1.5 million.

[2] Bernard Frieden and Arthur P. Solomon, *The Nation's Housing, 1975 to 1985.*

tended to form separate households more frequently than in the past.[3] And the "baby boom" children of the 1940s and 1950s are now starting families of their own. Another factor is that more couples are realizing that a house is an excellent investment. Many are becoming "trade-up" buyers and taking the profit from the sale of one home to buy another. Indeed, about 70 per cent of today's buyers are already homeowners.

It is first-time home buyers who feel the tightest price squeeze. They must raise enough money for a down payment, currently averaging about 25 per cent of the sales price, without the benefit of any gain from a previous house. Some families have to pool the earnings of both husband and wife to make the down payment. Among first-time buyers in 1975 and 1976, six of ten were families in which both spouses held jobs.

Effects of Various Factors on Housing Costs

The price of a new home is determined by a complex mixture of economic forces. It includes the cost of labor, lumber and other commodities, the growing scarcity of usable land near many cities, and the prevailing mortgage and tax rates. The chief economist for the National Association of Home Builders, Michael Sumichrast, calculates that the two leading causes of higher prices are costlier land and construction financing. Taken together, these two factors make up about 40 per cent of the cost of a new home.

Land accounted for only about 11 per cent of the price of a new home soon after World War II, but today the figure is almost 30 per cent. Land developers attribute much of the increase to environmental codes and regulations. "Ten years ago, we could buy land and open a model in four to five months...," Maryland builder Milton Kettler has said. "Today it takes two to three years before we can put a shovel into the ground. The cost of carrying land over this extended period has increased enormously."[4] J. D. Caswell of the Georgia Homebuilders Association testified before a Senate subcommittee in February that the cost of satisfying federal, state and local building regulations added approximately 16 per cent to the cost of a new home.[5]

While land and construction financing account for a larger share of a new home's price tag, the traditional "hard costs" of labor and material account for relatively less, dropping from 69 per cent 30 years ago to 48 per cent today. This has happened for

---

[3] See U.S. Bureau of the Census report, "Household and Family Characteristics: March 1975," Series P-20, No. 291, February 1976. See also "Single-Parent Families," *E.R.R.*, 1976 Vol. II, pp. 661-680.
[4] Quoted by Michael Sumichrast in *The Washington Star*, March 11, 1977.
[5] Senate Select Small Business Subcommittee on Environmental, Rural and Urban Economic Development, at hearings in Atlanta, Feb. 16, 1977.

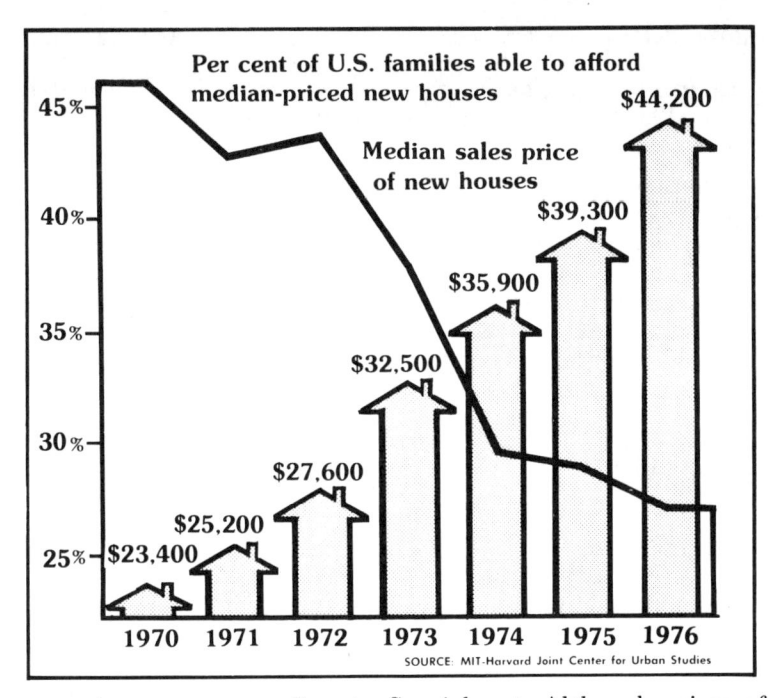

Per cent of U.S. families able to afford median-priced new houses

Year	Median sales price
1970	$23,400
1971	$25,200
1972	$27,600
1973	$32,500
1974	$35,900
1975	$39,300
1976	$44,200

SOURCE: MIT-Harvard Joint Center for Urban Studies

several reasons, according to Sumichrast. Although prices of lumber, plywood, brass and brick have increased faster than the average of all commodities, such other items as paint and plumbing and heating fixtures have not kept pace. Changes in construction, design and engineering also have helped hold costs down, even though the quality of construction may have suffered.

Doors, for example, are no longer solid but hollowed out and stuffed with cardboard. Slate roofs have been replaced by asphalt shingles, which are faster to install and easier to replace. Water lines are likely to be made of plastic instead of steel or copper. And drywall has replaced plaster. The other half of the "hard costs"—that going for labor—has declined, according to Sumichrast, due to (1) the development of standardized and prefabricated construction methods, (2) increased productivity resulting from mechanization, and (3) better tools.

Buyers' Resistance to 'No Frills' Housing

About three years ago, home builders decided to try a "back to basics" approach to construction in an attempt to build more affordable homes. Smaller houses were built, minus such expensive "extras" as cedar-lined closets, fireplaces, second bathrooms, two-car garages and finished basements. Some builders have had success with these lower-priced models, called "no frills" homes. In Dallas, for example, basic homes costing $26,500 to $28,000 are selling to many young people with annual family incomes of $13,000 to $20,000. And in several cities in Florida, a basic three-bedroom model which sells for about $19,000 is being grabbed up by retired citizens.

For the most part, however, builders attending the National Association of Home Builders convention in Dallas in January agreed that the "no frills" house has fizzled. "We've had a tough time selling what I thought was good for people," explained John C. Hart, the association's outgoing president. "We built houses for $25,000 to $35,000, houses in which the buyers could let inflation build their equity so they could trade up to a bigger, better one. But buyers just turned their noses up at them."[6] According to Robert Levenstein, executive vice president of Kaufman & Broad Inc., a leading developer of the "no frills" concept: "Housing's equivalent to the Pinto is no longer the answer. We're building slightly larger houses with more amenities that the trade-up buyer wants."[7]

The failure of the "no frills" experiment is explained by the fact that most persons buying houses today have sizable incomes or are young people who expect to become more affluent. Both groups prefer houses with the accessories. American families of average income who want lower-cost housing increasingly are renovating older houses rather than buying new ones. But even the cost of older houses has moved further away from the average family's reach. In 1970, about 45 per cent of American families could afford the cost ($23,030) of a median-priced, existing house. Six years later, the figure was down to 36 per cent. The cost of a median-priced, existing house, meanwhile, had risen to $38,100.

Restoration Through Urban Homesteading

One federal program that has made older houses more available is urban homesteading. Abandoned homes acquired by the federal government, usually through defaults on federally backed housing loans, are turned over to local governments and sold for nominal sums—usually one dollar—to families who agree to renovate the structures and live in them for at least three years. The cost of restoration usually runs from $3,000 to $20,000 and low-interest federal loans are available to help meet the expense.

The idea of urban homesteading was first conceived in 1968 by Philadelphia City Councilman Joseph E. Coleman. The first city to enact a program, however, was Wilmington, Del., which gave away 10 houses in August 1973. Three hundred persons applied for the giveaways. One year after the successful Wilmington experiment, Congress approved the Housing and Community Development Act calling for, among other things,

---

[6] Quoted by Lew Sichelman in *The Washington Star*, Jan. 28, 1977.
[7] Quoted by Robert L. Simison in *The Wall Street Journal*, Jan. 28, 1977.

Housing Outlook

an experimental urban homesteading program. The Department of Housing and Urban Development (HUD) was authorized $5-million to pay for the cost of transferring about 1,000 repossessed houses, in need of repair, to various local governments. Over 20 cities have already participated in the program, and more federal funds are on the way.

One criticism of the federal urban homesteading program is that it caters primarily to middle-income families and ignores lower-income groups who cannot finance the cost of renovation. Last year, in fact, Los Angeles Mayor Tom Bradley declined to participate in the program because he thought it would not aid the city's poor. In New York City, however, the Urban Homesteading Assistance Board has reached low-income groups by offering advice on financing and giving technical assistance. Although the private, nonprofit agency as a rule does not lend or donate money for restoration, it occasionally advances money to help get a project going.

'Do-It-Yourself' Housing; Mobile Homes

Besides restoring existing buildings, there are other ways to get around the high cost of new homes. Some families are building their own homes with "do-it-yourself" kits, some of which contain heating, plumbing and electrical supplies as well as basic frame materials. Others are turning to factory-built, mobile homes. One of the most popular types of mobile homes today is the "double wide" model that looks very much like a custom-built house. Generally priced at less than $25,000, this model comes with a pitched roof, aluminum siding, shutters and downspouts.

It is made of two sections bolted together and is placed on a concrete foundation, which increases the owner's chances of

Annual Housing Starts
(in thousands)

Year	Total	Year	Total
1959	1,553.7	1968	1,545.4
1960	1,296.1	1969	1,499.5
1961	1,365.0	1970	1,469.0
1962	1,492.5	1971	2,084.5
1963	1,634.9	1972	2,378.5
1964	1,561.0	1973	2,057.5
1965	1,509.7	1974	1,352.5
1966	1,195.8	1975	1,171.4
1967	1,321.9	1976	1,546.8

SOURCE: U.S. Bureau of the Census

Manufacturers' Shipments of Mobile Homes

Year	Thousands of Units	Year	Thousands of Units
1965	216.5	1971	496.6
1966	217.3	1972	575.9
1967	240.4	1973	566.9
1968	318.0	1974	329.3
1969	412.7	1975	212.7
1970	401.2	1976*	249.9

* Preliminary

SOURCE: U.S. Bureau of the Census, from figures provided by the Manufactured Housing Institute

getting a regular home mortgage rather than a mobile-home loan. Double-wide units also often have three or four bedrooms and two and one-half baths—all the comforts of a modern home built on-site. "Mobile homes have been providing nearly 20 per cent of the nation's output of shelter and more than 90 per cent of new housing priced below $20,000," stated *Fortune* magazine last year. "If mobiles were generally counted as one-family houses, a lot less would be heard about families of modest means being priced out of the housing market."[8]

Another relatively low-cost alternative to the purchase of a new home was described by Robert L. Williams, a college teacher in North Carolina, in *Money* magazine. Williams wrote that when he and his wife found the house of their dreams, though in very poor condition, the owner told them it was worth only about $10 but that the land, which had been rezoned for commercial use, was worth about $50,000. Williams bought the house for $10 and moved it to his own lot 20 miles away. In all, the remodeling, moving and land purchase came to about $15,000.

According to Williams, the cost of moving a house is determined by its size, construction and location. Distance makes little difference. However, "If the route of a move takes you under a lot of power lines, costs can get out of hand," Williams wrote. "Costs also run high where winters are severe, because foundations must be sunk deep enough to rest on earth that won't swell in a frost."[9] The best source of information on houses available for moving is the state highway department, which is among the first to know when houses are condemned for public works projects.

---

[8] Gurney Breckenfeld, "Is the One-Family House Becoming a Fossil?" *Fortune*, April 1976, p. 87.

[9] "How to Buy a $50,000 House for $27,000," *Money*, January 1977, p. 38.

Government's Role in Housing

THE STATE OF the nation's housing has been of vital concern to the federal government ever since the 1930s. Before that time, Congress had appropriated money to investigate city slums and had helped build housing for defense workers during World War I. But it was not until the Great Depression that the government began to assume a major role in the housing field, when it set out to stimulate and stabilize the economy through emergency housing and mortgage measures. Starting with passage of the Federal Home Loan Bank Act under President Hoover in 1932, the federal government steadily increased its housing activities.

In 1933, the first year of the New Deal, the Home Owners' Loan Corp. was organized to curb the rising trend of mortgage foreclosures, by granting long-term mortgage loans at low interest rates to those in urgent need of funds to protect their home investments. A year later the Federal Housing Administration (FHA) was established to encourage building and to increase the supply of mortgage funds by providing banks and other private lending institutions with government insurance against a loss on mortgage home loans. The FHA program was set up to encourage lenders, not buyers, to invest in home mortgages. If home owners failed to make their payments, they were not bailed out. The guarantee was given to the lender. This arrangement enabled lenders to make virtually risk-free loans on new and used homes and on repair work that was covered by FHA guarantees. The lender was therefore willing to accept low down payments and long-term mortgages.

In an effort to increase the supply of mortgage funds, the Federal National Mortgage Association was chartered by the federal housing administrator on Feb. 10, 1938, as a subsidiary of the Reconstruction Finance Corporation. The FNMA, known as "Fannie Mae," bought mortgages to release more capital into the mortgage market, or sold its mortgages when money was plentiful. These transactions, in turn, tended to counter the prevailing economic situation in the mortgage market, thus providing stability. Fannie Mae became a private corporation in 1968 and two years later was authorized by the Emergency Home Finance Act to buy conventional mortgages.

Despite government assistance, housing production sagged during the depression-ridden 1930s and for the first half of the 1940s, when industry concentrated on wartime needs. This concentration drew millions of households into urban areas, creating a housing shortage. The end of World War II in 1945 brought the GI's home, and frequently into marriage, creating millions of new households in quest of a place to live. By now the housing shortage was acute.

Postwar Assistance to Overcome Shortages

In the postwar years, the extent and form of government assistance to housing was a matter of controversy and debate. Most programs, however, survived opposition and were gradually liberalized. Although the federal role in housing grew to considerable proportions, the number of federally assisted housing units amounted to less than one-fourth of all private non-farm housing units built from 1945 through 1965.[10]

The Housing Act of 1949, in particular, significantly broadened the federal role in housing and set as a goal "a decent home and a suitable living environment for every American family." Private enterprise and state and local governments, in partnership with the federal government, were to take the lead whenever possible in meeting this goal. The act established a $1-billion program of federal urban renewal assistance to localities in clearing and redeveloping slums. It also revived and broadened the public housing program, authorized a housing census every 10 years and launched a program of economic and technical research in residential construction and finance.

In the years following the 1949 act, housing legislation was approved to meet new and specific needs. In 1950 the Veterans Administration was authorized to make direct home-purchase or repair loans to veterans living in small communities where private financing was not available. In the same year, a program of federal assistance in providing college housing was initiated. The Housing Act of 1954 carried urban renewal beyond slum clearance and fostered comprehensive federal and local cooperation to ensure sound community development.

During the Eisenhower administration, there were many conflicts in Congress between Democrats who favored a speedup of federal housing programs, particularly for low-income groups, and Republicans who favored slower advances or, in many cases, cutbacks. The Democrats clearly won out in 1961, during the Kennedy presidency, with a housing act that expanded all federal housing programs and extended federal activity into other areas. The 1964 Housing Act, called a "bare-bones" law by some, continued housing programs enacted in 1961, with a few minor changes.

---

[10] All types of home ownership, whether directly assisted or not by the federal government, are encouraged by the nation's tax laws. Home owners, for instance, may deduct the interest on mortgage payments from taxable income they report to the Internal Revenue Service. Home builders, who typically borrow heavily to finance their projects, enjoy a similar benefit.

Housing Outlook

Anthony Downs, who has written extensively on housing policy in the context of social history, observes that by 1960 a balance between supply and demand for housing had been restored in most metropolitan areas "for households with reasonably good incomes." This situation prevailed until mid-decade, when the Vietnam War buildup began diverting the construction industry away from home building. And the urban riots of 1965-68 began focusing attention upon the continuing problem of low-income urban households, especially those in the racial ghettos.[11]

Focus on the Urban Poor in the Late Sixties

The riots shifted federal housing policies toward the expansion of housing for America's urban poor, largely through a new set of subsidy programs. Congress enacted four major housing laws in 1965-68 during the Johnson presidency which, taken together, constituted the most far-reaching achievements in housing and urban development in decades.

The first two laws, both passed in 1965, authorized rent supplements to help poor people afford decent housing and established a Department of Housing and Urban Development, thus giving Cabinet-level status to the government's housing activities and bringing increased attention to federal efforts to solve urban problems. The third law, in 1966, established a model cities program intended to pump extra federal funds into needy cities. All three laws were highly controversial. Their central programs—rent supplements and model cities—were vigorously opposed by Republicans and conservative Democrats. Although this coalition was unable to prevent adoption of the programs, it succeeded fairly well in keeping funding at a low level.

The Housing and Urban Development Act of 1968 was the broadest of all. It contained 17 titles covering not only housing but also a variety of related activities including interstate land sales, mass transit and flood insurance. The basic part of the 1968 legislation was directed at home ownership and rental assistance. The homeownership plan (Section 235) provided a federal subsidy to lower interest rates on mortgages for low-income families. Generally, the program was limited to families with income of $3,000 to $6,500 annually, but exceptions were possible in high-cost areas and for very large families.

In 1976, eligibility under the homeownership plan was extended to families with incomes up to 95 per cent of the median

---

[11] See Anthony Downs, "The Impact of Housing Policies on Family Life in the United States Since World War II," *Daedalus* (journal of the American Academy of Arts and Sciences), spring 1977, p. 166.

income for a particular area. Maximum limits on the amounts of mortgage loans eligible for subsidies under the program were also increased to between $25,000 and $33,000, depending on family size and geographical cost factors. HUD Secretary Patricia Roberts Harris has proposed raising these limits even higher.

The 1968 act also established the Government National Mortgage Association (GNMA—"Ginny Mae") to subsidize the interest cost of mortgages on housing built under the various subsidy programs. These mortgage loans are made by private mortgage lenders or sometimes by the association itself, at interest rates below the prevailing yield in mortgage markets. Private mortgage lenders then sell these mortgages to GNMA at face value and it resells them to FNMA at a lower price that will bring the effective yield on the mortgages into line with current market yields. This arrangement, called the Tandem Plan, allows GNMA to limit its cash outlays to the difference between the price at which it buys the mortgages from private lenders and the price at which it sells them to FNMA.

Another aid to the housing credit market was the 1970 Emergency Home Finance Act, which, in addition to giving "Fannie Mae" the authority to buy conventional mortgages,

Nationwide Average Interest Rates on Home Mortgages

Effective Rate* on Conventional Loans

Year	New Homes	Existing Homes
1968	6.97%	7.03%
1969	7.81	7.82
1970	8.45	8.36
1971	7.74	7.67
1972	7.60	7.51
1973	7.95	8.01
1974	8.92	9.01
1975	9.01	9.21
1976	8.99	9.11
1977 January	9.05	9.03
February	8.99	9.00
March**	8.97	8.95

* Equals contract interest rate plus initial fees and charges amortized over a 10-year period.
** Preliminary

SOURCE: Federal Home Loan Bank Board

also created the Federal Home Loan Mortgage Corp. FHLMC, under the direction of the Federal Home Loan Bank Board, has authority to buy, hold and sell mortgages within limits similar to those established for FHA and with authority to borrow funds and issue mortgage-backed obligations.

Attempts to Alleviate 1973-74 Credit Crunch

In 1973, the homebuilding industry entered its worst slump since World War II.[12] Mortgage money dried up, under the impact of "tight-money" policies imposed by the Federal Reserve Board to fight inflation, and housing starts dipped close to 1970 levels. "The decline of housing starts in 1974 was a gruesome replay of a classic pattern," explains a study on home mortgage financing, prepared by the National Forest Products Association: "Inflation rises, the federal government tightens its monetary policies, credit in general becomes tight, interest rates skyrocket, savings are withdrawn to invest in high-paying short-term securities, mortgage money that is so dependent on savings dries up, home buyers and builders are unable to obtain mortgage money, new construction tumbles, orders for building materials decline, and all the industries dependent upon homebuilding nose dive into recession. It is not until monetary restraints ease, interest rates decline, and savings again swell that enough mortgage credit reappears for homebuilding to reverse its slide."[13] Two previous housing slumps brought on by tight credit occurred in 1966 and 1969.[14]

President Nixon had, early in 1973, declared a moratorium on major federal housing subsidy programs. Terming existing housing programs "failures," he said "our principal efforts should be directed toward determining whether a policy of direct cash assistance—with first priority for the elderly poor—can be put into practical operation." Consequently, the President requested authority to experiment more widely with the direct cash payment approach. The Nixon proposals met a chilly reception from the National Association of Home Builders and its allies in Congress. At the end of 1973, the federal housing program remained in limbo, with the moratorium on most subsidy programs still in effect and no new legislation to replace them. In the meantime, he outlined steps for easing the tight mortgage market. Several of his proposals, including a tax credit for lending institutions, required congressional approval.

The Housing and Community Development Act of 1974, the first major piece of housing legislation since 1968, included some but not all of Nixon's proposals. On FHA-guaranteed

---

[12] See "Housing Credit Crunch," *E.R.R.*, 1973 Vol. II, pp. 735-756.
[13] "Everything You Always Wanted to Know About Home Mortgage Financing," prepared by the National Forest Products Asociation, 1975, p. 1.
[14] See "Private Housing Squeeze," *E.R.R.*, 1969 Vol. II, pp. 511-530.

Per cent of increase, 1970-1976

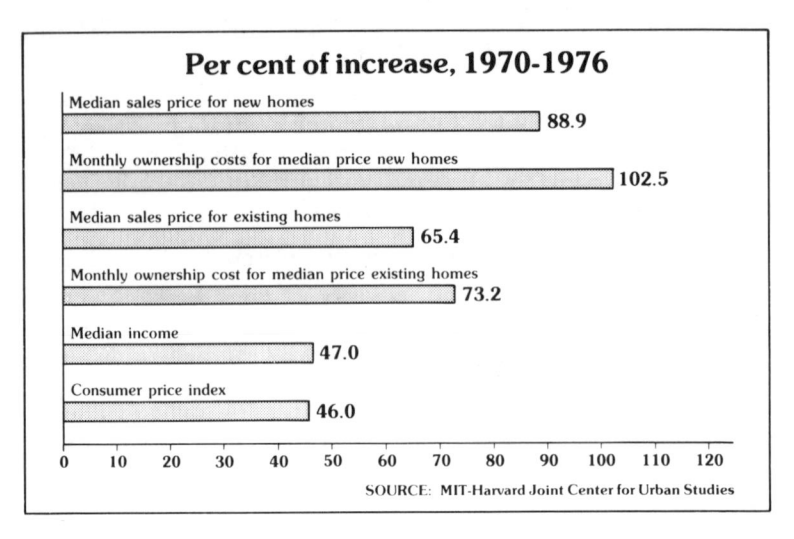

Category	%
Median sales price for new homes	88.9
Monthly ownership costs for median price new homes	102.5
Median sales price for existing homes	65.4
Monthly ownership cost for median price existing homes	73.2
Median income	47.0
Consumer price index	46.0

SOURCE: MIT-Harvard Joint Center for Urban Studies

mortgages, the new law raised the maximum to $45,000 from $33,000, reduced the required cash down payment and gave HUD authority to set flexible interest rates. The new act also consolidated 10 urban aid programs into a single three-year $8.6-billion program of block grants for community development and established a new rental assistance program (Section 8) for low- and moderate-income families.

Congress approved the 1974 act in August, but by then it was becoming apparent that the action so far—both administrative and congressional—was having only modest effect on the housing market. President Ford, in office two months, asked Congress on Oct. 8 to pass emergency legislation to let GNMA buy conventional mortgages—those not insured by the federal government—as well as mortgages backed by the FHA and VA. The legislation was signed into law Oct. 18, making $3-billion available immediately for mortgage purchases.

By the spring of 1975 the nation's two-year economic recession had ended, according to the reckoning of government economists, and by that fall the housing industry had begun to move out of its slump. The number of new housing starts reached 1.5 million units in 1976, up from 1.1 million in 1975, although the recovery was uneven geographically. The Northeast showed the slowest and weakest improvement. Demand for single-family homes was strong in many parts of the country during 1976, although some areas reported a continued backlog of unsold homes and condominiums.[15]

Buying reached frenzied levels in southern California, where the market is still heated, and developers had to resort to

---

[15] In a condominium, the resident owns his unit of a building and has an undivided interest in common areas and facilities like halls, basements, lobbies, recreation areas and swimming pools. Owners have title to their units and are taxed separately on them.

Housing Outlook

lotteries in some cases to determine who could and could not buy the new homes offered for sale. Although mortgage credit was generally available in 1975 and 1976, interest rates remained high. According to figures from the Federal Home Loan Bank Board, the average interest rates on mortgages have dropped below 9 per cent nationally since the beginning of this year. But many economists and analysts have predicted higher rates toward the end of the year because of an expected greater demand for home loans.

Influences on Housing Trends

ONE REASON for optimism among home builders this year is support from the new Carter administration, which has announced plans to strengthen federal housing subsidy programs. In congressional testimony on Feb. 24,[16] HUD Secretary Patricia Roberts Harris requested a three-year extension of the block grant program for community development beyond the expiration date of Sept. 30, 1977, the end of the current fiscal year. Her request of $4-billion in fiscal 1978 for the program represented an increase of $750-million over the existing level and a $500-million increase over the amount proposed in the budget President Ford sent to Congress in January before leaving office.

In addition, the new Secretary has pledged particular support for low- and moderate-income groups and has promised to work to revitalize American cities. "We must affirm, as a nation, that a decent home is a right and that adequate shelter is a basic commodity equivalent to food and clothing in the spectrum of human needs," she said in a speech before the National Housing Conference in Washington, D.C., March 7, 1977. The Carter administration has set a goal of providing 400,000 public housing units for low-income persons in fiscal 1978.[17]

The new administration is also expected to endorse new methods of ensuring a more stable supply of mortgage money. This includes experimenting with new mortgage-finance techniques, such as those that already have been proposed in Congress. One of these, the so-called "graduated payment" mortgage, allows first-time home buyers to make smaller monthly payments in the early years and larger payments later on. This plan presumes that the homeowner's income will in-

---

[16] Before the Housing and Community Development Subcommittee of the House Banking, Finance and Urban Affairs Committee.

[17] See "Administration Targets Aid to Aging Cities," *Congressional Quarterly Weekly Report*, March 5, 1977.

crease in future years. A study by the Congressional Budget Office said: "While there are disadvantages in slow initial build-up of equity and some risk of future incomes falling short of expectations, the plan has the powerful advantage of improving affordability for the key first-time purchaser group without involving direct federal expenditures."[18] Another idea being considered is to let the homeowner defer his or her mortgage payments. Although similar to graduated-payment mortgages, deferred-payment mortgages involve partial payment of costs by the government.

Another idea, introduced by Sen. Edward W. Brooke (R Mass.) this year in his Young Families Housing Act, would allow first-time buyers to set up tax-exempt savings accounts called "individual housing accounts" and accumulate funds for down payments. Some banks already are offering "variable interest rate" mortgages, which usually allow a borrower to begin with a rate lower than that of standard loans. The rate is then adjusted over the years in accordance with the prevailing market.

Reaction from lenders to "variable interest rate" mortgages has been mixed. "It's all right when you're reducing rates," Joseph Lipton of Dade Federal Savings and Loan in Miami has explained, "but when you go up you'll get a lot of complaints."[19] In testimony before the Senate Budget Committee on Feb. 24, 1977, Donald M. Kaplan, chief economist of the Federal Home Loan Bank Board, had this to say about alternative mortgage instruments in general: "We, at the board, do feel that ...[they] are a needed and important addition to this nation's housing finance system, and that borrowers should be given a wider choice of home financing arrangements. However, when everything is said and done, we expect that the traditional, fixed-rate-level-payment mortgage...will continue to be the predominant instrument which will serve the needs of most home buyers the best."

Changes in Household Size, Demographics

What will be the housing needs of the future? According to the Joint Center for Urban Studies, housing demands are likely to remain strong through the 1970s but level off in the early 1980s. The authors of this forecast also see a change occurring in the size of the average household. "In the 1950s and 1960s, the housing industry focused on building large, single-family houses to accommodate the parents and children of the baby boom," MIT Professors Bernard Frieden and Arthur Solomon have

---

[18] "Homeownership: The Changing Relationship of Costs and Incomes, and Possible Federal Roles," Congressional Budget Office, January 1977, p. 43.

[19] Quoted in *U.S. News & Word Report*, Sept. 6, 1976.

> ### Buying Versus Renting
>
> It is conventional wisdom that owning a home is more economical than renting one. But a recent study by *U.S. News & World Report** suggests that the case for renting is much stronger than it used to be. The magazine notes that rents, on the average nationally, have increased only about 26 per cent in the past five years while the costs involved in homeownership have gone up 57 per cent.
>
> The magazine calculated that rent and utilities for a three-bedroom house average $341 a month, some $150 less than a homeowner would pay in mortgage costs (assuming 9 per cent rate of interest), taxes, utilities, upkeep and insurance. A traditional argument for homeownership is that interest paid on the mortgage is tax deductible. But if the money used for a down payment were invested in high-grade utility bonds, the study said, the earnings might outweight the tax benefits.
>
> Still, the incentives for buying a home are powerful. Homeowners know they can stay indefinitely where they are. And they do not have to worry about rent increases. Moreover, in many places the value of a home has risen far faster than inflation.
>
> * Issue dated April 25, 1977

said. "In the early 1970s, there was a surge of apartment building to meet demand from young singles and couples—the baby boom children growing up." According to their study, the principal demand by the early 1980s will be for moderate-sized homes to accommodate smaller families—the families of the baby boom children who are now adults.

The housing picture of the future will also be affected by two changing migration patterns in the United States: (1) the rapid population growth in the "sun belt" states of the South and Southwest, and (2) the population shift from large metropolitan centers across the country to smaller cities and towns.[20] From 1970 to 1975, the population of the southern regions of the country increased 5.1 million, outpacing the gains recorded by all other regions combined. According to Joint Center projections, this trend will continue in the coming decade. Even in the sun belt, however, only a few large metropolitan areas are experiencing large population growth.[21] In fact, some big southern and western cities are actually losing population. Large metropolitan areas across the nation lost 1.2 million people in the first half of this decade, while non-metropolitan areas reversed their population losses of the 1960s and gained 1.5 million inhabitants.

---
[20] See "Rural Migration," *E.R.R.*, 1975 Vol. II, pp. 581-600, and "Mobility in American Life," *E.R.R.*, 1973 Vol. I, pp. 335-351.
[21] Phoenix, Tucson, Dallas, Houston, San Diego, Miami, Fort Lauderdale, Tampa and Orlando are notable examples.

The trend toward smaller families coupled with the rising cost of energy could lead to a change in housing styles. "The large suburban home of the last decade may go the way of the large homes of the 1920s," Thomas C. Marcin, an economist at the Department of Agriculture, has written. "New smaller, energy-efficient, but fully equipped houses may become popular in the future, while luxury townhouses or cluster-houses with amenity packages and open spaces could offer an attractive substitute for detached single-family housing."[22]

Construction Techniques and Fuel Prices

New methods of construction may also become popular, particularly the assembly-line modular unit method whereby whole units of rooms are plugged into each other like building blocks. This type of construction, which already is widely used in Scandinavia and Eastern European countries, is cheaper than the traditional stick-by-stick on-site method, partly because labor costs are less. It is also quicker, and developers do not have to tie up capital for a long time.

One reason—perhaps the principal one—for the dearth of mass-produced housing is that there are several thousand different local building codes in the country. In the words of the National Commission on Urban Problems, "What goes in one town won't in another...."[23] In addition to building codes, the zoning laws of many municipalities forbid or limit mobile homes and similar prefabricated structures.

Nevertheless, some inroads have been made. Geodesic dome structures, originally conceived by R. Buckminster Fuller, are reported to be popular among buyers of new homes. These structures, which are prefabricated, are considered more energy-efficient than conventional, rectilinear houses. According to one estimate, the energy bill for geodesic homes is only one-third to one-half as much as that for traditional houses with equal floor space.[24] The rising cost of fuel no doubt will be important in future housing trends. A home that is well insulated and relatively compact will have market appeal. Solar energy may ultimately be the homeowner's answer to high heating bills but so far its usefulness has been quite limited. In December 1976, the Energy Research and Development Administration, in releasing its most comprehensive study on solar energy to date, announced that "solar heating can now compete economically

---

[22] Thomas C. Marcin, "The Effect of Declining Population Growth on Housing Demand," *Challenge*, November-December 1976, p. 33.

[23] National Commission on Urban Problems, *Building the American City* (1968), p. 21. The commission headed by former Sen. Paul H. Douglas (D Ill.) was appointed by President Johnson to conduct a study, ordered by Congress in 1965, of building and housing codes, zoning, tax policies and development standards. The commission issued a series of reports before concluding its work in 1969.

[24] See *Time*, March 14, 1977, pp. 34-35.

Housing Outlook

with electric baseboard heating for well-insulated new homes in 13 major population centers throughout most of the United States."[25] ERDA later acknowledged that its conclusion was based on several assumptions not applicable in all situations.

Among the barriers to the use of solar energy in the home are building codes, financing constraints, tax laws, construction methods, labor requirements, and the difficulty of installing solar equipment in existing homes. Another complicating factor is the question of "sun rights" and solar zoning. What happens when a tree or new garage puts the solar collector of the house next door in the shade? These are matters yet to be resolved.[26]

Despite the problems, solar energy seems destined for fuller use in future homebuilding. ERDA is going ahead with plans for its long-delayed Solar Energy Research Institute, and other government support is expected. HUD has announced a $4.6-million solar testing project that will provide $400 grants to 10,000 homeowners or builders who wish to install solar water heaters.[27] According to Sheldon Butt, president of Solar Energy Industry, "in five years, we will see more than 1,800,000 solar water heaters in operation and 60,000 space heating installations. And in 10 years, 5,500,000 water heaters and well over 1,000,000 homes heated and cooled by the sun's energy."[28] Arthur D. Little Inc., an industrial consulting firm involved in several solar energy projects across the country, has predicted that solar water heaters for family residences will be offered by mass merchandisers within three to five years.

In the meantime, home builders and government officials continue to study the housing demands of this decade. "There is already a critical shortage, and the crisis is deepening," Leon Weiner, president of the National Housing Conference, said in a speech to the conference on March 6, 1977. "Soon five families will be competing for every four apartments and homes available in many cities, driving up home prices and rents." According to the Joint Center for Urban Studies, from 20.2 to 22.6 million new housing units will be needed between 1975 and 1985 to meet a 12 million increase in household growth and to replace physically obsolete housing. Even after the upturn of 1976, the Center noted, housing starts are 20 per cent below the number necessary to meet these demands. Whether the building industry will be able to catch up, without further pushing moderate- and low-income families out of the new home market, remains a crucial question.

---

[25] "An Economic Analysis of Solar, Water and Space Heating," December 1976.
[26] See "Solar Energy," *E.R.R.*, 1976 Vol. II, pp. 825-842.
[27] The grants will be distributed by 10 states: Connecticut, Massachusetts, New Hampshire, Rhode Island, Vermont, Delaware, Maryland, New Jersey, Pennsylvania and Florida.
[28] Quoted in *Realtors Review*, April 1977, p. 9.

Selected Bibliography

Books

Aaron, Henry J., *Shelter and Subsidies,* The Brookings Institution, 1972.
de Leeuw, Frank, *The Web of Urban Housing,* The Urban Institute, 1975.
Fried, Joseph P., *Housing Crisis U.S.A.,* Praeger Publishers, 1971.
Frieden, Bernard J. and Marshall Kaplan, *The Politics of Neglect: Urban Aid from Model Cities to Revenue Sharing,* Massachusetts Institute of Technology Press, 1975.
Solomon, Arthur P., *Housing the Urban Poor: A Critical Evaluation of Federal Housing Policy,* Massachusetts Institute of Technology Press, 1974.
Taggart, Robert, *Low-Income Housing: A Critique of Federal Aid,* The Johns Hopkins Press, 1970.

Articles

Breckenfeld, Gurney, "Is the One-Family House Becoming a Fossil?" *Fortune,* April 1976.
Downs, Anthony, "The Impact of Housing Policies on Family Life in the United States Since World War II, *Daedalus,* spring 1977.
"Home Mortgages with Variable Rates—How They're Working," *U.S. News & World Report,* Sept. 6, 1976.
"Housing in the Recovery," *Federal Reserve Bulletin,* March 1977.
"How to Keep Down the Cost of Buying a Home," *U.S. News & World Report,* March 21, 1977.
Marcin, Thomas C., "The Effect of Decling Population Growth on Housing Demand," *Challenge,* November-December 1976.
"Solar Energy is No Longer Just a Dream of the Future," *Realtors Review,* April 1977.
Williams, Robert L., "How to Buy a $50,000 House for $27,000," *Money,* January 1977.

Reports and Studies

Advisory Commission on Intergovernmental Relations, "Trends in Metropolitan America," February 1977.
Congressional Budget Office, "Homeownership: The Changing Relationship of Costs and Incomes, and Possible Federal Roles," January 1977; "Housing Assistance for Low and Moderate Income Families," February 1977.
Doyle Dane Bernbach Inc., "The United States Housing Market, 1975-1985," December 1976.
Editorial Research Reports, "Housing Credit Crunch," 1973 Vol. II, p. 735.
Joint Center for Urban Studies, "The Nation's Housing, 1975 to 1985."
National Commission on Urban Problems, *Building the American City,* Praeger Publishers, 1968.
National Forest Products Association, "Everything You Always Wanted to Know About Home Mortgage Financing," 1975.
Welfeld, Irving H. "America's Housing Problem," American Enterprise Institute, October 1973.

MANDATORY RETIREMENT

by

Nona Baldwin Brown

	page
ELDERLY'S PUSH FOR WORK RIGHTS	165
Congressional Action to Raise Age 65 Cutoff	165
Similar Moves by States and in Industry	166
Size of 'Gray Power' Lobby; Its Arguments	168
Business, University Oppositon to Change	170
POPULATION AND INCOME FACTORS	171
Origins of Making 65 the Retirement Age	171
Continuing Growth of the Elderly Population	173
Sources of Income for Retired Americans	174
Experience of Firms With Older Workers	176
FORCES SHAPING RETIREMENT ISSUES	177
Social Security Financing in Future Years	177
Growing Trend Toward Early Retirement	178
Legal-Right Questions Before the Court	179
Demographic Imperative: An Aging Nation	181

Nov. 11
1977

Editor's Note: The Senate and House in April 1978 reconciled their differences and cleared the legislation raising the mandatory retirement age for most non-federal workers to 70, up from 65. Most of the provisions became effective Jan. 1, 1979. However, the new law would permit until Jan. 1, 1980, any mandatory retirement requirements under collective bargaining agreements that were signed before Sept. 1, 1977. And the new law also would allow, until July 1, 1982, colleges and universities to force the retirement of tenured faculty members at age 65.

The then-pending Supreme Court ruling discussed on pages 168 and 169, *McMann v. United Air Lines,* has since been issued. By a 7 to 2 vote, the court on Dec. 12, 1977, upheld the airline's retirement plan which requires employees to retire at age 60. The plan was put into effect before Congress in 1967 enacted the Age Discrimination in Employment Act.

MANDATORY RETIREMENT

"TO LIVE is to work." The old aphorism, the credo by which Justice Oliver Wendell Holmes explained why he remained on the Supreme Court at age 90, the philosophic underpinning for the American work ethic, has suddenly become a political slogan for the nation's older citizens. With it, they have embarked on a fight to eliminate mandatory retirement for age from gainful employment as an immutable climax to productive years. In the process, they have raised far-reaching constitutional and economic questions: Is an extended working life a civil right? a personal necessity? or very possibly, an economic necessity for the nation? Politics and demographics may soon forge answers to these questions.

Congress, which normally recoils from sharp changes in existing programs, moved with unexpected speed this year to raise from 65 to 70 the age at which most workers can be compelled to retire. In less than five months from its final formulation in the House in June, both chambers overwhelmingly approved legislation to effect this change. The vote was 359 to 4 in the House and 87 to 6 in the Senate. The bills differed in some major respects but both versions agree in amending the Age Discrimination and Employment Act of 1967, which established legal protection against discriminatory employment practices for people of ages 40 through 64. The new legislation (HR 5383) moves that upper age limit to 70.

Passage was preceded by several sets of hearings before both Senate and House committees—notably the House Select Committee on Aging, under the chairmanship of 77-year-old Claude Pepper (D Fla.)—dealing with the mandatory retirement issue. The House Education and Labor Committee, which initiated the legislation, drew heavily on evidence compiled by the Select Committee. In its report, the Education and Labor Committee said:

> Increasingly it is being recognized that mandatory retirement based solely upon age is arbitrary and that chronological age alone is a poor indicator of ability to perform a job. Mandatory retirement does not take into consideration actual differing abilities and capabilities....[1]

---

[1] Report on Age Discrimination in Employment Act of 1977, House Committee on Education and Labor, July 25, 1977, No. 95-527, Part I, p. 2.

However, HR 5383 did not totally abandon the compulsory age concept despite some strong philosophic support for the idea. On this matter, the report said:

> The committee has considered removing the upper age limit entirely but has decided that an increase to age 70 at this time is the best course of action. The age 70 limit is a compromise between some who favor removing the age limit entirely and others who are uncertain of the consequences of changing the present age 65 limit. Experience with the age 70 limit would give us more data and other facts to better evaluate the pro and con arguments on eliminating mandatory retirement entirely.

Opposition to the legislation did not surface until the Senate, which lacked Congressman Pepper's enthusiasm for the issue, began its consideration. Organized labor backed off from its original criticism *(opposite page),* but the business community and the universities mounted intensive lobbying campaigns, based primarily on a dislike of sudden change in their retirement systems and fear that later retirement would block employment and promotion opportunities for younger people. The Senate version of HR 5383 therefore contained exceptions for highly paid executives and tenured university professors.

Whatever the final bill contains in detail—to be worked out in a House-Senate conference committee—it seems certain that President Carter will be handed a measure that will move the legal basis for mandatory retirement from age 65 to age 70. It also seems certain he will sign it, despite reported misgivings of some Cabinet advisers. Even in the Department of Labor, where support for the Pepper measure has been voiced publicly, there are many questions about its impact on chronic youth unemployment, sex discrimination and shifting consumer patterns.

Similar Moves by States and in Industry

Congress was not alone in what it did: this year three state legislatures—in Maine, New York and California—also debated measures modifying or eliminating retirement for age. The Maine lawmakers overwhelmingly approved a bill to remove the age factor for public employees, including school teachers, and then overrode Gov. James B. Longley's veto. The new law will go into effect July 1, 1978. New York legislation to eliminate age as a factor in both public and private retirement plans won approval in the Assembly but not the Senate.

California may provide the first large-scale test of the idea of eliminating age as a basis for compulsory retirement. The state legislature, after long and frequently acrimonious debate, voted to ban mandatory retirement at any age for both public and private employers, and Gov. Edmund G. (Jerry) Brown Jr.

> ### Organized Labor's Neutrality
>
> Organized labor ended up in a position of benign neutrality on the issue of forced retirement for age, after lining up initially with the U.S. Chamber of Commerce and other major business groups as the heavy hitters for the opposition. The AFL-CIO formally stated this opposition to both Senate and House committees because of fear that many labor-negotiated pension plans with mandatory age retirement provisions might be jeopardized by raising or eliminating the age limit. Labor wanted a special exemption, on the ground that these plans were voluntary agreements.
>
> From the beginning, according to an analysis by A. H. Raskin of *The New York Times*,* many labor leaders were uncomfortable over this stance. The alliance with big business bothered them. The fact that AFL-CIO President George Meany is 83 was an embarrassing contradiction—which led Meany to an unaccustomed sidelines position. Some major unions, such as the steelworkers, were fundamentally opposed to mandatory age retirement and, Raskin said, "historically, organized labor has viewed with hostility any form of forced retirement."
>
> When the House Committee on Education and Labor added a special proviso to the Pepper bill, allowing two years for union pension contracts to be revised to meet any new age standards, the AFL-CIO fell silent. The federation decided "to let nature take its course" instead of pursuing a losing political battle against the nation's elderly, Raskin reported. In addition, Lane Kirkland, the AFL-CIO Secretary-Treasurer and heir-apparent to Meany, let it be known that it was a mistake for labor to seek a special exemption.
>
> *Sept. 21, 1977

signed the measure into law. Its provisions are already in effect for state workers; for the private sector, they become effective Jan. 1, 1978.

Twelve other states[2] have laws dealing with age discrimination in employment. For the most part these follow the pattern of the 1967 federal law that protects workers of ages 40 through 64. Cities that have taken similar action on behalf of their employees include Boston, Seattle, Los Angeles and Portland, Ore. "The public is for it," Seattle Mayor Wes Uhlman has said. "They see it as patently unfair to tell a person they can't work, especially with our Puritan ethic that says if you won't work, you're not worth anything."

In the private sector, the most striking event was an announcement in August by Connecticut General Insurance Corp.

---

[2] Alaska, Connecticut, Florida, Hawaii, Illinois, Iowa, Maryland, Montana, Nevada, New Jersey, New Mexico and South Carolina.

that most of its 11,900 employees no longer had to retire at 65. "Some of our employees want to continue their careers with the company beyond...normal retirement age," said the announcement, "and we recognize what a valuable resource they are." Connecticut General did make one exception: officers and field office managers are still required to retire at 65. "We did that," said company spokesman Donald Illig, "because we didn't want it to appear that there was any blocking of the [executive] pipeline."

The issue is also stirring in the courts. The Supreme Court will hear at least one case this term, *McMann v. United Air Lines,* on the right to work beyond a certain age. It involves the forced retirement of airline pilot Harris McMann of Fairfax, Va., at age 60 under the terms of United's pension plan. McMann is McMann is arguing that such action contravenes the Constitution's due process and equal protection clauses, and furthermore that it is illegal under the Age Discrimination in Employment Act of 1967.

Another case which may reach the court, *Bradley v. Vance,* involves mandatory retirement at age 60 for personnel of the U.S. Foreign Service. The U.S. Court of Appeals for the District of Columbia has ruled against the government, saying that since Civil Service personnel need not retire until age 70, the Foreign Service system "is patently arbitrary and irrational" and therefore unconstitutional. The appeals court did not object to mandatory retirement for age *per se.*[3]

Size of 'Gray Power' Lobby; Its Arguments

As the bills against "ageism" moved through Congress and state legislatures this year, opinion on both sides of the argument solidified and lobbying and political pressures mounted. The "gray power" lobby organized better and earlier than did the foes of the legislation. Spokesmen for elderly groups have testified frequently in recent years on the problems and needs of the elderly, speaking to Senate and House committees that were understandably sensitive to the 23 million potential voters who are now 65 or older.

The lobby has consisted of such disparate colleagues as actors John Wayne and Ruth Gordon, the Gray Panthers, the National Association of Retired Federal Employees, the National Council of Senior Citizens, the National Council on the Aging, the American Personnel & Guidance Association, and—the heavyweight among them, claiming a membership of 10 million—the American Association of Retired Persons/National Retired Teachers Association.

---

[3] *Bradley v. Vance,* U.S. District Court for the District of Columbia, Civil Action No. 76-0085, Memorandum dated June 28, 1977.

"Last month, I reached mandatory retirement age. I am still here. Anybody want to make something of it?"

Drawn by Joe Mirachi; © 1977   The New Yorker Magazine, Inc.

These groups argued that mandatory age discrimination is costly to the nation and its old people. According to Professor James Schulz of Brandeis University, the national economy is deprived of at least $4.5-billion a year in lost income and purchasing power. Moreover, severe financial hardships are imposed on many retirees whose pension incomes are usually well below their earlier earnings. "Indeed," said the Senate report,[4] "for some, the opportunity to continue working has become a question of economic survival." It is further argued that there is no scientific reason for age 65 to have become the traditional retirement age *(see p. 171),* and that mere actuarial or administrative convenience is no reason for keeping it.

While making these practical and economic arguments for their position, supporters of the legislation generally leaned more heavily on ethics and human rights. Dr. Arthur Flemming, head of the U.S. Commission on Aging, said mandatory age retirement runs counter to the "Judeo-Christian ethic of dignity and worth of the individual." Claude Pepper stated the case this way: "Mandatory retirement is the cruel euphemism camouflaging age discrimination and forced unemployment.... It severs productive persons from the livelihood, shears their sense of self-worth and squanders their talents."[5]

"Mandatory retirement infringes on a basic right: the right to be judged on ability, not merely on age," Rep. Paul Findley (R Ill.), a cosponsor of the 1977 legislation, wrote in *The New York Times* on Sept. 14. This thought is echoed in arguments that forced retirement because of age is discriminatory and uncon-

---

[4] Report on HR 5383 of the Senate Committee on Human Resources, No. 95-493, issued Oct. 12, 1977.

[5] Speech to the National Council of Senior Citizens, Washington, D.C., June 6, 1977.

stitutional. Still another point made by backers of the legislation is that the loss of a job is a stress-producing event for the individual. The American Medical Association is cited in the Senate report as saying "there is ample clinical evidence that physical and emotional problems can be precipitated or exacerbated by denial of employment opportunities."

And finally, there is the political argument—no less powerful because it is implied rather than openly stated. The 23 million Americans 65 or older represent a big voting bloc. It is also known from election statistics that older people are more likely than others to cast a ballot on election day. The House Republican Research Committee said last July: "This is the type of people-oriented issue with which the GOP must be identified if it is to broaden its support base with the electorate." Democrats are equally interested. Indeed, public opinion seems to support the aims of the "gray lobby." A national poll of 1,603 persons conducted Oct. 26-27 by *The New York Times* and CBS News indicated that 52 per cent of the people want the law to forbid mandatory retirement below age 70 while 37 per cent do not, the newspaper reported Nov. 4.

Business, University Opposition to Change

Faced with a lost cause in the House, opponents of change mustered their arguments for the Senate. Businessmen and university spokesmen led the lobbying, citing primarily the economic and practical problems that might ensue from a five-year extension of the customary 65-year retirement age. Congress is moving too fast, they said. Such "drastic change" should not be enacted without further study. What business needs is less regulation, not more. George Skoglund, speaking for the Bank of America, said: "The underlying problem is that these laws constitute more and more regulation, more of government looking on and telling us how to manage."

Opponents said further that retirement at age 65 had become so deeply embedded in American society—through Social Security, many labor union contracts and private pension plans—that it would be too disruptive to change it. No one knew what costs or problems would follow. They also argued that:

> Extending the working years would slow down promotions and thereby thwart bright young people whose ideas and stimulation are necessary for growth.
>
> Without mandatory retirement at 65, corporations would be forced to make tough—and possibly humiliating—decisions on who is able to do his job, instead of letting the calendar solve the "deadwood" problem.
>
> It would be costly and difficult to manage pension funds and estimate employment costs, if there were no fixed date when employees would become entitled to benefits.

Mandatory Retirement

Having to make individual judgments about older workers would lead to a burst of age-discrimination lawsuits.

Keeping older employees would worsen the unemployment situation, specifically hurting young people, women and Affirmative Action programs. Spokesmen for both the National Association of Colored People and the Urban League joined the opposition on this basis.

Rebuttals to these arguments surfaced quickly and in various forums—speeches, press releases and political debate. They made these points:

If "ageism" is unfair and possibly unconstitutional, then discriminating against the elderly to benefit youth does not justify it.

The notion that older people could stay at work only at the expense of younger workers is false.

Mandatory retirement is just a crutch for the incompetent manager," asserted Mayor Wes Uhlman, "a tool used by the manager who doesn't want to do what any good manager should be able to do, that is: deal with an employee on a personal basis...."

The glut of Ph.D.'s is more responsible for scholarly unemployment than any possible impact of a change in the retirement age could be.

Population and Income Factors

THE MODERN history of mandatory retirement and the use of age 65 as the magic number are both traced to Germany's famous Iron Chancellor, Otto von Bismarck. In the late 19th century, socialist turmoil beset many European governments and none was more hard-pressed than that of the conservative German chancellor. Hoping to stave off socialism, he instituted in 1889 the modern world's first comprehensive social insurance program, including both health insurance and an Old Age and Survivors Pension Act. Bismarck picked 65 as the year when old age began—cynics say because he knew that life expectancy then was only 45 years, so the government would not have to pay out much money.

Other European countries followed suit, most of them designating that same age. By the start of World War I, 10 European countries and several British dominions had adopted economic protection plans for the aged. Action lagged in the United States. While a few private pension plans were adopted, and New Jersey instituted a pension plan for teachers in 1896, it

U.S. Population
(in millions)

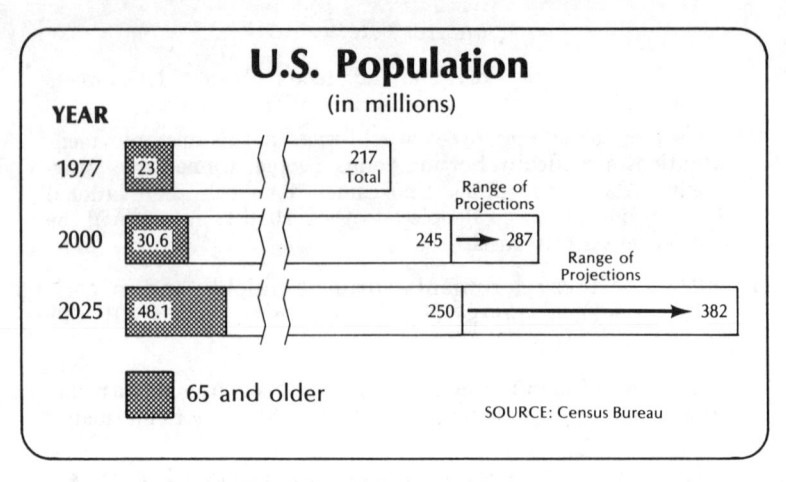

YEAR	65 and older	Total	Range of Projections
1977	23	217 Total	
2000	30.6	245	→ 287
2025	48.1	250	→ 382

SOURCE: Census Bureau

was not until after World War I that the movement toward pensioning elderly workers gained momentum. By 1931, 17 states and the territory of Alaska were providing old age insurance of some sort. But it was not until the Depression that major headway was made at the national level. Old age and unemployment insurance became major issues in the 1932 presidential campaign. After Franklin D. Roosevelt became President, he summoned experts to help develop the program which ultimately became the Social Security Act of 1935. Again, age 65 was used as the touchstone.[6]

Some say that age was selected quite casually, borrowed from the European precursors. Wilbur J. Cohen, then a congressional aide and later Secretary of Health, Education and Welfare (1968-69), wrote in his book *Retirement Policies Under Social Security* that there was very little consideration, pro or con, about the age when Social Security payments should begin. Robert J. Myers, one of the program's architects and for 20 years its chief actuary, recalls:

> "At the time, the Townsendites [followers of Dr. Francis E. Townsend, a California physician] were arguing that every American should collect a pension of $200 a month at 60, the money to be raised by a federal sales tax. But we knew that age was too low, because even with a smaller benefit than Dr. Townsend was advocating, the cost would have been enormous. At the time, too many people were working well beyond that age. We thought briefly about setting the age at 70, but decided that would be politically untenable, being so far above the age the Townsend Plan was agitating for. So we compromised on 65."[7]

Several big corporations—Eastman Kodak, General Electric, Standard Oil of New Jersey—had also picked 65 as the retire-

---

[6] While benefits were made available at 65, there was no provision in the act requiring retirement at that age. Congress amended the act in 1956 to permit women, and in 1961 to permit men, to retire at age 62 at 80 per cent of the monthly benefits that otherwise would be provided at 65.

[7] Quoted in *Dun's Review*, October 1977, p. 32.

Mandatory Retirement

ment year for pensions they had recently instituted. And so the pattern spread. Thus, after World War II, when retirement pension systems became a major goal of organized labor, the twin features of compulsion and age 65 became firmly implanted in major industries.

Unions were willing to accept forced retirement, usually at 65, for their workers in exchange for improved pension benefits—and lately, for the right to retire even earlier with full pensions. Corporations liked the personnel and bookkeeping tidiness of a flat rule for everybody: 65 and out. So even when pension-retirement plans are company-initiated, rather than the result of labor-management negotiations, the formula has been widely followed. According to Department of Labor estimates, some 21 million workers are now covered by private industry retirement plans, and 41 per cent, or 8.5 million, are affected by mandatory age retirement.

Continuing Growth of the Elderly Population

Much has changed in the working population since Bismarck's day. Not only is life expectancy longer in America today[8] but the entire age-mix of the population is tilting upward. Rep. Robert F. Drinan (D Mass.) has calculated that in terms of health and life expectancy, age 83 today is equivalent to what 65 was in Bismarck's time. The change is so striking that "graying of America" and the mobilization of "gray power" for "gray rights" are terms that have entered the political lexicon.

The specifics are these: of the nation's population in 1900, only 4.07 per cent (3.1 million people) was 65 or older; the percentage is now 10.8 and the number stands at 23 million. The Census Bureau projects an elderly population of 30.6 million in the year 2000 and 48.1 million in 2025, less than 50 years away. At that time the elderly may account for as much as 19.2 per cent of the total population, if one set of assumptions about national fertility proves to be correct.[9] If so, the nation's median age—now about 27—will rise by then to 41.8.

A population age-distribution chart shows a huge bulge in the age 20-34 category, a consequence of the postwar "baby boom" children now coming to maturity and into the job market. The baby boom reached its peak in the late 1950s and has been followed in recent years by a sharp drop in the birth rate and a consequent drop in the numbers of youngsters in the country.

---

[8] Life expectancy from birth is 68.7 for males and 76.5 from females; for those who reach 65, men can expect to live 13.2 years longer and women 17.5 years longer.

[9] The bureau makes a series of projections, each made on probable future fertility rates and other factors. See its publication *Projections of the Population of the United States 1975-2050*, Series P-25, No. 601, issued October 1975.

Teenagers and children made up nearly 40 per cent of the population in 1960 but may not account for 30 per cent in 2025.

The population profile half a century into the future is expected to show a huge bulge at the middle- and upper-age levels, the ages at which retirement from the job market becomes likely. A shrinking portion of the population will be working and feeding money into the giant pension systems. Within 50 years, one person will be drawing Social Security benefits for every two workers paying into the system. The ratio now is 3 to 1 and in 1950 it was 7 to 1.

Sources of Income for Older Americans

As Social Security legislation came into being, the principal problem with the elderly was poverty among people who had never earned very much or been able to save for the future. Even five years ago, one-fourth of the people over 65 had incomes below the official poverty level.[10] Today that figure has dropped to 15 per cent (it is 12 per cent for the general population); both Social Security benefits and private pensions have been fattened by inflation escalators. Studies indicate that the need today is not so much to avoid destitution as to maintain a decent living standard.

At the same time, the educational level of the elderly group has been rising. Where, a generation ago, many people over 65 were scarcely literate and only one out of five had a high school diploma, according to calculations made by *U.S. News & World Report*,[11] today one in three is a high school graduate and a great many have college degrees. Thus, observers note, the elderly today tend to be people accustomed to acting and doing, experienced in organizing, and self-confident enough to voice their concerns in the political forums.

It is difficult to get a precise picture of America's 23 million elderly citizens. It is equally difficult to find out much about the total "retired" population—which includes many people under 65. But a partial picture does emerge from available statistics and gerontological research. In the labor force today, 2.7 million workers are over 65 and one million of them are over 70. How many are holding or seeking part-time jobs is not known.

According to a recent White House survey,[12] 35 million Americans now get some sort of pension from either public or private sources, or both. The annual bill is now running around $133-billion, with the Social Security system paying $75-billion of that amount to retired workers or their survivors. As of June 1977, some 21.5 million of these recipients were over-65 retired

[10] Currently $2,964 for an individual.
[11] Issue of Oct. 3, 1977, p. 56.
[12] Cited in *Dun's Review*, October 1977, p. 83.

Mandatory Retirement

workers and their dependents.[13] The average Social Security benefit to retired workers that month was $240.17. While definitive figures are not available, it appears that more than half of all retirees do not have private pensions to supplement their Social Security income. There are also indications that, while retirees with two pensions may be receiving approximately half of their pre-retirement earnings, those on Social Security alone have only about a 40 per cent replacement of their generally lower earlier incomes.[14]

For many people, retirement is a much sought-after goal, a chance to get away from the daily work grind and to do all the pleasant things postponed through the working years. Most retirees, in fact, have retired as soon as they felt they could afford to, sometimes nudged by health problems. In a massive study of retirees conducted for the National Council on the Aging, 61 per cent said they chose to retire and 65 per cent said they had no desire to work any longer.[15]

There are differing opinions, however, on whether retirees are stimulated or traumatized by the end of regular work and earnings. "The key is psychological," remarked Paul Jackson, a consulting actuary in Washington. "It used to be when someone 55 retired, people looked at him a little funny if he hadn't had a heart attack or wasn't missing a leg.... Today, they look at him and say, 'Gee, he's got it made.' "[16]

The so-called trauma of retirement is "a myth without a shred of evidence to support it," asserts George Maddox, director of the Center for the Study of the Aging and Human Development at Duke University. Dr. Robert Atchley at the Scripps Foundation Gerontology Center at Miami University in Ohio, has observed: "In 12 years of research involving 5,000 people, I have not been able to document any serious psychological difficulties produced by retirement per se. ...A lot of people are anxious in anticipating retirement but most [of their fears] are not founded in fact."

On the other hand, Dr. Robert N. Butler, director of the National Institute on Aging, said: "For a significant number, retirement can be devastating. Many don't know what to do with themselves; they're jumpy and depressed. I call it the 'Willy Lohman' syndrome."[17] Statistics do show that the suicide

---

[13] Some 11.8 million recipients are under 65, including 1.8 million retired workers. Others are disabled workers or survivors and dependents. See *Social Security Bulletin*, October 1977, p. 1.
[14] Report of the House Select Committee on Aging, August 1977, Cmte. Publ. 95-91, pp. 25-29.
[15] "The Myth of Aging in America," 1975, study conducted by Louis Harris and Associates, Inc.
[16] Quoted by Jerry Flint in *The New York Times*, Oct. 2, 1977.
[17] Butler and Atchley are quoted by Lois Timnick in the *Los Angeles Times*, Sept. 10, 1977.

rate for white males age 65 to 69 is high: 36.5 per 100,000 population compared with a rate of 16 for all white males. But whether this phenomenon is related to post-retirement depression, to individual health problems, or to the cumulative effects of some chronic condition like alcoholism is not well documented yet. The American Medical Association says flatly that the "sudden cessation of productive work and earning power often leads to physical and emotional illness and premature death."[18]

In another aspect of the picture, considerable evidence has been amassed indicating that older workers are not necessarily the incompetent, deteriorating "deadwood" that personnel managers sometimes imply. Two studies referred to by the Senate Committee on Human Resources made this point. A New York survey of 33 state agencies in 1974 compared workers over and under age 65 with regard to absenteeism, punctuality, on-the-job accidents and overall job performance. It concluded that older workers were "about equal to and sometimes noticeably better than younger workers." The University of Illinois came to a similar conclusion in a study it had conducted earlier. "There was no specific age at which employees become unproductive and that satisfactory work performance may continue into the eighth decade," this study reported.

Duke researchers have found that older workers actually tend to be sick less frequently than others, although their illnesses are more likely to be serious and they are slower to recover. Senility affects only 15 per cent of all older people, usually as a corollary of some debilitating disease, it was further found. "The characteristics they seem to suffer most from," said Dr. Maddox, "is the tendency of society to treat them as though they are all alike."[19]

Experience of Firms With Older Workers

Forced retirement for age is not a universal practice. Companies that do not require it include Banker's Life and Casualty of Chicago, the Paddock Corp. of Arlington Heights, Ill., and even the huge steel industry where blue-collar workers have traditionally opposed mandatory age retirement. Their experience seems to bear out the picture of usefulness among those older people who want to keep on working.

The steel industry copes with the matter of competence and productivity of its workers by requiring annual physical examinations. "We don't have any problems with a worker staying on past 65 if he can pass the physical," a U.S. Steel Corp. official has said. "In fact, his productivity is probably greater." Not everyone shares this view. An oil company official

---
[18] Quoted in the Senate Committee on Human Resources' report *(see footnote 4)*, p. 4.
[19] Quoted by Ken Ringle in *The Washington Post*, Sept. 18, 1977.

remarked: "Let's face it. People's productivity begins to drop as they get older. You'd have a messy situation with no mandatory retirement forcing out the non-producers."[20]

Sen. S. I. Hayakawa (R Calif.), 71, and Ambassador Ellsworth Bunker, 83, who both support mandatory age retirement in principle, see it as a means of enabling older people to embark on second careers. Hayakawa, a former educator, revels in his new political life: "It is scary but extremely exhilarating. If you have ceased to be ready to face the frightening, then you become old." Ambassador Bunker, who recently completed negotiating a new Panama Canal treaty, has said: "I don't think there is any age limitation on a person's usefulness. It depends entirely on the individual."[21]

Forces Shaping Retirement Issues

FINANCIAL PROBLEMS of the Social Security system have provided an ominous background for the forced retirement issue. In the early 1970s, an accelerating trend toward early retirement and a recession-induced increase in the number of older people who lost their jobs combined to boost Social Security expenditures. The system is now paying $85-billion a year to retired and disabled persons, their survivors and dependents. Those benefits will rise to $180-billion by 1985, according to current projections.

Social Security payments exceeded income by $1.2-billion in 1975, by $3.2 billion in 1976 and, it is anticipated, $5.6-billion this year. The gap is currently made up by drawing on the Social Security Trust Fund reserves. But this fund, which stood at $40-billion in 1975, is expected to be exhausted by 1983. Clearly, the government will not let the Social Security system go bankrupt, so Congress this year has also been wrestling with various proposals for refinancing Social Security and insuring its stability well into the next century. Both the House and Senate have passed bills increasing Social Security taxes and benefits. Differences between the two bills are to be worked out in a House-Senate conference.[22]

The question has arisen, naturally, as to whether the Social Security system would benefit if the working years were extended and more people waited until later to start drawing benefits. The House Education and Labor Committee report

---

[20] Quoted in *Business Week*, Sept. 19, 1977, p. 39.
[21] Hayakawa and Bunker are quoted in *Time*, Oct. 10, 1977.
[22] It is likely that the conferees may not iron out their differences until early in the 1978 session of Congress.

said: "No estimate has been made of the possible effects of the [retirement age] legislation on Social Security outlays or receipts because of lack of recent and reliable information to make such an estimate...." However, the report went on to say that "some Social Security savings are likely to result...because some workers will forego private pensions and part or all of their social security benefits in order to continue working." The report of the Select Committee on Aging carries this point further, saying:

> With the ratio of workers to beneficiaries dropping significantly over the years, and the projected shortages in the trust funds, the economy and the country would seem better served if older workers who want to work and are able to work were permitted to do so.

Secretary of Commerce Juanita M. Kreps has wondered whether it might not be advisable, in view of both actuarial and population trends, to consider moving the age of entitlement to full Social Security benefits gradually from 65 to 68. This, she said, would "enormously reduce the Social Security burden." The outcry against such a "breach of faith" with present and future retirees was loud and immediate, although there is evidence that her suggestion is gaining some acceptance. In September, there was a Republican effort to revive the Kreps proposal, and some favorable editorial comment has appeared.

Growing Trend Toward Early Retirement

Since the early 1960s, the trend toward early retirement—well before age 65, and today even before age 60—has picked up momentum. In 1956 only 2.2 per cent of all Social Security benefits were paid to people under age 65. By 1972, the figure was above 50 per cent. Of the new awards made in 1974, some 72 per cent were for reduced benefits under age 65.

The trend has been furthered by a growing number of large union-negotiated pension plans that encourage early retirement by offering full pensions after a given length of time—often 30 years of work by age 55. The auto and steel workers have been leaders in the "30 years and out" drive. At General Motors, Congress was told, the average retirement age for wage earners was 67 in 1954 and for salaried workers it was 63. Today, they both retire at 58 or 59. Only 11 per cent of the salaried workers at General Motors stay on the job long enough to reach mandatory retirement age, and a mere 2 per cent of the blue-collar workers do. At Ford, more than 89 per cent of all employees retire before age 65, and only 2 per cent stay to the mandatory retirement age of 68. The federal government, with its 70-year age limit for most employees, reported that in 1976 the average age for all retirees was 58.2 years.

Mandatory Retirement

It appeared to the House Select Committee on Aging that most people opting for early retirement are those receiving both private pension and Social Security benefits. They retire as soon as they can afford to so they can "go for the good life." A Social Security survey in 1968 did show that more than half of the early retirees questioned said that health was the reason for quitting work early, but there is no data correlating this finding with pension levels. The House Select Committee, in reporting the survey, concluded nonetheless that "the primary reason for the trend toward early retirement would seem to be eligibility for a pension connected with a desire for leisure time to pursue other interests."

Why, then, the push for eliminating mandatory age requirements, when so few workers wait to be pushed out? John Martin, former head of the U.S. Commission on Aging, responds: "We don't want this legislation passed because we want all people over 65 to work. We just want to have the choice of working, like anyone else."

Legal-Right Questions Before the Courts

The immediate question of raising the mandatory retirement age to 70 is almost settled. But long-range questions remain and will undoubtedly surface in many ways. There is, first, the question of the constitutionality of age discrimination. Court cases decided so far have not upheld the thesis that "ageism is like sexism or racism," or, as some describe it, the last great constitutional barrier to full civil rights by all citizens. The Supreme Court, in upholding a Massachusetts law permitting the forced retirement of a state police officer at age 50, said in 1976 that the elderly "have not experienced a 'history of purposeful unequal treatment' or been subjected to unique disabilities on the basis of stereotyped characteristics not truly indicative of their abilities." The elderly, in other words, are not a "suspect classification" like blacks or women.[23]

The McMann case now before the Supreme Court *(see p. 168)* will not necessarily rest on the constitutional issue, but it is important for other reasons. Although the pleading mentions discrimination under the due process and equal protection clauses of the Constitution, the plaintiff's principal argument focuses on the Age Discrimination and Employment Act of 1967, in which a provision on pension plans is in dispute. United Air Lines, the defendant, interpreted the provision to exempt pension plans already in effect which required retirement at 65. If the Supreme Court were to uphold United's position, pension plans now in existence might conceivably be exempt from current legislation changing the mandatory retirement age.

---

[23] *Massachusetts v. Murgia,* 427 U.S. 307 (1976).

> **Federal Retirement Rules**
>
> Most employees of the federal government are required to retire at age 70, but there are many exceptions. While 70 applies to Civil Service personnel, 60 is the retirement age in the Foreign Service. And for FBI agents it is 55.
>
> Congress imposes no age limit on membership. Twenty-one of the 100 senators and 38 of the 435 representatives are 65 or older.* At 81, Sen. John L. McClellan (D Ark.) is the oldest member of Congress, followed by Sen. Milton R. Young (R N.D.), who turns 80 on Dec. 6. Five of the nine members of the Supreme Court are over 65: Chief Justice Warren E. Burger (70) and Associate Justices William J. Brennan (71), Thurgood Marshall (69), Harry A. Blackmun (69) and Lewis F. Powell Jr. (69).
>
> Likewise, no upper age limit is imposed on the President. Only two Presidents took office when they were 65 or older—Buchanan (65) and William Henry Harrison (68)—but several remained in office after reaching 65. Eisenhower served till age 70 and became the oldest man to hold the office.
>
> *Two others become 65 before the end of the year—House Speaker Thomas P. (Tip) O'Neill Jr. (D Mass.) and Rep. Clement J. Zablocki (D Wis.).

In contrast to the Supreme Court's ruling in the Massachusetts case last year, the House Select Committee concluded in its report that age "should be as protected a classification as race and sex." The argument "that everyone ages and no particular group is singled out for discrimination ignores the fact that discrimination solely on the basis of age is wrong," the committee reasoned. "If mandatory retirement because of age...is not to be declared unconstitutional by the courts, then Congress should act to make such practice illegal."

The current legislation directs the Secretary of Labor to undertake a study of the economic effects of total elimination of age criteria for retirement, and to report back to the Congress within two years. One question to be answered is: How big an impact on the labor market will result from raising, or voiding, the mandatory retirement age limit? The Department of Labor estimates that perhaps 200,000 workers might be added each year to the labor force, which currently stands at 98 million. Other estimates have been as low as 125,000. A Sears Roebuck employee poll indicated that one-third or more of the elderly would like to work if they could obtain jobs—a finding that suggests to some the number could be as high as 2.8 million. The critical question is whether these added workers would be absorbed into the job market or whether they would cause a commensurate jump in unemployment.

How can pension plans, both public and private, find adequate funds in the future if the trend continues toward earlier retirement and higher benefits? General Motors, for example,

Mandatory Retirement

has found a situation similar to that facing Social Security: in 1967 the ratio of GM workers to pensioners was 10 to 1, but by the early 1990s it is expected to be only 2 to 1.

Can management cope with the uncertainties that may result from increasing or eliminating mandatory age retirement? In objecting to current legislation, many corporate representatives cited experience rather than statistics. The general feeling in Congress seemed to be that both the human and financial aspects of the situation were quite manageable. Only time would tell whether pension costs would rise or fall, or whether payrolls would be affected by having proportionately more highly paid older workers.

Demographic Imperative: An Aging Nation

"It's a scary thing," Allen Selmin, 71, a member of the Tennessee Commission on aging, has said. "With people living longer and no work force coming on, you're going to have fewer people working and more and more old folks. It can't keep up. The answer is you can't retire them. You'll have to have them work until they die or until they're too sick."[24] Selmin was speaking of a future that is only 40 or 50 years away, as the demographic charts indicate.

Peter Drucker, social scientist and prominent writer on the problems of the elderly, wrote recently that "except perhaps in the event of a truly catastrophic depression, labor supply for the traditional blue-collar jobs will increasingly be inadequate even if present blue-collar workers are willing to stay on the job beyond age 65.... We will have to consider what incentives we need to encourage people...to postpone retirement...."[25] The concern is focused on what will happen when today's young people of the baby boom reach their sixties. If they all retire—early or even at 65—the number of supporting workers will be too low and the tax level required for pension support too high to be politically tolerable.

What lies ahead, then, may well be something more than today's gray rights' advocates have had in mind. The January 1977 *Morgan Guaranty Survey* said: "Working life in this country in the future may well grow longer rather than shorter, as many Americans have blithely assumed. About the time today's 35-year-olds reach the age when their parents retired, an added stretch of years on the job may be required." This, observers noted, would simply mean a return to the work force characteristics of the first decade of this century, when two-thirds of all American workers over age 65 stayed at their jobs.

---

[24] Quoted by Katherine Barrett in Memphis *Commercial-Appeal*, July 4, 1977.
[25] Peter Drucker, writing in *The Wall Street Journal*, Sept. 15, 1977.

Selected Bibliography
Books
Atchley, R. C., *Sociology of Retirement*, John Wiley & Sons, 1976.
Butler, Robert N., M.D., *"Why Survive? Being Old In America,"* Harper & Row, 1976.
Cohen, Wilbur J., *Retirement Policies Under Social Security*, University of California Press, 1957.
Drucker. Peter, *The Unseen Revolution*, Harper & Row, 1975.

Articles
Colamosca, Anne, " 'Gray Rights' Retirement Fight," *Dun's Review*, October 1977.
Congressional Quarterly Weekly Report, Sept. 3, 1977, pp. 1874-1878.
Eglit, Howard, et al., "Is Compulsory Retirement Constitutional?" *The Civil Liberties Review*, fall 1974.
Flint, Jerry, series of articles in *The New York Times*, July 10, Aug. 11, Sept. 24, Oct. 2, 1977.
Ladd, Everett Carl Jr. and Seymour Martin Lipset, "Many professors would postpone retirement if law were changed," *The Chronicle of Higher Education*, Nov. 7, 1977.
Maddox, George L. and Gerda G. Fillenbaum, "Work after Retirement," *The Gerontologist*, Vol. 14, No. 5, October 1974.
Maddox, George L. and Linda K. George, "Subjective Adaptation to Loss of Work Role: a Longitudinal Study," *Journal of Gerontology*, 1977, Vol. 32, No. 4.
McCraw, M. Louise, "Budgets for Retired Couples Rose Moderately in 1976," *Monthly Labor Review*, October 1977.
"Now, the Revolt of the Old," *Time*, Oct. 10, 1977.
Shapiro, Harvey D., "Do Not Go Gently...." *The New York Times Magazine*, Feb. 6, 1977.
"The Ax for Forced Retirement," *Business Week*, Sept. 19, 1977.
U.S. News & World Report, "Big Fight over Retirement," Oct. 3, 1977; "New Retirement Rules: Their Impact on Business, Workers," Nov. 7, 1977.

Reports and Studies
Editorial Research Reports, "Plight of the Aged," 1971 Vol. II, p. 865; "Retirement Security," 1974 Vol. II, p. 967; "Pension Problems," 1976 Vol. I, p. 363.
House Committee on Education and Labor, report accompanying H.R. 5383, "Age Discrimination in Employment Act Amendments of 1977," Rept. 95-527, Part I, July 25, 1977.
House Select Committee on Aging, "Mandatory Retirement: The Social and Human Cost of Enforced Idleness," August 1977, Comm. Publ. No. 95-91.
Senate Committee on Human Resources, report accompanying H.R. 5383, "Amending the Age Discrimination in Employment Act of 1977," Rept. No. 95-493, Oct. 12, 1977.
Social Security Administration, "Beneficiaries Affected by Annual Earnings Test in 1973," Vol. 40, No. 9, September 1977.
United Nations General Assembly "Question of the Elderly and the Aged," Report of the Secretary General, Nov. 8, 1973.
William Mercer Inc., "Employer Attitudes Toward Mandatory Retirement," June 1977.

PHYSICAL FITNESS BOOM

by

Marc Leepson

	page
NEW ENTHUSIASM FOR EXERCISE	185
Factors Behind Physical Fitness Boom	185
Jogging, Marathon Running and Health	186
Cooper's System of Aerobic Exercises	188
Risk of Injury to Sports Participants	190
LEISURE TIME AND PURSUITS	191
Long Working Hours in Early America	191
Postwar Concern About Youth Fitness	192
Interest in Employee Exercise Programs	193
FUTURE OF FITNESS MOVEMENT	195
Mounting Sales of Athletic Equipment	195
Popularity of Sports Books, Magazines	196
Growth of Organized Exercise Classes	197
Benefits of Different Fitness Programs	198

**Apr. 14
1 9 7 8**

PHYSICAL FITNESS BOOM

NEVER BEFORE have so many Americans spent so much time, energy and money to get into shape and stay there. Tens of millions of men and women have made physical fitness an integral part of their lives, regularly setting aside time for tennis, swimming, bicycling, jogging and the like. Young affluent adults are in the vanguard of the movement, but nearly all segments of American society are participating in the physical fitness boom.

Exercise authorities are even encouraging parents to take their pre-schoolers to gym classes. At the other end of the age spectrum, senior citizens are active in sports and exercise activities that only a few years ago were thought to be the exclusive domain of the young *(see p. 197)*. One of the most important trends in the fitness craze is the marked increase in women sports participants.[1]

According to Richard O. Keelor, director of program development for the President's Council on Physical Fitness and Sports, "America is going through a physical fitness renaissance that can make a real dent in degenerative diseases, not to mention the quality of life." Keelor is one of many medical authorities who believe that exercise is a form of preventive medicine that leads to better physical and mental health.

Nearly half of all Americans — 47 per cent — now participate in some form of daily physical exercise, according to a Gallup Poll released Oct. 6, 1977. This is twice the percentage recorded in 1961. Sindlinger's Economic Service, a marketing and opinion research firm located in Media, Pa., estimates that 38.5 million adult Americans participate in swimming, 34.7 million play tennis and 27.7 million are regular bowlers — the three most popular sports in the United States *(see table, p. 187)*.

Many are turning to exercise for reasons other than physical conditioning. Long distance running, for example, has been used as a form of psychological therapy. Many say that running brings them tranquility, enabling them to forget everyday troubles. Running can be a "mental exercise, a kind of ambulatory yoga," Michael Fessier Jr. explained.[2] Moreover,

---

[1] See "Women in Sports," *E.R.R.*, 1977 Vol. I, pp. 329-348.
[2] Michael Fessier Jr., "Transcendental Running," *Human Behavior*, July 1976, p. 18.

physical conditioning is highly personal and, unlike team sports, non-competitive. The only goal is self-improvement. Exercising thus fits in with a social philosophy that has become prevalent in the 1970s, described by social critic Tom Wolfe as the "Me Decade" and by others as the "New Narcissism." Improving physical appearance frequently is part of this preoccupation with self.

Then, too, physical fitness has become a chic pastime in places like New York City, Chicago and Los Angeles. Seventy-five-dollar designer suits for running have replaced rumpled cotton sweat suits for many. And movie stars' publicity photos are likely to show the actor or actress dressed in the latest jogging or tennis attire.

Government statistics indicate another reason for the fitness boom. The amount of leisure time available to Americans has increased significantly in recent years. According to a 1977 Commerce Department survey,[3] the average American's leisure time increased 11 per cent between 1965 and 1975. The increase in leisure time was reported among all races, age groups and education levels. The biggest increases were among non-whites, young adults and those who had completed 13 to 15 years of schooling. While the study indicated that watching television has become the leading leisure activity, it also reported that Americans are spending more leisure time on recreation than ever before.

Even though unprecedented numbers of Americans are exercising regularly, many others choose not to exercise at all. The non-exercisers tend to be older, poorer and less educated than those who exercise. Most medical experts believe that lack of exercise is a contributing factor in obesity. And there is ample evidence that a sizable part of the U.S. adult population is overweight.[4] The Department of Health, Education and Welfare's National Center for Health Statistics reported last November that the average male was from 20 to 30 pounds overweight and the average female was 15 to 30 pounds heavier than she should be.[5] Medical research has established a strong link between obesity and several diseases, including heart disease, the nation's leading cause of death.

Jogging, Marathon Running and Health

The most visible sign of the new fitness boom is the large number of people who jog along the nation's roads and in parks and athletic fields. About 5 per cent of the population — from 8

---

[3] "Social Indicators 1976," December 1977.
[4] See "Obesity and Health," *E.R.R.*, 1977 Vol. I, pp. 453-472.
[5] National Center for Health Statistics, "Height and Weight of Adults 18-74 Years of Age in the United States, 1971-1974," Nov. 30, 1977.

The Top Ten Adult Participation Sports
(in millions)

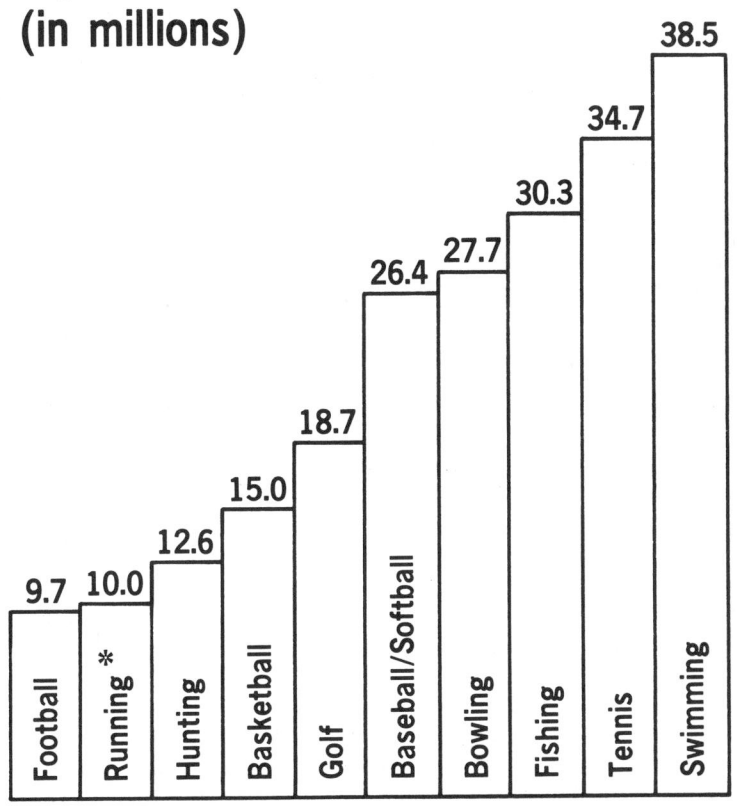

Sport	Millions
Football	9.7
Running*	10.0
Hunting	12.6
Basketball	15.0
Golf	18.7
Baseball/Softball	26.4
Bowling	27.7
Fishing	30.3
Tennis	34.7
Swimming	38.5

SOURCE: Sindlinger's Economic Service, January 1978
*Estimated

ATKINSON

to 10 million Americans — are regular joggers, according to Bernard L. Galdieux Jr. of the National Jogging Association (NJA). Membership in the NJA, an organization dedicated to physical fitness and health through running or jogging, has been increasing rapidly. There are some 20,000 members today, up from about 8,000 a year ago.

Local running clubs also have had an upsurge of members. The Road Runners Club of New York City, which sponsors or stages long-distance races in the New York City metropolitan area, has grown from 250 members in 1953 to 6,700 members today. The club is affiliated with 120 chapters across the country. "When this club started ... it was a place for people to find someone to run with," Road Runners President Fred Lebow said recently. "Now people are going into running because of health...and a lot of people get mental therapy out of it."[6]

Many joggers participate in competitive activities, such as the marathon — the 26-mile, 385-yard endurance test for runners. Marathons and other long-distance races, once few in number, have gained participants and spectators in the last few years. The oldest such American race, the Boston Marathon, drew a record field of 2,933 runners last year. Canadian Jerome Drayton won the 81st annual race in 2 hours, 14 minutes and 46 seconds. Of the 126 women starters, Miki Gorman of Los Angeles came in first in 2 hours, 48 minutes and 44 seconds.

The New York City Marathon, sponsored by the Road Runners Club, had 4,823 entries in its second annual running last year. This was the largest field of marathon runners ever assembled. The 1977 Honolulu Marathon attracted a record 3,050 entrants — including 619 women, the largest number to compete in any marathon. The Newark, N.J., Distance Run, consisting of four- and 12-mile races, drew some 2,000 participants in its fourth annual race on Feb. 12. San Francisco's 7.8-mile Bay-to-Breakers Race had only about 100 participants when it began in 1963. By 1967, some 5,000 runners entered the contest; last May, 12,000 finished the race. In Tampa, Fla., the Gasparilla Distance Classic, a 15,000-meter event, is held concurrently with a 5,000-meter "Run for Fun." This year's Run for Fun, held Feb. 13, drew 1,216 runners, including Mayor Bill Poe.

Cooper's System of Aerobic Exercises

Many observers of the running boom credit a former Air Force physician, Kenneth H. Cooper, with spurring much of today's interest in jogging and running. Cooper developed a theory of exercise called aerobics in the early 1960s. With publication of his book *Aerobics* in 1968, Cooper's exercise system became widely

---

[6] Quoted in *The New York Times,* Feb. 9, 1978.

> ## Running vs. Jogging
>
> **Rory Donaldson** of the National Jogging Association: "This debate rages on with purists on both sides. No answer satisfies everyone. There are two popular definitions which may help. Jogging is a pace slower than seven minutes per mile. When you cover a mile in less than seven minutes you're running. Two. A 'runner' is one who competes against others. A 'jogger' only competes against herself. You can see, therefore, that a person may be a jogger one day and a runner the next." *(Guidelines for Successful Jogging* [1977])
>
> **Robert Anderson,** publisher of *Runner's World:* "Joggers run for a reason — to lose weight, to stay in shape. If running itself is the climax for you, I'd call you a runner." *(The Washington Post,* March 2, 1978)
>
> **Frank Shorter,** Olympic Gold Medal winner who averages 17 miles of running a day: "Jogging is once or twice around the block in your baggy high-school sweats. Running is when you measure time or distance and strive for goals." *(Business Week,* Nov. 7, 1977)
>
> **Bernard L. Gladieux Jr.,** managing editor of *Jogger,* a National Jogging Association publication: "Distinctions between running and jogging are not very helpful. Jogging is running, but it's generally thought to be running long, slow distances. Its goal is elevation of the pulse rate to a level that is consistent with your level of fitness, age and capability."

popular. Cooper's theory is that aerobic exercises — those which induce the heart to work harder, expanding the blood vessels and stimulating increases in oxygen-bearing blood flow — are the key to physical fitness. Aerobic exercises increase the consumption of oxygen by increasing the vehicles for supply and delivery — the lungs and heart. In doing so, the exercises improve the overall condition of the body, and, according to Cooper, build resistance to illness and disease.

Cooper's system begins with field and treadmill tests to determine a person's fitness level. Then a progressive weekly exercise program is designed. The most common aerobic exercises are walking, jogging, bicycling, swimming and rope skipping. These activities can be used for long periods of sustained physical activity. Cooper believes that persons with coronary artery disease are able to live longer if they follow a prescribed aerobic exercise program. At his Aerobics Center in Dallas, Texas, students — including many with histories of heart disease — have run more than 1.4 million miles since the center opened in 1971. There have been no fatalities.

"Until a few years ago it was the conventional [medical] wisdom that strenuous exercise was bad for you," explained Dr. Paul Milvy, a biophysicist and epidemiologist at Mt. Sinai

School of Medicine.[7] But medical thinking has changed significantly. Many doctors now prescribe vigorous exercise for those who have had heart attacks. Not too many years ago the same doctors would have told their patients to take life easy, get plenty of rest and avoid even walking up stairs.

In spite of the success Cooper and other physicians have had with heart patients, it has not yet been proven conclusively that regular physical exercise can prolong life and protect against heart disease. Hundreds of scientific tests in recent years have focused on the relationship between exercise and heart disease. Most of them tended to show that persons who exercised were healthier and had lower incidences of heart disease than those who did not exercise. But science thus far has been unable to answer the pivotal question about those who exercise: Do they have fewer physical ailments because they exercise or do they exercise because they have fewer physical ailments? There is, however, widespread agreement in medical circles that those who exercise generally are healthier than those who do not.

Risk of Injury to Sports Participants

Everyone concerned with the fitness movement advises beginners to proceed slowly. Those who have not exercised for several years should consult a physician before embarking on any conditioning program. Males over 30 usually are cautioned to take a thorough physical examination, including an electrocardiogram and stress tests. "Some people play a sport to get in shape when in fact, very often they should get in shape to play the sport," declared Dr. Robert P. Nirschl, an orthopedic surgeon who is chairman of the Virginia Medical Society's committee on sports medicine.[8]

Both novice and experienced exercisers face many potential physical injuries. "Runner's knee," an inflammation of the cartilage behind the kneecap, is a common ailment among joggers. Shin splints, the aching of inflamed muscles or tendons in the lower legs, is often caused by running on hard pavement. Other foot injuries, such as inflammation of the Achilles tendon and bone spurs of the heel, are common because of the constant pounding involved in running.

Doctors have uncovered what is believed to be a benign kidney condition in many joggers — athletic pseudonephritis, or "jogger's kidney." The symptoms are abnormal levels of protein, red blood cells and other substances in the urine. The condition is caused by a reduction of blood flow to the kidneys during an hour or more of jogging. The condition cures itself

---

[7] Quoted by C. P. Gilmore in "Taking Exercise to Heart," *The New York Times Magazine,* March 27, 1977, p. 38.
[8] Quoted in *U.S. News & World Report,* Feb. 27, 1978, p. 40.

within two days, but doctors do not know whether it leads to permanent kidney damage.

Joggers are not the only ones vulnerable to specialized physical injuries. "Tennis elbow," the inflammation of the tendon joining the forearm muscle to the outside of the elbow, is a painful side effect for many tennis players. And those starting out in any exercise program often are bothered by strains, bruises and muscle aches, especially in legs and feet. Outdoor exercising, like jogging and bicycling, can cause skin irritations due to wind and cold weather. In addition, clothing frequently rubs against sensitive parts of the body, causing painful soreness in areas such as the nipple.

These physical maladies range from mild irritations to painful disabling injuries. But a carefully thought-out exercise program can minimize most of the potential dangers. Everyone who exercises agrees that the potential benefits of regular exercise — especially for those who live largely sedentary lives — far outweigh the risks of physical injury.

Leisure Time and Pursuits

BEFORE THE industrial age, most Americans depended on physical movement to survive. Dawn to dark working hours were prevalent on farms and in businesses well into the 19th century. Until the mid-19th century, leisure was largely confined to "society" in the eastern cities and the South. The rich migrated to summer resort areas in the Northeast while southern families repaired during the summer months to family cottages at various Virginia springs.[9] For most Americans, though, the only leisure time came on Sunday, a day of rest in keeping with the biblical injunction.

As the nation became more industrialized, many Americans no longer needed to expend themselves physically to arrange the necessities of everyday life. The average workweek in industry declined from an estimated 69.7 hours in 1850 to 47.7 hours in 1930. But the six-day workweek still prevailed. By 1929, it is estimated that only 5 per cent of the American labor force was working five-day weeks. The steel industry, manned largely by immigrant labor, did not give up the 12-hour day until 1923. By the end of the 1920s, the eight-hour day with a Saturday half-holiday had become the standard. On the eve of the Depression the average worker in manufacturing put in 44 hours a week.

---

[9] See "Leisure Business," E.R.R., 1973 Vol. I, pp. 145-163.

The average for other workers was closer to 48 hours. The Depression and the national mobilization effort of World War II left little leisure time for most Americans.

Postwar Concern About Youth Fitness

Postwar prosperity brought with it fuller employment and more leisure time. Within a decade after the war, studies began to show the effects of a prosperous society on the physical condition of the American people. Drs. Hans Kraus and Sonja Weber of New York University completed a study of the fitness of schoolchildren in 1954. The results of their work shocked many Americans. Nearly 58 per cent of the American schoolchildren who were tested failed a battery of six simple muscular fitness tests. Only about 9 per cent of the Italian, Swiss and Austrian children examined by Kraus and Weber failed the same tests.

Kraus said that the main difference between the American and European children "is the fact that European children do not have the 'benefit' of a highly mechanized society; they do not use cars, school buses, elevators or other labor-saving devices. They must walk everywhere.... Their recreation is largely based on the activities of their bodies. In this country, the children are generally conveyed in private cars or by bus, and they engage in recreation as spectators rather than as participants."[10]

Concern about the findings was so widespread that President Eisenhower met with government leaders, medical researchers and sports figures at the White House in June 1955 to discuss youth physical fitness. The next year at the President's Conference on the Fitness of American Youth in Annapolis, Md., some 150 fitness experts recommended that the President form a special committee on youth fitness. President Eisenhower responded by creating the President's Council on Youth Fitness on July 16, 1956. The council was set up to help design and implement physical fitness programs in the nation's schools.

President Kennedy broadened the council's scope in 1961. He appointed Charles B. (Bud) Wilkinson, football coach and athletic director at Oklahoma University, to be a special consultant on physical fitness and to supervise the council's activities. The council started new programs to develop testing standards and began a series of physical fitness clinics for teachers, administrators and recreation personnel. The idea was to influence physical education teachers in public schools to design new types of athletic training programs that placed more emphasis on physical fitness than on team sports. Marked improvements

---

[10] Quoted by James A. Michener, *Sports in America* (1976), p. 67.

in physical fitness testing results appeared between 1958 and 1965.

But a 1976 study conducted by the University of Michigan for the U.S. Office of Education found that the physical fitness of American schoolchildren did not improve between 1965 and 1975. In 39 out of 40 categories, fitness performances of boys and girls remained unchanged during the decade. The one bright spot was that more girls than boys showed improvement, especially in endurance tests. The President's Council cited two reasons for the leveling off of the overall physical fitness of America's schoolchildren: (1) many schools cannot afford adequate physical fitness programs and (2) students who have the choice tend to choose physical education programs that do not contribute significantly to fitness.

The President's Council began to promote fitness for adults in 1962. Today the council — now called the President's Council on Physical Fitness and Sports — runs public information programs and works with state and local governments and other organizations to promote the development of physical fitness facilities and programs. The council runs clinics, sponsors seminars and works with businesses to set up employee fitness programs.

Interest in Employee Exercise Programs

Many white-collar workers and executives lead totally sedentary lives. They begin each weekday with an automobile ride to work, sit for eight or more hours at a desk, drive home and spend the evening sitting in front of the television set. The President's Council on Fitness and Sports estimates that American businesses lose $25 billion a year from the premature deaths of employees and an additional $3 billion because of employee illness. Hundreds of business leaders in the United States and Canada think that lack of exercise is partly responsible for these problems. Many have set up programs to encourage employees to exercise.

The President's Council works with federal agencies to establish employee health fitness programs. The council helped set up or redirect fitness programs in 11 government agencies last year, including programs at the Department of Justice, the Central Intelligence Agency and the White House. The council develops training concepts, and helps with layout, facility design, equipment selection and staff employment.

The Justice Department's fitness program concentrates on coronary high-risk employees. A screening system, including stress tests, is used to determine the type of exercise program to be developed for each employee. The council noted that a large

> ### President Carter's Fitness Regimen
>
> President Carter has made exercise a part of his daily routine. He plays tennis several times a week and swims in the White House pool at least twice a week. Like President Truman, who took brisk morning walks near the White House (his morning "constitutionals"), President Carter also enjoys long walks, especially at the presidential retreat in Camp David, Md. Camp David also is equipped with tennis courts, a swimming pool and bowling alley.
>
> The President once jogged regularly, but he no longer does so. He does not use the elevators at the White House, preferring instead to walk up and down the stairs. Carter also bowls several times a week in the White House bowling alley and regularly rides a stationary bicycle for about ten minutes in the morning.
>
> The President, who ran cross country and played intramural football while a cadet at the U.S. Naval Academy, does not smoke and is not a regular drinker. White House physician William M. Lukash said recently that the President is in good physical shape.

percentage of "high risk individuals were returned to normal or near normal ranges in terms of cardiovascular risk" after taking part in the program.[11]

The American Association of Fitness Directors in Business and Industry is affiliated with the President's Council. The association helps private industry set up employee fitness programs. The 300-member group, formed in 1974, is headed by W. Brent Arnold, manager of physical fitness and recreation for Xerox Corp.'s International Center for Training and Management Development in Leesburg, Va. "Well over a thousand corporations and businesses have set up some type of physical training program for employees," Arnold told Editorial Research Reports. "Around 75 corporations employ full-time people to head fitness programs."

The Canadian government also is involved in developing employee fitness programs. Recreation Canada, a branch of the federal health and welfare department, has helped set up fitness programs for the Post Office and Department of Public Works in Ottawa. Recreation Canada's manager of fitness programs, Sandy Keir, last year called for a national law to force corporations that employ people in sedentary jobs to set up exercise facilities.

Rockwell International Corp. has one of the most elaborate employee fitness programs in the United States. The corporation has built several recreational facilities for employees, including a 16-acre site in El Segundo, Calif., which consists of a

---
[11] "Annual Report of the Activities of the President's Council on Physical Fitness and Sports," September 1977, p. 9.

gymnasium, rifle range, tennis courts and lighted softball diamonds. The Kimberly-Clark Corp. of Neenah, Wis., has spent some $2 million on its employee fitness program. The company conducts programs on nutrition, mental stress, alcohol and drug abuse, as well as physical fitness.

"Kimberly-Clark has a substantial investment in its employees," Darwin E. Smith, chairman and chief executive officer, said recently. "To us, it is simply good business sense to keep them feeling well, which not only keeps them on the job but even helps them do a better job."[12]

Other company fitness programs are not as extensive or costly as Kimberly-Clark's or Rockwell International's, but still provide adequate exercise opportunities. Johns Manville, the building products manufacturer, recently installed a $17,000 gymnasium in its Denver offices. Employees must pass a physical examination before using the facility and then follow a specified exercise program. Almost half of the 1,500 employees at Johns Manville's Denver offices have used the gymnasium.

The Canadian firm of James Richardson and Sons built an employee exercise area, complete with running track, on the 34th floor of an office building in Winnipeg. Bankers Life & Casualty Co. in Chicago encourages its employees to work out in a community center gymnasium across the street from the firm. Those who regularly use Northern Natural Gas Co.'s fitness center in Omaha reportedly lose significantly fewer days at work due to illness than those who do not exercise there. Exercise is a good way to work off office tension, many businesses have found, in addition to increasing employees' physical and mental strength. According to magazine publisher Malcolm Forbes, exercise by employees "gives the whole firm a sense of team spirit."[13]

Future of Fitness Movement

MANY OBSERVERS of the fitness movement are convinced that it is not a passing fad. "I've wondered whether the fitness movement was just another flash-in-the-pan American craze — whether today it's fitness, tomorrow it's some new therapy, diet, political movement, or whatever," Richard Kipling, director of The Sports Project of Santa Barbara, Calif.,

---

[12] Quoted by Jack Martin in "The New Business Boom — Employee Fitness," *Nation's Business*, February 1978, p. 68.

[13] Quoted in *Newsweek*, May 23, 1977, p. 79.

told Editorial Research Reports. "But I've watched this thing closely for three years now and it looks like it's become part of a new American life-style. It certainly fits Americans' vision of themselves as vigorous, healthy, active and on the go."

One measure of the movement's impact is sporting goods sales. The National Sporting Goods Association reported a strong increase in sales in 1976 — the latest year for which statistics are available. Between 1975 and 1976 sporting goods sales increased 15.2 per cent, reaching a record $12.1 billion. The association estimates that sporting goods sales for 1977 will be about $13 billion.[14] One of the highest sales increases — 18 per cent — came in exercise equipment. Warm-up suits led the way with $132 million worth of sales in 1976. Exercise equipment sales continued to increase in 1977.

Running and athletic shoes also have had record sales years recently. Some 45 million pairs of specialized athletic shoes were sold in 1976, up from 18.2 million pairs in 1974, according to *The Wall Street Journal*. Retail sales amounted to some $700 million. Today's running shoes sell from under $10 to as high as $50, and there are about 175 different styles from which to choose. "The total running shoe business, whether for people who run or people who want to look like they run, is really on fire," said Robert Schott, a vice president of Uniroyal, which makes Pro-Keds athletic footwear.[15]

Popularity of Sports Books, Magazines

There are hundreds of books currently in print concerning physical fitness. James F. Fixx's *The Complete Book of Running* has been a nationwide best seller for months — an unprecedented accomplishment for a book of that nature. Magazines devoted to participant sports also have been very successful in recent years. *Runner's World* magazine, founded in 1966, has led the way. The monthly magazine published in Mountain View, Calif., has increased its circulation from around 35,000 three years ago to over 200,000 today. *Runner's World* is known as the runner's "bible" and its tests and recommendations on running shoes are consulted by thousands of readers. *Running Times,* a monthly in its second year of publication, is No. 2 with a circulation of 9,000. A new magazine, *The Runner,* is scheduled to begin monthly publication in September 1978. The magazine, which projects a circulation of 50,000, will be published by *New Times* magazine publisher George A. Hirsch.

---

[14] According to a consumer survey based on interviews with 32,000 families conducted by Irwin Broh and Associates, Des Plaines, Ill., for the National Sporting Goods Association of Chicago. See Thomas B. Doyle, "The 1977 Market," *Selling Sporting Goods,* June 1977.

[15] Quoted in *The Wall Street Journal,* July 20, 1977.

> **Exercise for the Elderly**
>
> One sign of the physical fitness boom is that increasing numbers of senior citizens are becoming active in sports and exercise programs. Fitness classes for the elderly have been started in most American cities, according to C. Carson Conrad, executive director of the President's Council on Physical Fitness and Sports. Conrad, who is 66 years old, has conducted workshops on exercise for the elderly in 12 states and 32 counties or cities in the last year alone.
>
> Older citizens, of course, must be extremely careful with exercise programs. They should avoid quick movements in sports like tennis. But a properly designed fitness program with careful supervision can help older people physically and mentally. There are many physical activities older people can take part in, including calisthenics, yoga, tennis, jogging and gymnastics.
>
> Larry Lewis, who jogged until a few months before his death at 106, once said: "Old means dilapidated and something you eventually get rid of like an old automobile or a refrigerator. You're like a violin, a portrait, a wine. You mellow, but you never grow old."

There are also magazines about other participant sports, including soccer, bicycling, cross-country skiing and volleyball. San Francisco's *City Sports Monthly* magazine is written solely for participant sports enthusiasts in that city. Its success and growth in the past year have prompted its backers to consider publishing sports magazines like it in other cities.

Growth of Organized Exercise Classes

The increasing number of organized exercise classes for adults at YMCAs, health clubs and spas is another indication of the growing American fitness movement. *U.S. News & World Report* estimated recently[16] that there are some 3,000 health clubs and spas around the country with "several million" members. Full-time membership in the nation's YMCAs has grown 16 per cent in the last 10 years, while attendance at exercise programs increased 26 per cent between 1971 and 1976, according to Lloyd Arnold, the YMCA's national director of health and physical education.

In the last several years YMCAs nationwide have shifted their emphasis from exercises that provide strength, power and endurance to those that stress cardiovascular conditioning. Many YMCAs offer total fitness programs based on aerobic exercises. The Bethesda-Chevy Chase, Md., YMCA, for example, uses choreographed dance routines in its "Aerobics in Motion" program that promote improvement in cardiovascular response while toning muscles and improving endurance and coordination.

[16] Feb. 27, 1978, p. 39.

**Calories Per Hour
Expended in Certain Sports**

Running (10 mph)	900	Horseback riding	
Scull-rowing (race)	840	(trotting)	350
Bicycling (13 mph)	660	Badminton	350
Squash and		Walking (3¾ mph)	300
handball	600	Swimming (¼ mph)	300
Skiing (10 mph)	600	Rowboating	
Hill climbing (100		(2½ mph)	300
ft. per hr.)	490	Lawn mowing	
Water-skiing	480	(hand mower)	270
Tennis	420	Lawn mowing	
Wood chopping		(power mower)	250
or sawing	400	Golf	250
Table tennis	360	Canoeing (2½ mph)	230
Roller-skating	350	Gardening	220
Volleyball	350	Walking (2½ mph)	210
Square dancing	350	Bicycling (5½ mph)	210

Source: *Today's Health,* May 1972.

The exercise explosion has induced many to try different types of exercise. Yoga exercise now is offered at evening adult education classes, YMCA programs and specialized yoga centers, among many other places across the country. There are many branches of yoga, the Hindu philosophy of living which dates from the Middle Ages. The exercises, called Hatha yoga, are designed to attain bodily and mental control. Hatha yoga — the "yoga of force" — stresses relaxation, breathing and bodily postures, such as the headstand and the shoulder stand. Those who follow yoga claim that it can prevent disease, as well as help cure existing diseases, both mental and physical. Many Americans practice yoga exercises merely for the physical benefits, such as improved flexibility, coordination and muscle strength.

Benefits of Different Fitness Programs

The question of what type of exercise to choose is an important one. "Not all sports return equal rewards," James M. Michener has written, "and some kind of comparison between them is essential."[17] Medical and fitness experts differ as to the relative benefits of different kinds of exercising. Dr. Kenneth Cooper breaks down the various kinds of exercise into three broad categories: (1) those designed to provide rest and relaxation, (2) those designed to condition the cardiovascular and pulmonary systems, and (3) those designed to build muscles

---

[17] Michener *op. cit.,* p. 69.

Sports Activities Graded by Dr. James A. Nicholas
(highest possible score is 63)

Archery	28	Hiking	18
Auto racing	45	Hockey	54
Badminton	40	Ice Follies	51
Ballet	55	Jai alai	52
Ballroom dancing	27	Jockey Riding	52
Baseball	44	Judo	51
Basketball	50	Karate	50
Bicycling	36	Lacrosse	38
Big-game hunting	45	Modern dancing	28
Billiards	27	Motorcycling	37
Bobsledding	39	Mountain climbing	47
Bowling	29	Paddleball	42
Boxing	51	Polo	50
Bridge	26	Rodeo	49
Bullfighting	55	Racing	46
Calisthenics	33	Rugby	52
Canoeing	37	Sailing	43
Camping	23	Scuba diving	37
Circus acts	48	Skiing	41
Cricket	44	Snowmobiling	38
Curling	36	Soccer	44
Diving	45	Surfing	50
Equestrian	46	Swimming	39
Fencing	49	Table tennis	34
Field hockey	36	Tap dance	37
Figure skating	41	Tennis	42
Fishing, deep-sea	33	Tumbling	45
Football	56	Volleyball	44
Golf	39	Water polo	44
Gymnastics	50	Yachting	46
Handball	37		

Source: *Sports Medicine*, September-October 1975.

and contour the figure.[18] It is essential for someone starting an exercise program to determine which kind of exercise he or she needs the most. "Exercise should be prescribed for the individual more carefully than any drug," said Dr. Herman K. Hellerstein of Case Western Reserve University in Cleveland.[19]

One of the more thorough comparisons of the effects of different exercises was devised by Dr. James A. Nicholas, an orthopedic surgeon and medical school professor who is director of the Institute of Sports Medicine and Athletic Trauma at Lenox Hill Hospital in New York City. Dr. Nicholas's study breaks down the factors that come into play in different physical

---
[18] Kenneth H. Cooper, *The Aerobics Way* (1977), p. 195.
[19] Quoted in *Newsweek*, May 23, 1977, p. 82.

activities into three broad categories: (1) physical factors such as endurance, reaction time and strength; (2) mental factors such as intelligence, creativity and alertness; and (3) environmental factors such as playing conditions and equipment. The Nicholas scale rates 61 different sports and other physical activities. The highest possible rating is 63 points.

Although Dr. Nicholas has cautioned that the findings are "subject to many continuous changes, as the knowledge of sports medicine grows,"[20] the chart provides a useful comparison of the effects of differing activities. Football was the most demanding of the 61 sports, scoring 56 out of 63 points *(see box, p. 199)*. Ballet and bullfighting followed with 55 points. Of the more popular sports, basketball scored 50, tennis 42, baseball 44 and golf 39. The highest scores in the physical-reaction category went to ballet, hockey and boxing, followed closely by basketball, bullfighting, fencing, football, gymnastics and judo.

"Exercise should be prescribed for the individual more carefully than any drug."

Dr. Herman K. Hellerstein
of Case Western Reserve University

A sport that many participants practice for exercise is racquetball, which is widely believed to be the nation's fastest growing sport. There were no commercial racquetball facilities in the country in 1970. Today there are about 750, according to the U.S. Racquetball Association of Skokie, Ill. The sport has grown from some 50,000 participants in 1970, when it was played mostly on the West Coast, to more than five million today. The National Sporting Goods Association reported a 25 per cent increase in the sale of racquetball rackets between 1975 and 1976, and estimated another 25 per cent sales increase for 1977.

The game was invented in California in 1949. Racquetball's rules are essentially the same as handball's; however, players use a small racket to hit a green, vulcanized rubber ball. The court is the same size as a regulation handball court, but racquetball is played off of the four walls or ceiling. There are several reasons why the game has become so popular. For one thing, it is easy to learn. "Anybody can play it, anybody 8 to 80,

---

[20] James A. Nicholas, M.D., "Risk Factors, Sports Medicine and the Orthopedic System," *Sports Medicine,* September-October 1975, pp. 254-255.

Physical Fitness Boom

anybody old enough to walk and young enough to run," said Chuck Levy, national director of the U.S. Racquetball Association.[21] Most people can learn racquetball's fundamentals and begin playing after a five-minute lesson. Men and women can play together. It is estimated that about 40 per cent of all racquetball players are women.

There is no question that the number of Americans exercising regularly is at an all-time high. It is doubtful that every American adult will soon be a regular jogger or tennis player. But with an increasing number trying to stay in shape through serious exercise programs, those who choose not to participate may soon become an out-of-shape minority.

---

[21] Quoted in *The New York Times*, Feb. 13, 1978.

▼▼▼

Books

Anderson, James L. and Martin Cohen, *The West Point Fitness and Diet Book,* Rawson Associates, 1977.
Cooper, Kenneth H., *Aerobics,* Evans, 1968.
—*The Aerobics Way,* Evans, 1977.
Donaldson, Rory, *Guidelines for Successful Jogging,* National Jogging Association, 1977.
Eckholm, Erik P., *The Picture of Health,* W. W. Norton, 1977.
Fixx, James F., *The Complete Book of Running,* Random House, 1977.
Leonard, George, *The Ultimate Athlete,* Viking, 1975.
Michener, James A., *Sports in America,* Random House, 1976.
Satchidananda, Swami, *Integral Yoga Hatha,* Holt, Rinehart, 1972.

Articles

Gilmore, C. P., "Taking Exercise to Heart," *The New York Times Magazine,* March 27, 1977.
"How to Enjoy Sports — and Avoid Injury," *U.S. News & World Report,* Dec. 29, 1975.
Jogger (publication of the National Jogging Association), selected issues.
"Keeping Fit in the Company Gym," *Fortune,* October 1975.
Lang, John S., "The Fitness Mania," *U.S. News & World Report,* Feb. 27, 1978.
Martin, Jack, "The New Business Boom — Employee Fitness," *Nation's Business,* February 1978.
Penney, Alexandra, "Keeping Fit in California," *The New York Times Magazine,* Jan. 8, 1978.
Runner's World, selected issues.
Steward, Hartley, "Fitness: The Great Canadian Shape-Up," *Maclean's,* Jan. 24, 1977.
Waters, Harry F., et al., "Keeping Fit: America Tries to Shape Up," *Newsweek,"* May 23, 1977.

Reports and Studies

"Annual Report of the Activities of the President's Council on Physical Fitness and Sports," September 1977.
Editorial Research Reports, "Obesity and Health," 1977 Vol. I, p. 453; "Women in Sports," 1977 Vol. I, p. 329; "Nutrition in America," 1973 Vol. II, p. 583; "Leisure Business," 1973 Vol. I, p. 145.
"Half of Americans Now Exercise Daily," The Gallup Poll, Oct. 6, 1977.
U.S. Department of Commerce, "Social Indicators 1976," December 1977.

INDEX

A

Abortion
Decline in child-bearing - 70
Public funds question - 46
Teenage - 43, 45, 47
Adoption
Bachelor fathers - 76
Single-parent homes increase - 65, 66
Affirmative action. See Minorities
Ageism. See Mandatory Retirement
Aid to Families with Dependent Children (AFDC)
Federal welfare funds - 16, 45, 74
Alcoholism. See Drug Abuse

B

'Baby Boom' (Postwar)
Age-distribution chart - 173
Housing demands - 146, 158
Mid-1950s peak - 15, 50
New baby boom theory - 18, 19
Youth unemployment problem - 106
Bachelor fathers. See Single-Parent Families
Battered wives. See Domestic Violence
Birth control. See Family Planning
Blacks
Affirmative action - 96, 97
Breakdown in family structure - 9, 51, 71
Growth in one-parent families - 65, 66
Teenage pregnancy - 54
Women in the work force - 92, 94, 98
Youth unemployment - 105, 108
Broken homes. See Divorce

C

Carter, President Jimmy
Education Department proposal - 137
Family planning, sex education - 48, 58
Family policy - 15, 63
Housing programs - 157
Physical fitness - 194
Student assistance - 130, 139
Teenage pregnancy - 46
Youth unemployment - 105, 109, 119

Child Care
Changing attitudes toward child-rearing - 6
Child Abuse
Abuse-prone parents profile - 35
Adolescent pregnancies problem - 44
Diminishing influence of parents on teens - 10, 11
Generational theory of violence - 31
Increased attention from the government - 24, 25
Nationwide statistics - 23
New efforts to help abusers - 35
Preventing abuse and treating abusers - 36
Telephone reporting lines - 37
Child-Support Decrees
Parent-locator service - 75
State enforcement programs - 74
Custody
Joint custody arrangements - 78
Methods for avoiding custody - 69
State laws awarding to fathers - 76
Tax deductions - 76
Day-care centers shortage - 68, 77, 101
Day-care tax deduction - 76
Disciplinary measures used by parents - 33
Extension of the age of dependency - 11
Federal role debate - 16, 46, 75
Society's mixed views on physical punishment - 33
Childless marriages - 8, 18
'Couple-families' - 18
Crime. See Juvenile Delinquency; Domestic Violence

D

Discrimination
Affirmative action for minorities - 96, 97, 134
Anti-discrimination Laws
Age Discrimination and Employment Act (1967) - 165
Civil Rights Act (1964) - 96
Equal Pay Act (1963) - 95
Fair Labor Standards Act (1938) - 95
Continuing fight for job equality - 98
Laws protecting single parents - 77, 78
Liberalization of courtship and sex mores - 13
Pay gap between men and women - 86, 87
(See also) Supreme Court

Divorce. See also Single-Parent Families
  Changing social standards - 4, 13, 70, 71
  Child-support decrees. See Child Care
  Emotional and social issues - 68, 69
  Growth in one-parent families - 3, 64, 65, 70
  Money problems of single mothers - 66, 67, 74, 84
  Nationwide statistics (1867-1950) - 14
  Rising U.S. rates - 3, 5, 64
Domestic Violence
  Battered husbands - 27
  Child abuse. See Child Care
  Emergency Shelters
    Federal funding legislation - 25, 26
  Generational theory of violence - 31
  Marital rape - 30
  Murders in the family (table) - 25
  Self-defense pleas in wife-husband killings - 29
  Tolerance for violence in family setting - 32
  Wife-battering Cases
    Changes in police attitudes - 26, 27, 28
    Nationwide statistics - 11, 23
    Special aid programs for abusers - 37, 38
    State laws aiding victims - 27, 28
    Therapy for troubled couples - 38, 39
Drug Abuse
  Teenage alcoholism - 11

E

Education
  Affirmative action - 97, 134
  Alternatives to college - 140
  College Tuition Aid
    Carter program - 130, 136, 137
    Congressional debate - 126, 136
    Federal programs - 131, 132
    Opposition to tax credit plan - 128
    Student loan defaults - 138
    Veterans' assistance - 133
  Education for parenthood - 36
  Faculty retirement age - 170
  Head Start - 75
  Pay gap between men and women - 89
  Physical fitness - 185, 197
  Sex education. See Family Planning
  Underemployment of college graduates - 118
Employment. See also Youth Unemployment
  Anti-discrimination laws. See Discrimination
  Employee exercise programs - 193
  Family Protection Proposals
    Company day-care centers - 77
    Fair part-time job opportunities - 17
  Flexible work schedules - 17, 77
  Women in the workplace. See Women

F

Family Planning
  Birth Control
    Decline in childbearing - 70
    Laws affecting access - 57
    Supreme Court rulings - 52, 57
    Teenage attitudes - 54
  Federal Intervention
    Criticisms of family planning strategies - 48
    Family Planning Services Act (1970) - 52
    Teenage pregnancy and welfare dependency - 51
  Growing interest in population problems - 52, 53
  Planned Parenthood Federation of America
    Adolescent pregnancies epidemic - 45
    Family planning funds cutback - 48, 49
  Sex Education
    Contraception through radio - 57
    Criticism of a contraceptive orientation - 58
    Failure of school-based programs - 56
  Teenage Pregnancy Prevention
    Carter budget recommendations - 46, 47, 48, 49
    Criticism of administration's effort - 48
Family Stress. See also Divorce; Domestic Violence
  Black families deterioration - 9, 71
  Child-rearing Strain
    Childless marriages increase - 8
    Decline in childbearing - 70
    Diminishing influence of parents on teens - 10
    Disciplinary measures used by parents - 33
    Emergency 'hot lines' - 37
    Financial burden - 9, 10, 125
  Disillusionment with parenthood - 8
  'Emotional violence' - 24
  Emphasis on 'self-fulfillment' - 7, 8
  Impact on children - 31, 72, 73
  Inadequate income - 17, 66, 74, 85
  Lessening of religion's influence - 70
  Redefinition of family roles - 3, 4
  Rise of working wives - 5, 97
  Therapy techniques for troubled couples - 38
  World War II dislocations - 15
Ford, Gerald R. - 156

G

Government Programs
Carter family policy proposals - 15
Carter student assistance program - 130, 139
Child-care programs debate - 75
Concern for battered women - 24, 26, 27
Concern for welfare of pregnant teens - 43, 46
Federal aid for higher education - 132
Federal intervention in family planning - 48, 51
Federal role in job creation - 106, 112
Fragmentation of programs - 16
Government support of traditional family life - 71
Government's role in housing - 151
Laws dealing with child abuse - 25
Laws dealing with sex discrimination - 45, 98
Physical fitness programs - 192, 194
Social Security program - 172

H

Housing Outlook
Climbing Costs
Buying vs. renting - 159
Do-it-yourself housing, mobile homes - 149
Economic factors - 146
Failure of 'no-frills' experiment - 147
Home mortgage interest rates (table) - 154
Trends (1970-76) - 147, 156
Government's Role
Depression-ridden 1930s - 151
Postwar programs - 152
Subsidies, model cities in 1960s - 153
'Tight-money' policies, 1973-74 credit crunch - 155
Influences on Housing Trends
Carter subsidy programs - 157
Changes in household size, demographics - 158
Construction techniques and fuel prices - 160

I

Illegitimate children - 9, 43, 44, 47, 51, 66
Income security. See Retirement and Pensions; Social Security

J

Johnson, Lyndon B. - 52, 96, 153
Juvenile Delinquency
Broken homes linkage - 73
Consequences of unemployment - 106
Diminishing influence of parents on teens - 11
Effects of physical punishment on children - 34

M

Mandatory Retirement
Age Discrimination and Employment Act of 1967
Business, university opposition to change - 170, 176, 177
Congressional amendments - 165
Organized labor's neutrality - 167
Supreme Court case *(McMann v. United Air Lines)* - 168, 179
'Ageism'
Constitutionality of age discrimination - 179
'Gray power' lobby - 168
Federal retirement rules - 180
Origins of 65-year retirement age - 171
Pension cost uncertainties - 180, 181
Poll reports - 170, 175, 180
Population and Income Factors
Age-distribution chart - 172
Growth of elderly population - 173
Sources of income for older Americans - 174
Social Security financing problems - 177
State laws eliminating age for retirement - 166, 167
Trauma of retirement - 175
Marital rape - 30
Minorities. See also Blacks; Women
Affirmative Action
Education - 97, 134
Employment - 96

N

National Organization for Non-Parents (NON) - 10
Nixon, Richard M. - 53, 71, 155

P

Parents Anonymous - 37
Physical Fitness Boom
  Future of Movement
    Benefits of programs - 198, 199
    Growth of exercise classes - 197
    Mounting sales of athletic equipment - 195
    Popularity of sports books, magazines - 196
  Leisure Time and Pursuits
    Employee exercise programs - 193
    Increase in leisure time - 186
    Long working hours in early America - 191
    Postwar concern about youth fitness - 192
  New Enthusiasm for Exercise
    Carter's fitness regime - 194
    Cooper's system of aerobic exercises - 188
    Exercise for the elderly - 197
    Factors behind boom - 185
    Jogging, marathon running and health - 186
    Risk of injury to participants - 190
    Running vs. jogging - 189
    Top ten participation sports - 187
Planned parenthood. See Family Planning
Public Health Services Act of 1970
  Population research and family planning services - 48

R

Religious cults - 11
Retirement and Pensions
  Compulsory retirement. See Mandatory Retirement
  Federal retirement rules - 180
  Pension Plans
    Early retirement trends - 178
    Opposition to retirement age change - 170, 173
  Social Security benefits. See Social Security

S

Single-Parent Families
  Anti-discrimination laws - 77
  Bachelor fathers - 76
  Child adoption increase - 65
  Child-care tax deductions - 76
  Emotional and Social Issues
    Black family instability - 9, 71
    Impact of divorce on children - 10, 11, 73
    Joint custody arrangements - 78
    Loneliness - 68
    Public prejudice - 72
  Money Problems
    Child-rearing and education costs - 9, 10, 125
    Child-support payments default - 67, 74
    Day care expenses - 68, 75, 77
    Inadequate income - 74
    Mean family income (table) - 74
    Median income of single working mothers - 68
    Sex discrimination - 77, 78
  Public Policy Implications
    Debate over federal role - 75
    Low-income housing development - 78
    Search for missing parents - 74, 75
    Support payments collection - 75
    Welfare programs - 16, 74
  Rising Divorce Rates
    Increase in one-parent homes - 3, 5, 63, 64, 70
    Juvenile delinquency linkage - 11, 73
    Lessening influence of religions - 70
    Separation problems - 69
Social Security System
  Family income support proposals - 17
  Financing Problems
    Growing trend toward early retirement - 178
    Refinancing proposals - 177, 178
  Social Security Act of 1935 - 172
  Spouse abuse shelters - 26
Supreme Court
  Abortion (Planned Parenthood of Missouri v. Danforth) - 57
  Age discrimination (McMann v. United Air Lines) - 168, 179
  Contraceptives (Griswold v. Connecticut) - 52
  Corporal punishment (Ingraham v. Wright) - 34
  Equal pay (Corning Glass Works v. Brennan) - 95
  Job segregation (Griggs et al. v. Duke Power Co.) - 96
  Mandatory retirement (Bradley v. Vance) - 168
  Pregnancy pay (General Electric v. Gilbert) - 99
  School financing cases (box) - 129

T

Teenage Pregnancy Epidemic
School-Age Parents
Administration response to problem - 46
Birth rates (age 15-19) - 51
Births in 1977 (table) - 47
Grim prospects faced by young mothers - 44, 45
Outcome of teenage pregnancies (chart) - 45
Teenage unemployment rates - 84
Sex education. See Family Planning
Social and Public Policy Factors
Early puberty - 49
Fertility patterns - 50
'Illegitimacy' ratio - 51
Inadequate use of birth control - 54, 55
Increased sexual activity among teens - 53
Poverty and unplanned childbearing - 51

U

Unemployment. See Youth Unemployment
Unmarried Couples
Increase (1970-1975) - 4
Public housing for unwed and homosexual couples - 18

V

Veterans Affairs
College tuition assistance - 133
Postwar housing assistance - 152
Student loan defaults - 138

W

Women. See also Single-Parent Families
Age at Marriage
Impact of the Depression - 14
In Colonial America - 12
In 1975 - 70
Mid-1950s - 15
Rise in teenage marriages - 50
Domestic responsibilities - 6, 12, 17, 44, 69, 88, 100
Rights Movement
Demand for protection in family crises - 24
Push for suffrage - 13, 92
Self-fulfillment
Changing attitudes toward child-rearing - 7
'New narcissism' - 8, 186
Sex discrimination. See Discrimination
Wife battering. See Domestic Violence
Womanhood as a vocation - 92
Working Women
Affirmative action - 96, 97
Anti-discrimination laws - 77, 95
Assertiveness training - 101
Back-to-work movement - 5, 6, 83
Child care. See Child Care
Civil War job opportunities - 91
Immigrant labor - 91
Industrial workers' militancy - 92
Opinion polls - 86, 94
Pay gap between sexes - 68, 74, 86, 89
Pregnancy pay ruling - 99
Psychic barriers to advancement - 100
'Secretary trap' - 101
Share of U.S. labor force (table) - 93
Shift to professional and blue-collar jobs - 89
World War II job market - 94

Y

Youth Unemployment
Expanding Size of Problem
Consequences and causes of unemployment - 105
Disdain for work ethic - 111
Federal work programs - 106
Special difficulties facing black youngsters - 108
Youth unemployment in Europe - 109
Federal Role in Job Creation
Civilian Conservation Corps and NYA - 113
Job Corps controversy in 1960s - 116
World War II job openings - 115
Implications for the Future
Different views as to problem's severity - 119
Grim prospects faced by young mothers - 44
Minimum wage debate - 117
Projected teenage population decline - 120
Underemployment of college graduates - 118
Unemployment Rates
1950-1977 - 107
1974-1976 - 84